T0088085

# HEINRICH HIMMLER

Heinrich Himmler

ROGER MANVELL AND HEINRICH FRAENKEL

# HEINRICH HIMMLER

## THE SINISTER LIFE OF THE HEAD
## OF THE SS AND GESTAPO

Greenhill
Books

Skyhorse Publishing

Greenhill Books/Lionel Leventhal Ltd
Park House, 1 Russell Gardens
London NW11 9NN
www.greenhillbooks.com

Skyhorse Publishing, Inc.
307 West 36th Street, 11th Floor
New York, NY 10018
www.skyhorsepublishing.com

British Library Cataloguing-in Publication Data
Manvell, Roger, 1909–1987
Heinrich Himmler
1. Himmler, Heinrich, 1900–1945    2. Nazis – Biography
I. Title II. Fraenkel, Heinrich, 1897–1986
943'.086'092
ISBN 978-1-85367-740-3

Library of Congress Cataloging-in-Publication Data
Manvell, Roger, 1909–1987.
Heinrich Himmler : the SS, Gestapo, his life and career / Roger Manvell and Heinrich Fraenkel.
p. cm.
Includes bibliographical references and index.
Originally published: London: W. Heinemann, 1965.
ISBN 978-1-60239-178-9 (pbk.: alk. paper)
1. Himmler, Heinrich, 1900–1945.    2. Nazis—Biography.
3. Nationalsozialistische Deutsche Arbeiter-Partei. Schutzstaffel Biography.
4. Germany—Politics and government—1933–1945.
I. Fraenkel, Heinrich, 1897–1986. II. Title.
DD247.H46M3 2007
943.086092—dc22
[B]      2007016953

10

# Contents

# Illustrations

# ABBREVIATIONS

In addition to the familiar S.S., the *Schutzstaffeln* or Protection Squads, the following abbreviations are also used frequently throughout this work:

S.A. – the *Sturmabteilungen* or Assault Sections

S.D. – the *Sicherheitsdienst* or Security Service

# Introduction

This study of Heinrich Himmler completes the trilogy of biographies we have written about Hitler's principal assistants in the establishment and control of the Third Reich. The general desire to understand the exact nature of this régime and of the individuals who created it has become more pressing during the past few years, now that both Germany and the world outside have to a great extent overcome the shock to our common humanity inflicted by the Nazis, which either paralyzed or inhibited clear thinking during and immediately after the war. While the Germans have had to come to terms with themselves as the society which enabled Hitler to win control of the state and to establish a modern form of tyranny that eventually covered almost the whole of Europe, the other European powers and the United States have also had to search their consciences in order to discover to what degree they connived at the consolidation of Hitler's rule.

Our aim in writing these biographies, as well as our other book *The July Plot* which examines the German resistance movement in its weaknesses as well as in its strength, has been to discover as much as we could of the real nature of the men who helped to create Nazism and to examine all the facts known about them. We are opposed to the sensational kind of interpretation which classes Hitler, Göring, Goebbels and Himmler simply as 'monsters', a term used largely by the popular press to separate these much-hated men from ourselves and so comfort their readers. But the fact remains that these 'monsters' and their colleagues were for a considerable while circulating freely in both German and European society. They were liked or disliked, despised or feared, accepted socially or avoided in just the same way as other politicians, diplomats and soldiers. The Nazi leaders cannot be voided from human society simply because it is pleasanter or more convenient to regard them now as outside the pale of humanity. The thousands of men and women who worked with them were for the most part their admirers or their willing colleagues, while the influential Europeans and Americans who either actively favoured them or else tolerated them as a rather grim necessity in European politics who should not be opposed by any show of force, are not so far removed from those who actively cheered them in the streets.

The Nazi Party, as Alan Bullock has pointed out in his admirable biography of Hitler, had no political philosophy; their attitude to power was solely that it was something to be won by any means that could be improvised, irrespective of the moral issues involved. It was Hitler's utter unscrupulousness in handling the political leaders of other countries that preyed on their weakness and took a contemptuous advantage of their traditional sense of values in diplomacy. This lack of scruple is by no means uncommon in many human activities. Indeed, his unscrupulous brilliance was the very aspect of Hitler's character that excited widespread popular admiration and sympathy between 1933 and 1938, both inside and outside Germany.

The nature of the régime and of the public reaction to it sprang directly from the characters of the men who created it. Though this is in a sense true of all régimes, none in recent history has been so hastily and casually constructed as Hitler's Third Reich. Both policy and administration were largely concocted as a result of the individual whims of the various leaders, and of intuitive decisions taken at random in response to the mood of the moment or an urgent need to out-smart some opponent. The sufferings of the German people and those they were led to inflict on others twenty years ago were largely the result of the personal psychology of Hitler and of the three men whose lives we have attempted to reconstruct and interpret.

In each case we have tried to approach the task of writing these biographies with as little prejudice as possible. We have described in turn the development of Goebbels, Göring and Himmler through their childhood and adolescence; we have shown how they came to join the Nazi Party and discussed the particular contribution they made to it during its early formative period. There could scarcely have been three more different men than these in temperament and social background, nor could the particular parts they played in supporting Hitler during the years of his power have been more divergent. It has been a profound and at times a shattering experience to retread the familiar path of German history from 1923 to 1945 and interpret it as it was conceived and to a large extent actually created by these men, each of whom in varying degrees formed an individual empire in his own image within the larger empire built by Hitler.

We contend that the twelve years of Nazi rule in Europe offer us as clear a warning for the future in human terms as the explosion of the two atom bombs over Hiroshima and Nagasaki. It was the Nazis themselves who finally forced us to use violence against them when the provocation offered by their actions became too outrageous to be endured. But far too many people favoured what they stood for at the time, or still hanker after their memory today, for us to be sure the warning has been more than superficially taken by the world as a whole. For this reason alone it seems to us necessary to tell the story of these men's lives without bias or false emphasis, in order to show as precisely as possible what drove these leaders of a great country to behave in the way they did, and what, above all, they have in common with the rest of us, who profess now so readily to detest them.

It has been an illuminating experience for Heinrich Fraenkel to discuss in Germany the character and actions – or often the inaction – of Himmler with men and women who had to work closely with him. In preparing this biography, as with those of Goebbels and Göring, we have gone wherever possible to the sources of first-hand evidence. We have also been greatly assisted by Himmler's daughter Gudrun and his brother Gebhard, both of whom entertain memories of him which remain affectionate. They still find it very hard to reconcile the image of the man they knew so intimately with the public image of Himmler which was inspired by a fear and a hatred that became universal. It has been our task to try to achieve this reconciliation, to try to understand why this simple, unassuming man became a mass-murderer convinced of the essential rightness of his actions.

Himmler's contribution to the theory and practice of Nazism was that of a conscientious pedant who had always hankered after being a soldier but had ended by becoming a policeman. His brief career as a commander-in-the-field at the end of the war proved a complete disaster, though not in his own view, since he had to be induced to resign. But in its own strict terms, Himmler's career as Hitler's Chief of Police was a triumphant success, and it could be argued that Nazism found its most complete and practical expression in the repressive activities of Himmler's secret forces. During the war the work of the S.S. and the Gestapo became by far the surest weapon in the exercise of Hitler's tyranny. It was the extension of this work into the field of mass extermination in order to fulfil a false dream of racial purity which obsessed both Himmler and his master, that made the system become unmanageable. It was destroyed in the act of undertaking the slaughter of others under Himmler's direct instruction. Death choked itself through its own excesses.

In the curious grouping of rival ambitions that gradually surrounded and isolated Hitler during the final maniacal period of his rule, Himmler's power was the most secret, Göring's the most flamboyant, and Goebbels's the most self-proclaimed. Goebbels's vociferous contribution was that of the eternal campaign-manager who wanted to be acknowledged the dictator of Germany's civilian life while Hitler controlled the war. His volatile, egocentric nature demanded the satisfaction of constant public appearance and constant flattery; he enjoyed being at the centre of a whirlpool of incessant action. He wanted above all to be recognized both by Hitler and the German people as the second man of the Third Reich, Hitler's indispensable manager-of-state.

For Göring the failure of the Luftwaffe meant the passing of his personal glory as the most popular and colourful figure in the Nazi régime, the jovial air-ace. Alternately elated and deflated by his drug addiction, he also needed to feel indispensable and enjoy the satisfaction of collecting endless offices of state from the master of whom he stood in so great an awe that eventually it verged on panic. Depressed by the failure of the Luftwaffe, Göring turned increasingly to the consolation of his great art collection, amassed by gift, by purchase, but most of all by plunder, until it reached at the end of the war an estimated value of £30 million. In spite of this gradual fall from Hitler's favour, he remained until the last days the Führer's nominal successor; his real power declined after 1943 in the eyes of everyone except himself as he became increasingly self-indulgent and less and less involved in the direction of the war or the conduct of the economy.

It remained for Himmler, the idealist without ideals, at once the most diffident and the most pedantic man in the Nazi hierarchy, persistently uncertain of himself and yet perpetually militant and power-loving, to accumulate in secret the ultimate control of Germany. Looked at from his own point of view, it was Himmler's personal tragedy that while loving the thought of power so dearly he proved so utterly incapable of using it to any positive ends once he had acquired it. It remained a dead weight in his hands and a constant source of anxiety. While the very mention of his name struck terror into the hearts of millions of people, he himself was nervous to the point of timidity and became utterly speechless if Hitler chose to reprimand him. He cowered behind his own autocracy, and lost all powers of initiative in the face of personalities stronger or more persistent than himself, especially those on whom he came to depend, such as Heydrich, Schellenberg or Felix Kersten, his masseur, the only man who could relieve him of the chronic cramp in his stomach which was exacerbated by worry and despair. Yet it was Himmler who towards the end held most of what trump cards there were left in the hands of Nazi Germany, and who was regarded by many as the certain successor if Hitler collapsed.

The more one learns about the character and behaviour of these men, the more extraordinary does it seem that less than a quarter of a century ago they would have become under Hitler the joint masters of Europe and have held a great part of the world to ransom. Yet this, as we all know, is what happened. To us it seems best now to regard this black history as a warning. In our new world there are many emergent states and many longer established nations without the natural self-discipline to resist men similar in nature to the Nazi leaders should they emerge and either stride or slip to power. Such men are not always easy to recognize for what they are until it is too late. This certainly was the case with Himmler. Hitler at first appeared an absurd fanatic, Goebbels a posturing mob-orator, Göring a good-natured ass, Himmler a nonentity. Yet none of them proved to be what they had seemed, or they would never have won by their wits alone the supreme power in a great nation.

Our aim in writing this series of biographies is therefore to examine what particular qualities they and the men they chose to serve them actually possessed. Also, the reasons for their ultimate failure are as significant and absorbing as the explanation of their initial success. Within the space of only eight years they rose from insignificance and comparative penury to become the absolute masters of Germany. Twelve years later they were dead and utterly discredited. This story is unique in modern history, and it happened not in some lawless period of the past but in the middle of our own century.

Heinrich Fraenkel has made numerous visits to Germany on research for this book. He has interviewed many people, some of them
prominent in the S.S. or former members of Himmler's staff who
have asked to remain anonymous. Owing to Himmler's methodical
nature, vast quantities of private papers, official correspondence
and secret memoranda have survived and are held in the various
official archives we have indicated. Many new facts have come to
light during the past two years from captured documents recently
handed over by the American government to the German Federal
Archives at Koblenz. These and other files have been studied and
what they have shown has helped to complete this portrait of
Himmler.

Although this is the first detailed biographical study of Himmler,
we must express our great indebtedness to the published works of
Gerald Reitlinger, whose researches into the activities of the S.S.
and the extermination of the Jewish people in Europe, which he
published in his two books *The Final Solution* and *The S.S.*, have been
indispensable to us in that they throw so much light on Himmler
himself. Willi Frischauer's study of Himmler has also been useful
in points of detail, though his book is devoted at least as much to
the S.S. and its activities as to Himmler the man.

We have received valuable assistance from Fraulein Gudrun
Himmler, Himmler's daughter, and from Gebhard Himmler,
Himmler's elder brother; also from the former S.S. General Karl
Wolff, at present serving a sentence following his trial in Munich,
where he was visited on a number of occasions by Heinrich Fraenkel.
Others who have kindly given us significant information include Count
Schwerin von Krosigk, Hitler's Minister of Finance, Dr Otto Strasser,
who employed Himmler as an assistant during his initial work for
the Party, Dr Werner Best, who became during the Third Reich the
Governor of Denmark, Frau Lina Heydrich, widow of the former
S.S. leader, Josef Kiermaier, Himmler's bodyguard, Fraulein Doris
Mähner, one of Himmler's secretaries, Dr Riss, head of the Erding
Law Court, and Colonel Saradeth, both former fellow-students of
Himmler in Munich, Dr Otto John, Frau Irmgard Kersten, widow of
Felix Kersten, Himmler's masseur, and Colonel L. M. Murphy and
Captain Tom Selvester, the British officers in charge of Himmler
after his arrest. We must also acknowledge the generous help given
us by the staff of the Wiener Library in London, and in particular
by Mrs Ilse Wolff, and by the staffs of the German Federal Archives

at Koblenz (in particular Dr Boberach), the Institut für Zeitgeschichte at Munich (in particular Dr Hoch), the Berlin Document Center, the Rijksinstituut voor Oorlog Documentatie at Amsterdam (in particular Dr de Jong), and the International Red Cross Tracing Centre at Arolsen (in particular, Dr Burckhardt). Once more, we would like to thank Mrs M. H. Peters who undertook the arduous task of typing the manuscript of this book.

ROGER MANVELL

# I

# *Chaste Youth*

At the turn of the century, Professor Gebhard Himmler was already at the age of thirty-five a well-placed and well-respected schoolmaster in Munich. He was a studious, pedantic man, very conscious of the social prestige he had gained from the patronage of the Bavarian royal household of Wittelsbach. For when he had finished his education at the University of Munich, where he studied philology and languages, he had been appointed tutor to Prince Heinrich of Bavaria. Only after this period of service was finished had he taken up teaching in Munich.

In his restricted and very bourgeois world, he remained highly conscious of this link with a royal house. His surroundings, the heavy furniture, the ancestral portraits, the collection of old coins and German antiquities, all reflected his serious and respectable turn of mind and the need he felt to distinguish himself in middle-class society. His father had been a wandering soldier with only meagre resources, but his wife, Anna, who came from Regensburg, had brought him a modest amount of money, since her father was in trade. So it was in a comfortable second-floor flat on the Hildegardstrasse in Munich that Anna Himmler gave birth to her second son on 7 October 1900.[1] When their first child, Gebhard, had been born two years earlier, he had been named after his father, but for the second son the special privilege was reserved of being called after no less a person than Prince Heinrich himself, who graciously consented to act as godfather to the child of his old tutor. The draft of a letter dated 13 October 1900 and written in the Professor's immaculate script with its stiffly sloping loops still survives; in it he expresses the hope that the Prince will honour the family with his presence and partake of a glass of champagne. 'Our small offspring', writes the Professor, 'on the second day of his sojourn on this earth, weighed seven pounds and two hundred grammes.'²

The upbringing of the Himmler brothers – a third son, Ernst, was born in December 1905 – followed the routine of the period. With a schoolmaster for father, the masculine dominance natural in German households was all the more evident in their lives, especially when the boys attended their father's school in Landshut, the small town to which the family moved in 1913 on the Professor's appointment to a joint-headmastership.

Landshut is a pleasant place some fifty miles north-east of Munich with the water of the River Isar flowing through its centre. It had a castle and sufficient history to encourage young Heinrich's growing interest in national tradition and in the ancestral pictures and other mementoes his father collected to show their family's link with Germany's past. Professor Himmler did everything he could to encourage serious interests and self-discipline in his sons; he had a willing and assiduous pupil in Heinrich, who always remained devoted to both his parents in his own formal way. He was never to lose touch with them all their lives.

The first personal note by Heinrich to survive is a fragment of a diary he kept during 1910 in Munich. In a typical entry on 22 July he wrote: 'Took a bath. The thirteenth wedding anniversary of my dear parents.' It is a diary in which he simply adds up the smaller facts of his life from taking baths to going for walks, and he is careful always to show his respect for adults by entering their correct titles. The impression he gives already is that he has a painstaking primness of nature.³

The sections of Himmler's early diary that survive increase in length and scale during the later years of his youth, and so reveal more about his mind and character. The principal period they represent includes the first year of the war, when he was a schoolboy of fourteen in Landshut, and the period of his adolescence and young manhood in Munich, when he was from nineteen to twenty-two years of age, and then again when he was twenty-four. The total span of the diary covers ten important and formative years in his life, but the entries themselves are intermittent and survive in notebooks that cover only occasional periods of a few months in any detail. Nevertheless, they are of the greatest interest because they reveal so much of the nature of their author.

Although the war seems at first to have affected life at Landshut very little – Himmler's diary is full of the records of peaceful walks and church-goings, of working on his stamp collection and doing his homework – it is evident that the war news excited him sufficiently to make him enter up various events which he copied from the newspapers. Occasionally he bursts out into schoolboy slang. He notes on 23 September that Prince Heinrich has written to his father, and that the Prince has been wounded. But the initial German victories fill him with enthusiasm for the war, and on 28 September he says how he and a schoolboy friend 'would be so happy if we could go and slog it out' with the English and French. But principally he lives the normal life of a schoolboy – attending Mass, going out with his brothers to visit friends ('had tea with the Frau President, who was very gracious'), playing games and practising on the piano, for which it seems he had little aptitude. He pours scorn on the grumbling and timid people of Landshut who so dislike the war – 'all the silly old women and petty bourgeois in Landshut . . . spread idiotic rumours and are afraid of the Cossacks who, they think, will tear them limb from limb.' On 29 September he notes that his mother and father went to the railway station to help hand out refreshments to transports of wounded soldiers. 'The entire station was crowded with inquisitive Landshuters who cut up very rough and even began to fight when bread and water were given to seriously wounded Frenchmen who, after all, since they are prisoners, are worse off than our chaps. We took a walk in town and were frightfully bored.' On 2 October he is roused to enthusiasm by the mounting statistics of Russian prisoners. 'They multiply like vermin', he writes. 'As for the Landshuters, they are as stupid and chicken-hearted as ever.' 'Whenever there is talk about our troops retreating, they wet themselves,' writes Himmler, in an attempt to be vulgar, and he continues the following Sunday, after church, 'I use dumb-bells every day now so as to *get more strength*.' On 11 October, a few days after his fourteenth birthday, he refers to an army exercise in his locality, and how he 'would have loved to join in'.

The diaries of this earlier period already begin to reveal that, in spite of his frequent walks, his swimming, and other exercise, he is constantly complaining of heavy colds and suffering from feverishness and stomach upsets. He seems to have been a diligent, not brilliant, pupil at school; he refers frequently, among other subjects, to history, mathematics, Latin and Greek, and to the homework he has to do. He practised assiduously at the piano, but unlike his elder brother, he had no talent at all as a pianist; it was

years, however, before he asked his parents to allow him to give up
this impossible task. He was also studying shorthand, and began
in 1915 to use it for the entries in his diary. But after September
1915 he seems virtually to have given up the diary until a year after
the war, in August 1919, when the entries are suddenly resumed.

To judge from his schoolboy enthusiasm, Himmler's one idea
was to grow up and join the Army. His elder brother became
seventeen on 29 July 1915, and Heinrich records how on that very
day 'he enters the Landsturm', that is, the Reserve Army. 'Oh, how
I wish to be as old as that', writes Heinrich, 'and so able to go to the
front.'

He had to wait until 1917 before he too could volunteer. The
draft of a letter written by his father on 7 July survives to show how
he used his influence with the Bavarian royal household to ask that,
while his son might be regarded as a future officer-cadet, he should
at the same time be allowed to remain at school long enough to
matriculate before being conscripted. The application form he filled
in, dated 26 June, also survives; this was designed to secure his son's
eventual acceptance for training as an Army officer.

Himmler did not in fact formally matriculate until 18 October
1919, two days before he began the study of agriculture in the Technical High School of the University of Munich. Meanwhile in 1917
he had been called up; he served in the 11th Bavarian Infantry
Regiment, training at Regensburg, his mother's home town. Much
later, Himmler was to claim that he had led men into action during
the First World War,[4] but this does not accord with an application
for military papers that is still preserved in his own handwriting;
this is dated 18 June 1919, and makes it clear that Himmler had been
released from the Army on 18 December 1918 without having received the military documents due to him following the completion
of a course for officer-cadets in Freising during the summer of 1918,
and another as a machine-gunner in Bayreuth during September.
He needs these papers, he claims, because he is about to join the
Reichswehr, having served meanwhile in the local Landshut Free
Corps.

Himmler therefore did not qualify as an officer in time to serve
on the Western Front, but continued what military activities he
could after the Armistice in 1918. It is clear that in spite of his weak
health soldiering appealed to him, but meanwhile during the difficult
post-war years – Bavaria had for a while a Communist state govern-

ment during 1919, and the effects of inflation were soon to be felt – he had to qualify for some civilian occupation. It was then that he decided to study farming. By the time he resumed his diary more fully in August 1919, he was already working on a farm near Ingolstadt, a small town on the Danube to which the family were to move from Landshut during September, when Professor Himmler took up a post as headmaster.

Himmler's work as an apprentice farmer was not to last long; on 4 September he suddenly felt ill. At the hospital in Ingolstadt it was found he had paratyphoid fever. When he recovered he was told he must leave the farm for at least a year, and on 18 October he was accepted as a student in agriculture at the University of Munich. The diary also makes it clear that for the time being he had to give up his hopes of serving as a reservist either in the Army or in the Free Corps movement. He managed, however, to join the traditional student fencing fraternity.

Himmler was to remain a student in Munich until August 1922, when at the age of twenty-one he gained his agricultural diploma. What remains of his diary during this three-year period shows that he was anxious to live the life of the conventional student, persistently seeking out fencing partners until he had received the traditional cut in the face during his last term at college, and making enthusiastic friendships which enabled him to indulge in earnest intellectual discussions. He also believed in enjoying himself, and he even learned dancing in his youthful determination to become a social success. He found the dancing lessons troublesome: 'I'll be glad once I know it', he writes on 25 November. 'This dancing course leaves me absolutely cold and only takes up my time.'

He lived in rooms where no food was provided, and he took his meals at the house of a certain Frau Loritz, who had two daughters, Maja and Käthe. Although he went home frequently at weekends, and remained on close terms with his brother Gebhard, he soon fell in love with Maja in Munich. 'I am so happy to be able to call this wonderful girl my friend', he writes in October, and again the following month: 'had a long talk with her about religion. She told me a great deal about her life. I think I have found in her a sister.' Some of his entries are enigmatic: 'we talked and sang a little. It gives one plenty to think about later.' But apparently this slight love affair soon drifted into an unimpassioned friendship, even though in November he 'talked to Maja about relations between man and woman', and after a discussion on hypnotism he claims to himself that he has considerable influence over her.

It was, apparently, an uneasy time for him. He was restless, and dreamed of leaving Germany eventually and working abroad. Though he often had to work in the evenings, he began to study Russian in case his future travels took him east. His closest friend, apart from his brother Gebhard, was a young man called Ludwig Zahler, a companion from his days in the Army, with whom he talked endlessly, but whose character evidently disturbed him. 'Ludwig seems to me more and more incomprehensible', he writes, and then two days later, 'I have now no more doubts about his character. I pity him.'

He shows that he also had some doubts about himself. 'I was very earnest and depressed', he records in November, after an evening with Maja. 'I think we are heading for serious times. I look forward to wearing uniform again.' Less than a week later he confesses to himself, 'I am not quite sure what I am working for, not at the moment at any rate. I work because it is my duty. I work because I find peace of mind in working . . . and overcome my indecision.'

At the time he was writing these entries at odd moments in his diary, Himmler was only nineteen, but already he reveals qualities in his nature which were to remain unchanged throughout his life. Although he enjoys a narrow social life with a small circle of friends, he instinctively avoids any human relationship that commits him too deeply. The force that drives him is what he believes to be his duty, and this leads him to work hard at his studies, and force his un-healthy body to succeed in the accepted exercises, such as swimming, skating and, above all, fencing. His conventionalism becomes in itself a kind of passion; he is gregarious without any real warmth, and he is only prepared to seek the companionship of girls on the understanding no passion enters into his relationship with them. He still attends Mass, and, in his spare time, practises shooting with Gebhard and Ludwig against the future when he can, once more, 'wear uniform'. He is an ardent nationalist in politics, and seriously alarmed by events in the east.

The diaries lapse again between February 1920 and November 1921, and again between July 1922 and February 1924. The final phase of his life as a student followed much the same pattern, broken by minor military exercises as a reservist and clerical duties for a student organization known as *Allgemeiner Studenten Ausschuss*. His ambition to farm in the east has, however, changed; he considers Turkey now to be more suitable, and he travelled to Gmund, where he was later to establish his lakeside home on the Tegernsee, to meet a man who knew something of the prospects in Turkey. He is, however, still uncertain about his own character. In November 1921, in his twenty-second year, he writes: 'I still lack to a considerable degree that naturally superior kind of manner (*die vornehme Sicherheit des Benehmens*) that I would dearly like to possess.'

His relations with girls are still platonic. He mentions meeting a girl from Hamburg on the train, and remarks in his diary that she was 'sweet and obviously innocent and very interested in Bavaria and King Ludwig II'. His friend Ludwig, who worked in a bank, tells him that Käthe thinks he despises women, and Himmler says she is right. Then he adds:

'A real man will love a woman in three ways: first, as a dear child who must be admonished, perhaps even punished, when she is foolish, though she must also be protected and looked after because she is so weak; secondly, he will love her as his wife and loyal comrade, who helps him fight in the struggle of life, always at his side but never dampening his spirit. Thirdly, he will love her as the wife whose feet he longs to kiss and who gives him the strength never to falter even in the worst strife, the strength she gives him thanks to her childlike purity.'

Although he mentions many girls in his diary, it is with increasing primness and resistance. He still attends church, and he moralizes after eating in a restaurant on how the beauty of the waitress will inevitably lead to her moral downfall and how, if he had the means, he would love to give her money to prevent her from going astray. He mentions a coolness, even a breach, in his relations with Frau Loritz and Käthe, whose 'feminine vanity' he considers a waste of his precious time. In May 1922 he notes in the diary how shocked he had been to see a little girl of three permitted by her parents to 'hop round in the nude' before his shocked gaze. 'She ought at that age', he says, 'to be taught a sense of shame.'

The recollections of certain fellow students complete the portrait of Himmler in his youth that his diaries contain.[5] He is remembered as being meticulous in his studies and awkward in his social relationships. He wore his rimless pince-nez even when duelling, he recited Bavarian folk poetry rather badly, he avoided association with girls except those who expected to be treated with formality and politeness, and he never made love like his fellow students where love was to be found. He told his brother Gebhard he was determined to remain chaste until marriage, however much he might be tempted. Yet he was socially ambitious, putting himself forward as a candidate for various student offices for which he seldom received more than an unflatteringly small number of votes. The student society in which he tried most to shine was the Apollo club, which had a cultured rather than a sporting or merely beer-swilling membership. The members of Apollo were mostly ex-service men and senior graduates, and the president of the society at that time was a Jew, Dr Abraham Ofner. Although Himmler, a junior member of Apollo, was studiously polite to Dr Ofner and the other Jewish members, he was already strongly anti-Semitic in feeling, and he joined in violent discussions as to whether Jews should not be excluded from the society. In politics he is remembered as inflexibly right-wing, a natural if not very efficient member of the Free Corps formed to oppose the Communist infiltration into post-war Bavarian administration. We are left with a picture of a small man, prosaic and platitudinous, concealing his shyness under a certain arrogance. He disguised his fear of seeming unable to fulfil the hot-blooded life of a student by displaying excessive diligence in his work and making it quite clear he was determined to take part in the various right-wing, militaristic movements of that unsettled time. His exactness of habit seems to amount to a mania, for he never ceases to record when he shaves, when he has his hair cut, even when he has a bath. All these experiences take their due place alongside the duelling and the military exercises, and the serious discussions of religion, sex and politics. He notes down the comparative beauty of his dancing partners with exactly the same calm, meticulous cataloguing that he shows when he notes the cutting of his hair or the shaving of his beard:

'Dance. Was rather nice. My dancing partner was a Frau [lein] von Bück, a nice girl with very sensible opinions, very patriotic, no bluestocking and apparently quite profound . . . The girls were on average rather pretty, some close to beautiful . . . Mariele R. and I talked together for some time . . . Accompanied Fraulein von Bück home. She did not take my arm which, in a way, I appreciated . . . A few exercises, to bed.'

Himmler used his diary to castigate himself at those times when he seemed to fall short of his own very modest ideal. He complains that he talks too much, that he is too warm-hearted, and that he lacks self-control and a 'gentlemanly assurance of manner'. He enjoys helping people, visiting the sick and, occasionally, assisting and comforting old people, going home to visit the family: 'they think I'm a gay, amusing chap who takes care of things – Heini will see to it', he writes in January 1922. It is plain that, like many people, he sought recognition and a place in his social and family circle by involving himself as much as he could in other people's affairs. At the same time, a certain genuine kindness of heart has to be allowed him. But always he sought for popularity and for acceptance in student circles, though his primness of manner and his weak constitution, which prevented him from drinking beer without upsetting his stomach, led his fellow-students to look down on him and to make fun of his excessive diligence.

As a church-goer he remained regular in his habits at least until 1924, though the signs of religious doubt begin to appear much earlier in his diaries. 'I believe I have come into conflict with my religion', he writes in December 1919, 'but whatever happens I shall always love God and pray to Him, and remain faithful to the Catholic Church and defend it even if I should be expelled from it.' In February 1924 he is still attending church, but refers to his discussions of 'faith in God, religion, doubts (immaculate conception, etc.), confession, views on duelling, blood, sexual intercourse, man and woman'. The subject of sex exceeds even religion in its attraction, no doubt because of his conviction that abstinence from intercourse was morally binding before marriage. He seems to have remained virgin until the age of at least twenty-six, and he evidently experienced the pangs of unsatisfied sexual desire. After one of his frequent discussions of sex with his friend Ludwig, the bank clerk, he wrote in February 1922:

'We discussed the danger of such things. I have experienced what it is like to lie closely together, by couples, body to body, hot; . . . one gets all fired up, must summon all one's reasoning. The girls are then so far gone they no longer know what they are doing. It is the hot, unconscious longing of the whole individual for the satisfaction of a really powerful natural urge. For this reason it is also dangerous for the man, and involves so much responsibility. Deprived as they are of their will-power, one could

do anything with these girls, and at the same time one has enough
to do to struggle with one's self.'

Another tribulation was lack of money. He disliked increasingly
being dependent on his family for his maintenance, though he
learned how to eke out the allowances he received from his father,
and measure most carefully his very modest expenditure on clothes
and food. His letters to his parents that have been preserved show
how he enumerated each small detail of what had to be done in
the way of mending and repairs, as well as small needs for additional
sums of money. His letters are always respectful, affectionate and
formally gushing:

> 'your dear birthday letter . . . the tie should be mended on the
> left-hand side . . . unfortunately I must ask you, dear parents, for
> money; have only twenty-five of the last hundred marks, which
> included the monthly thirty . . . white shirts I never put on for
> work, so my things are really being saved enormously . . . the
> polka-dot tie I got for Christmas is torn in several places . . .
> heartfelt greetings and kisses.'

The character of the man is in everything he writes, as well as in
the fact that these letters, like so much else from the period – receipts,
lists, drafts, ticket-stubs, and so on – survived through his care the
holocaust of Germany.

Correctness was all. On 5 November 1921 he attends in hired
morning dress the funeral of Ludwig II of Bavaria; a few weeks
later he calls formally on the royal widow, who was the mother of
his godfather; on 18 January 1922 he takes part in a nationalist
student ceremony to commemorate the founding of the German
Empire. A week later, on 26 January, he attends a rifle-club meeting
in Munich with Captain Ernst Roehm, who, he says in his diary, is
'very friendly'. 'Roehm pessimistic about Bolshevism', he adds
laconically.

Roehm was still active in the Army. He was thirteen years senior
to Himmler and was soon to become the principal influence in
bringing him more fully into contact with politics. Along with his
elder brother Gebhard, Himmler was to join the local nationalist
corps led by Roehm and called the *Reichskriegsflagge*, the para-
military contingent which was later, in November 1923, to join
forces with Hitler in the Munich *putsch*.

Meanwhile Himmler had graduated on 5 August 1922. His studies at the Technical College had included chemistry and the science of fertilizers, as well as the generation of new varieties of plants and crops. His immediate need for work was relieved by an appointment as laboratory assistant on the staff of a firm in Schleissheim specializing in the development of fertilizers. Schleissheim is barely fifteen miles north of Munich; this meant that Himmler did not lose touch with the centre where Hitler was breeding his own particular form of nationalism which had already led to the formation of the National Socialist Party. Although Himmler could not have escaped knowing something of Hitler and his political activities in Munich, the first mention of him in what survives of the diaries does not occur until February 1924, five months after the *putsch*. Among the many rival or parallel nationalist groups of the period, Himmler, like Goebbels, was initially affiliated to a group that did not come immediately under Hitler's growing influence.

He was, however, already developing his anti-Semitism, a feeling common enough among the right-wing Catholic nationalists in the south. From 1922 anti-Jewish sentiment grows stronger in Himmler's diary, although on one occasion he softens a little towards a young Austrian-Jewish dancer he met in a night-club with a friend called Alphons, who had managed to persuade him to indulge in this most unusual expedition. He noted that she had 'nothing of the Jew in her manner, at least as far as one can judge. At first I made several remarks about Jews; I absolutely never suspected her to be one.' He made sentimental excuses to himself on her behalf, no doubt because she was pretty and gave him a pleasant shock by admitting she was no longer 'innocent'. He is less indulgent to a fellow-student and former fellow-pupil at school, a Jew named Wolfgang Hallgarten[6] whom he calls Jew-boy (*Judenbub*) and a Jewish louse (*Judenlauser*) because he had become a left-wing pacifist. From now onwards there are occasional references to the 'Jewish question' in the diaries.

This was in July 1922, shortly before he left college and began to earn his living. Official records show that he did not formally apply to join the Nazi Party until August 1923, four months before the unsuccessful *putsch*, in which he was to play a minor part as ensign to Roehm's contingent, the *Reichskriegsflagge*.[7] Roehm's men did not take part in the notorious march through the streets of Munich led by Hitler and Ludendorff; he had been made responsible for occupying the War Ministry in the centre of Munich. A photograph of Himmler survives in which he can be seen standing near Roehm holding the traditional Imperial standard and peering open-mouthed over the flimsy barricades of wood and barbed-wire. He had come specially from Schleissheim to take part in this exciting event, and its failure cost him his job though not his liberty.

The two days of the Munich *putsch* first brought together in a common action the future Nazi leaders, Hitler, Göring, Roehm and Himmler. But whereas Himmler stood in the background holding a flag, Göring, the former ace flier, marched beside Hitler and Ludendorff on 9 November, the day after Hitler's attempt at a *coup d'état* during a meeting addressed by leading Bavarian ministers in the hall of the Bürgerbräukeller, the great tavern of Munich. Roehm, by now a close associate of the Nazi movement, had agreed to march on the military headquarters of the Ministry of War on the Schoenfeldstrasse, where they barricaded themselves in with barbed-wire and set up machine-guns for their defences. It was the only successful action of the *coup*. Roehm and his men occupied the building and stayed there during the night of 8/9 November, while Hitler and his storm-troopers spent the hours of darkness in the grounds of the Bürgerbräukeller before the decision was reached to march on the centre of the city the following day and link up with Roehm, who alone among the leaders of the *putsch* did not behave like an actor in a melodrama. The march, which began around eleven o'clock, led by Hitler flourishing a pistol and Ludendorff looking grim and important, involved some three thousand storm-troopers crossing the River Isar and progressing for over a mile to the Town Hall in the Marienplatz. After this another mile had to be covered through narrow streets before the Ministry of War was reached. It was then that armed police finally stopped the march, and in the scuffle that followed Hitler was slightly injured and Göring badly wounded in the groin. Only Ludendorff strode on, oblivious of the bullets and sure of the iron weight of his authority. But he was arrested; Roehm and his men were forced to surrender some two hours later. They had been living in a state of siege in the Ministry since dawn, when infantry forces of the regular Army had put a cordon round the building.

The times were too uncertain for violent recriminations. The Nazi Party was banned; Himmler lost his job, and was forced to return home cap-in-hand. Home now meant Munich, to which the family had moved back in 1922. Roehm, whom Himmler still regarded with respect and affection as his superior officer, was confined like the other leaders of the unsuccessful *putsch*. On 15 February 1924, Himmler asked permission of the Bavarian Ministry of Justice to visit Stadelheim prison where Roehm was held. He rode out on his much-prized motor-cycle, taking with him some oranges and a copy of *Grossdeutsche Zeitung*. 'Talked for twenty-minutes with Captain Roehm', he recorded when he got back. 'We had an excellent conversation and spoke quite unreservedly.' They discussed various personalities, and Roehm was grateful for the oranges. 'He still has his sense of humour and is always the good Captain Roehm', remarks Himmler.

At the trial of the conspirators that followed on 26 February and lasted for over three weeks, Hitler acted as if he were the accuser, and the trial degenerated into a soft formality. Though Hitler was found guilty and served a nominal sentence, Roehm was completely discharged even though he too had been pronounced guilty of high treason. Hitler was confined in Landsberg castle; Roehm pursued his own plans for founding a revolutionary military movement while Hitler, dictating *Mein Kampf*, deliberately let his underground party disintegrate in his absence. By the time Hitler was released, owing to the favour shown him by the Bavarian Minister of Justice, Franz Gürtner, Roehm was no longer an acceptable figure in Hitler's party. By April 1925 he felt bound to send Hitler his resignation as leader of the storm-troopers.

Himmler meanwhile had also been active. Much to his family's annoyance, he refused to seek work: he wanted, he said, to leave himself free to engage in politics. Corresponding most closely to the disbanded Nazi Party were the nationalist and anti-Semitic groups of the extreme right known as the Völkische movement. Prominent among their supporters were Ludendorff, Gregor Strasser and Alfred Rosenberg; the Völkische groups were collectively a powerful element in the Bavarian government, and in 1924 they managed to draw sufficient support in the Reichstag elections to secure themselves thirty-two seats. Strasser, Roehm and Ludendorff were among those who became members of the Reichstag.[8]

The sight of such success naturally attracted Himmler. With time on his hands, he took part in the Völkische campaigns in Lower Bavaria. He began to gain experience as a member of a team of speakers at political meetings; he toured the smaller towns and the villages in the area of Munich and spoke on 'the enslavement of the workers by stock exchange capitalists' and on 'the Jewish question'. 'Bitterly hard and thorny is this duty to the people', he writes after difficult meetings in the countryside attended by peasants and communists. Along with the other speakers he would mingle with the audience and encourage individual argument. The groundwork of his initial political experience was therefore laid in the same hard school as that of young Joseph Goebbels, who was about to be drawn into the same sphere in politics and address similar political meetings in the industrial area of the Ruhr.

Hitler's name barely appears in the surviving diaries. On 19 February 1924 Himmler notes that he reads aloud to some friends from a pamphlet called *Hitlers Leben*, but with the departure of Roehm he had to find another leader to whom he might offer his services and from whom, if possible, also obtain paid work.

He rejoined the Nazi Party on 2 August 1925; it was during this period that he also joined the staff of Gregor and Otto Strasser, the Bavarian brothers who were among the principals in the reconstruction of the Nazi movement. The Strassers had a family druggist establishment in Landshut. They remained uneasy partners to Hitler who, after his release from Landsberg on 20 December 1924, began at the age of thirty-five to gather once more the reins of leadership into his own hands. While the Strassers were for compromise with other nationalist groups, Hitler was determined to lay the foundation of a new and vigorous political party over which he had full personal control. In the very month of his release from prison, the Nazi-Völkische alliance lost all but fourteen of its thirty-two seats in the Reichstag after the second election of the year, but Hitler, to the exasperation of the Strassers and Roehm, did not seem to care. Once he had obtained the removal of the ban on the Nazi Party, he was prepared to lose the support of the anti-Catholic Völkische groups. All that concerned him was to make a new start, to reform the Nazi Party under his own undisputed leadership. This he announced at the end of February 1925, and his platform included a virulent campaign against the Marxists and the Jews.

Himmler had obtained his appointment nominally as a secretary, but actually as a general assistant prepared to undertake any duties assigned to him. According to Otto Strasser, his brother welcomed Himmler because, as he put it, 'the fellow's doubly useful – he's got

a motor-bike and he's full of frustrated ambition to be a soldier'.[9]
He was responsible for surveying the secret arms dumps which were
kept concealed in the country districts away from the eyes of the
Inter-allied Control Commission. Himmler, aged twenty-four,
enjoyed this underground activity; it filled him, says Otto Strasser,
with nationalistic pride, and he preferred it to the office work which
he had to carry out for Gregor Strasser who, as well as being a
Reichstag Deputy, was in charge of Party activities in the district of
Lower Bavaria, a position he had held since 1920. Gregor Strasser
was a vigorous orator and a tireless organizer. At this stage Hitler
could not spare him and, in spite of the growing differences between
them, it was by mutual consent that the Strassers finally moved the
main sphere of their activities to the north. Otto Strasser, whose
particular flair was for journalism, moved to Berlin and founded
there the northern Party newspaper, the *Berliner Arbeiterzeitung.*

During 1925 Goebbels and Himmler met at Landshut during the
course of their work for the Strassers. It soon became apparent that
while Goebbels was the brilliant speaker and potential journalist,
Himmler's talent lay rather in desk-work and other, more pedestrian,
activities. It has been assumed, based largely on loose statements
made by Otto Strasser, that Himmler was displaced in the Strassers'
service by the vain and volatile young man from the Ruhr.[10] This
was far from the case. Goebbels, during his frequent visits south,
became increasingly fascinated by Hitler, who soon recognized his
talents and, during 1926, flattered him into accepting the difficult
post of Gauleiter, or party organizer, in Berlin. Previously, however,
Goebbels had spent the greater part of his time in the Ruhr when he
had not been engaged in special conference work for Strasser or
Hitler in other parts of the country. Himmler, on the other hand,
consolidated his own position in Lower Bavaria during 1925 to a
sufficient extent to be able to write as follows at the end of the year
to Kurt Lüdecke, one of Hitler's supporters who was soon to leave
for America:

'Dear Herr Lüdecke,
    Excuse my bothering you with this letter and taking the liberty
of addressing a question to you. Perhaps you know that I am
now working in the management of the district of Lower Bavaria
for the Party. I also help with editing the local "folk" journal, the
*Kurier für Nieder-Bayern.*
    'For some time I have entertained the project of publishing the

names of all Jews, as well as of all Christian friends of the Jews, residing in Lower Bavaria. However, before I take such a step I should like to have your opinion, and find out whether you consider such an undertaking rich in prospects and practicable. I would be very indebted to you if as soon as possible you would give me your view, which for me is authoritative, thanks to your great experience in the Jewish question and your knowledge of the anti-Semitic fight in the whole world.'[11]

According to Lüdecke, Gregor Strasser laughed when he was told of the letter, saying in effect that Himmler was getting fanatical about the Jews. 'He's devoted to me, and I use him as secretary', he added. 'He's very ambitious, but I won't take him along north – he's no world-beater, you know.'

Himmler's ambitious diligence, however, won him the position of Strasser's deputy as district organizer in Lower Bavaria, working of course under Hitler's shadow in Munich. He also became second-in-command of a small corps numbering some two hundred men and known as the *Schutzstaffel*, or S.S. The S.S. was originally a group formed in 1922 before the Munich *putsch* and called the Adolf Hitler Shock Troops, a special bodyguard of tough men who kept close to Hitler on public occasions and guarded him from attack. According to his official record Himmler had joined the S.S. in 1925, receiving the S.S. number 168. The reformed S.S. marched past Hitler at the second Party gathering in Weimar in 1926, and they were given a special 'blood-flag' for their services to their leader in the November *putsch*. These services had been to wreck the printing presses of the Social Democrat newspaper in Munich.

The main task for Himmler in the Party offices at Landshut, where a portrait of Hitler frowned down on his activities, was to increase the Party's supporters. His initial salary was 120 marks a month, and the local S.S. were sent out to collect subscriptions and canvas advertisements for the Party newspaper, the *Völkischer Beobachter*. In 1926 he was made Deputy Reich Propaganda Chief, and this gradual accretion of subordinate offices led to a modest increase in his salary. Yet he seems to have made little impression at this stage other than by being a willing and dutiful administrator. There are glimpses of him in Goebbels's excited diary during the period of Party expansion before he went to Berlin – on 13 April 1926, for example, during a speaking tour, he writes: 'with Himmler in Landshut; Himmler a good fellow and very intelligent; I like him'. On 6 July, 'ride on the motor-bike with Himmler'; and, on 30 October, 'Zwickau. Himmler, gossip, slept.'[12] Goebbels, aged twenty-eight and eaten up with vanity, regarded Himmler as the local manager of his star speaking tours.

He did, however, travel to Berlin, and it was during one of these visits to the capital in 1927 that he finally became involved with the woman whom he was later to marry. She was a nurse seven years older than himself; she was of Polish origin and her name was Margarete Concerzowo. Marga, as she was called, owned a small nursing-home in Berlin, and had unorthodox ideas about medicine which appealed to Himmler and excited afresh the discussions of his student days. She was interested in herbal cures and homoeopathic treatments, and their discussions set up a longing in Himmler to work once more in the open air. These two seemed at this stage in their relationship to be made for each other, in spite of the difference in their ages. Both worshipped efficiency, thrift and the rigorous neatness of a parsimonious life. Both felt they needed the comforts of marriage and domesticity, and both believed that their common interests in such matters as medicine and herbs amounted to love. Marga sold her nursing-home and decided to use the money to acquire a property in the country.

They married early in July 1928. One of Marga's coy and excited letters, written eight days before their marriage, survives in Himmler's carefully preserved files, and relates to the house and smallholding they bought with her money in Waltrudering, some ten miles outside Munich. In her joy at the thought of marriage, she hastily calculates what they are spending and whether or not they can avoid taking out a mortgage. In the margin Himmler coldly notes that her totalling is out by 60 marks. Nevertheless, Himmler, her 'naughty darling', will soon be hers, as she goes on to remind him.[13]

The smallholding at Waltrudering became a modest enterprise and was left largely in the hands of Marga Himmler. They kept about fifty hens, and they marketed produce and agricultural implements; it made a little money over and above Himmler's salary, which stood now at around 200 marks a month. The following year Marga gave birth to her only child, their daughter Gudrun.

This year, 1929, became the turning-point in Himmler's life. On 6 January Hitler issued an order appointing him Reichsführer S.S. in place of the commander Erhard Heiden, whose deputy he had been. It was a far-seeing appointment. Something in this clerk-like man with his military ambitions and scrupulous self-discipline must have revealed to Hitler that he had in him the kind of perfectionism necessary to create a reliable counter-force to the undisciplined mob of storm-troopers who roamed the streets in the name of the Nazis.[14]

# II

# *Reichsführer S.S.*

Though the appointment of Himmler to the command of the S.S. was for Hitler a matter of expediency, for the man himself it was a moment of fulfilment. He was now Reichsführer S.S. This new, high-sounding title was in itself a challenge to his tenacity and an inspiration to the particular vision germinating in his brain, his own interpretation of what Hitler, with his aid, might make of the German people in the distant future.

Himmler was now twenty-eight, a young man with a pregnant wife older than himself, and a modest smallholding. To be Reichsführer S.S. based on Munich was to be in command of less than 300 men, and there were limits even to this very minor place of power. In Berlin, the centre of radical action stirred up by Goebbels's violent propaganda, Kurt Daluege was also appointed by Hitler to be head of the local S.S. and empowered to operate independently of Himmler, who was in any case regarded, along with his force, as subordinate not only to Hitler but to the general organization of the S.A., the brownshirt Party battalions on the streets. The S.S. was in fact a force within a force, its special task nominally the protection of Hitler and other Nazi leaders at meetings, rallies and parades. But, according to Gunther d'Alquen, who was later to become editor of *Das Schwarze Korps*, the special journal of the S.S., Hitler had instructed his Reichsführer S.S. to make the corps into an utterly dependable body of carefully selected men.

Himmler was therefore able to indulge his vision. In spite of his sloping shoulders, his close-cropped hair, his neatly trimmed moustache and rimless pince-nez with its ear-chains suitable for a respectable clerk, he saw his unit of Black Guards as an *élite* band of warriors whose unique character would elevate them far above the street-ruffians of the S.A. They were to be made into Hitler's knights-at-arms.

This elevation of his men became Himmler's great obsession. The fact that he played comparatively little part in the day-by-day strategy and intrigue with which Hitler, Göring and Goebbels worked their way to power between 1929 and 1933 did not at this stage trouble him. He had his own bright, particular star to follow. His immediate ambitions in the Party were fulfilled for a while by his command of the S.S. and by the seat in the Reichstag that was allocated to him after the 1930 elections. His domestic ambitions, such as they might be, were fulfilled when his wife had given birth to their child, Gudrun, in 1929. Marga Himmler was attended by a Dr Brack, whose son, Dr Viktor Brack, was some twelve years later to take charge of Himmler's euthanasia programme, after first serving him in the capacity of a chauffeur.

The S.S. did not expand suddenly under Himmler's leadership. The years 1929 and 1930 represent primarily a period of preparation; the final stage of expansion came later, as we shall see, during 1931, when many thousands of men were added to the force. Their initial duties, when the S.S. had been summoned to roll-calls and allocated in groups to accompany various Party speakers to their meetings, were by then superseded; by 1931 the S.S. had other work, at once more secret and more spectacular.

The first substantial stage in the establishment of a permanent, *élite* corps came when Himmler issued, in January 1932, the notorious marriage code for the members of the S.S. The code was based on the principles outlined by Walter Darré in his book *Um Blut und Boden* (*Blood and Soil*), which was published under the auspices of the Party in Munich in 1929.

Darré was Hitler's agricultural expert, and he had come to believe in selective breeding as a result of his studies. He was born in the Argentine in 1895, and had been educated in England at King's College School, Wimbledon. He had for a while been a civil servant in the Prussian Ministry of Agriculture, but had been dismissed in 1929 after a disagreement with his colleagues. In the same year he published a book on the peasantry as the life source of the Nordic race. His ambition was to become Reich Minister of Agriculture, and this indeed is what he became in 1933.

Darré is of importance only because of the hardening influence he had on certain of Himmler's prejudices, which were later to develop into dire obsessions. Darré was some five years older than Himmler, and in a movement that found it expedient to encourage unscientific theories if the results arrived at were useful as propaganda, Darré became an accepted 'thinker' on behalf of the Nazis, closely linked with Alfred Rosenberg, one of the principal propounders of the myth which convinced the Party that the true Germans possessed a unique racial superiority.

Rosenberg was of German stock, but he had been born in the Baltic town of Reval and had studied architecture in Moscow before escaping to Germany at the time of the Russian Revolution. He had become editor of Hitler's journal *Völkischer Beobachter* in 1923. In his book *The Myth of the Twentieth Century*, published in 1930, he declared the humane ideals of Christian Europe to be a useless creed. What Europe needed, he said, was to be freed from the soft, abstract Christian principles derived from Asia Minor and the East, and to discover a new philosophy, which would be rooted once more in the entrails of the earth and recognize the racial superiority and cleanliness of Nordic man. 'A culture always decays', wrote Rosenberg, 'when humanitarian ideals . . . obstruct the right of the dominant race to rule those it has subjugated.' He saw in the German people the race endowed by nature with a true, mystic understanding, a 'religion of the blood'. Christianity, on the other hand, taught the decadent doctrine that all races shared an equality of soul, which the German race would soon show to be nothing but a vicious and insidious illusion.

In place of the meek and all-forgiving, Rosenberg created the ideal of the 'powerful, earth-bound figure', the 'strong peasant', and it was at this point that Darré, Rosenberg's disciple and Himmler's teacher, took over the spiritual education of his leader.

In *Blood and Soil*, Darré gave his reasons why the German race was so especially privileged. His assumptions were based on the essential nobility of the Nordic peasantry, whose blood was as rich and fruitful as the soil they tilled. So great was their virtue that the future strength of Europe depended on the survival of their stock; it was essential they should breed and multiply until their blond and shining youth outnumbered and outfaced the lurking, decadent Slavs and Jews, whose blood was poison to the human race and whose haunts were the healthless streets of towns and cities.[1]

Himmler's energies during this initial period were, as we have said, devoted to the theory and practice of the S.S. In 1931 Darré joined his staff to organize the department known as the Race and Settlement Office, *Rasse und Siedlungshauptamt* (R.U.S.H.A.). This office was set up to determine the racial standards required of good German stock, to conduct research into the surviving ethnic groups in Europe that could be claimed as German, and to decide all matters connected with the descent of individuals at home and abroad about whom there were any racial doubts. Darré remained in charge of this office with its increasing powers until 1938, though he was also, from 1933, Reich Minister for Food and Agriculture. It was with his aid that searching tests were devized for the brides of S.S. men and made obligatory in the notorious Marriage Law of the S.S., dated 31 December 1931 and coming into force the following day.

In its opening paragraphs, Himmler's Marriage Law insisted on the importance of maintaining the high standard of blood in the S.S.[2] The principal clauses that followed filled many unmarried S.S. men with dismay:

'Every S.S. man who aims to get married must procure for this purpose the marriage certificate of the Reichsführer S.S.

'S.S. members who though denied marriage certificates marry in spite of it, will be stricken from the S.S.; they will be given the choice of withdrawing.

'The working-out of the details of marriage petitions is the task of the Race Office of the S.S.

'The Race Office of the S.S. directs the Clan Book of the S.S., in which the families of S.S. members will be entered after the marriage certificate is issued.

'The Reichsführer S.S., the manager of the Race Office, and the specialists of this office are duty bound on their word of honour to secrecy.'

Himmler ended his Marriage Code with a defiant flourish:

'It is clear to the S.S. that with this command it has taken a step of great significance. Derision, scorn, and failure to understand do not move us; the future belongs to us!

(Signed) Heinrich Himmler'

Himmler's Marriage Code for members of the S.S. required every man who wanted to marry to obtain a certificate of approval for his bride in order that the purity of the Nordic stock which he already represented should be maintained unimpaired in the blood of his descendants.

The Office kept stud records for every S.S. man, who was issued with a genealogical or clan book (*Sippenbuch*)[3] which recorded his right and duty to mate with his chosen woman and procreate children by her. His bride and her parents were required to prove that they were free of all disease, mental or physical, and the girl was meticulously examined and measured by S.S. doctors who had to satisfy themselves that she could be suitably fertile. The Aryan blood of her ancestors, uncontaminated by Slav, Jewish or other inferior racial elements, had to be established as far back as 1750 for every woman marrying into the S.S.

Later Himmler was to set up a number of S.S. Bride Schools at which, in addition to their political education, the future wives of S.S. men were taught housewifery, the hygiene of childbirth and the principles of rearing their future children in the correct Nazi tradition.

The order, as inhuman as it was outrageous, lay at the heart of Himmler's future racial policy, and what seemed at first to be merely an absurdity to some of Himmler's own colleagues was later to become the poisonous root from which sprang the practice of compulsory euthanasia and the genocide of those he regarded as racially impure.

The significance of the S.S. Marriage Code must be understood in its proper light. It could be claimed that, in introducing eugenics and selective breeding among the restricted group of men in his charge, Himmler was anticipating a principle which civilized societies will be led to adopt in the future. He would most certainly have argued himself that this was so. But if such principles are eventually to be adopted, there must surely be every medical, psychological and social safeguard to ensure that the men and women who are bred represent in one way or another the widest capabilities and qualities latent in the human race. It is not necessarily to Himmler's discredit that he was ambitious to see the human race improved; but it was pernicious that he believed himself fit, together with a few unqualified and unscrupulous colleagues, to determine what the ideal human being should be. He had absorbed a few ill-founded theories and with the temerity of ignorance hastened to put them into immediate practice without taking any account of the cost in human suffering. Thus the men who had through various motives, either worthy and unworthy, joined the S.S. found themselves caught in a ludicrous trap, and had either to submit to Himmler's oppressive decrees or find methods of evasion which soon became common practice not only in the S.S. but in the whole of Nazi society as the oppression spread.

Himmler's ideal man was a fair-haired, blue-eyed, superhuman athlete whose values were derived from a medieval concept of relationship with the cultivation of the earth, a man who despised most developments in modern culture because he had no judgment in such matters, though like Heydrich, he might well play accepted music on the violin or read accepted books. He was a man who left all political and social judgment to his leaders, and gave them his unquestioning obedience. Though he might well be in private a kindly husband and an indulgent father, he was essentially a destructive man, ready to act on the vilest or most stupid orders that only served to show the prejudice and cruelty of his commanders. This image of the ideal man, primitive in his outlook and brutal in his behaviour, was the result of the racial intolerance of Rosenberg, Darré and Himmler, whose collective vision was blinded by the same false idea of past glories which bore no relation whatever to historic truth, to the needs of modern society, or to any future social order which might be called civilized.

It was in June of the year when Darré and Himmler were concocting their marriage code that a man arrived to help them who had all the appearance of a young Messiah. Himmler was approached by one of his staff, the Freiherr von Eberstein, with a request that he interview a young man who had recently joined the S.S. in Hamburg. His name was Reinhard Heydrich; he was of good family and had until recently been a lieutenant in the Navy. Heydrich was a godson of Eberstein's mother. Himmler agreed, then fell ill and cancelled the appointment. Heydrich took no notice of the cancellation and travelled overnight south to Munich, relying on Eberstein to arrange for him to see Himmler, who had returned to his poultry farm to recover from his sickness. Himmler agreed over the telephone that, since Heydrich had come to Munich, he should visit him in Waldtrudering.

The first meeting between these two men, whose strange relationship was to constitute the direst threat to the well-being of Europe that resulted from conquest by Hitler, took place on 4 June 1931. Himmler understood that Heydrich had been a naval Intelligence officer, and he had a particular, important task in mind which he felt might be carried out by a man with this kind of background and training. He wanted to establish an Intelligence or security service of his own within the S.S. to conduct secret research into those members of the Party, particularly among the leaders of the S.A., whose ambitions seemed hostile to his own, or whose presence degraded the ideals of the Party as he conceived them.

The young man who came down to Waldtrudering was of impressive appearance. He was tall and blond, blue-eyed and Nordic, with a model physique that corresponded exactly to Himmler's conception of what an S.S. man should be. His eyes, in fact, were of a peculiar lightness, piercing and hypnotic. Although there was some mistake in his records (he had been a code and signals officer in naval Intelligence, not an Intelligence officer), his handsome bearing and assurance of manner made an immediate impression on Himmler, whose diffidence of nature always made him nervous when he had to deal with men of a capacity greater than his own. In order to assert himself, Himmler set Heydrich a written test, like a schoolmaster sizing up an over-bright pupil; first he described to him the kind of Intelligence service he had in mind, and then invited Heydrich to outline on paper how he would set about organizing it. He gave him twenty minutes to complete the project, and Heydrich seized this chance to impress still further a man whose limitation of character he could already sense. Himmler read the paper and offered him a post on his personal staff as head of an entirely new department in the S.S., the *Sicherheitsdienst* (S.D.) or Security Service.

During the next ten years Heydrich was to create a network of power which was eventually to threaten not only his master but every other member of the Nazi leadership, including Hitler himself. This cold and brutally handsome man, three and a half years younger than Himmler, was the son of a distinguished teacher of music, who had once been a performer in opera and came, like Himmler's mother, from a musical family. Heydrich's second name was Tristan, and he had begun his own musical studies at an early age. He became an outstanding violinist, but his musical talents did not prevent him undergoing the strict training given to schoolboys at the school in Halle, where the family lived. He was brilliant at school, and it seemed that he could have succeeded equally well in an academic or musical career. He was also a skilled athlete and a notable fencer. His mother, who was a strict Catholic, brought her son up in the Catholic faith; scepticism, however, seems to have developed fairly early in his cold and cruelly intelligent nature, and the traditional faith of his family in German nationalism led him at the age of sixteen to join the nationalist Free Corps movement that spread throughout Germany after the First World War. He decided to abandon a career in music and train to become an officer in the Navy.

His character was already well developed. He was alert, filled with a nervous energy, restless, hard-working, strong-willed and intolerant. His lean face was hard and ruthless, and he had grown over six feet tall. As a naval cadet he soon mastered the technicalities of navigation and he charmed the wife of Commander Canaris, the First Officer of the training cruiser on which he was stationed, by playing to her on the violin. He was invited by Frau Canaris to form a quartet for the performance of chamber music. Meanwhile, his energetic mind turned to the study of languages, and he rapidly gained a fair knowledge of English, French and Russian. He also began to develop his lifelong taste for philandering. In 1926 he was promoted lieutenant, and in 1928, at his own request, he was made a signals and radio officer stationed at Kiel. Here one night at a ball held just before Christmas in 1930 he met a beautiful girl of nineteen, Lina Mathilde von Osten, who was as blonde as himself. Within three days they had become engaged, in spite of the fact that a scandal arose because another blonde girl, the daughter of a prominent industrialist, claimed he was in love with her and she with him. The industrialist, who, unfortunately for Heydrich, was a friend of the Grand Admiral Raeder, used his influence to have Heydrich dismissed the service when he refused to break his official engagement and marry the other girl. He was required to resign his commission in April 1931, and his fiancée insisted on maintaining her engagement to him in spite of the opposition of her parents now that he was disgraced.[4]

Heydrich took his dismissal very badly. He wept, the only time he ever did so in Lina's presence. He could think of no future for himself outside the services. But Lina von Osten had other ideas. She was a passionate Nazi, whose conversion had started when at the age of sixteen she had first heard Hitler speak at a meeting in Kiel. She knew all about the S.S., and believed that in this movement there should be a place for so talented and handsome an officer as her unemployed lover. He responded to her enthusiasm and joined the Party, and it was her resolution that eventually persuaded him to make the contact with Eberstein that led to his visit to Himmler in June.[5]

Himmler, though in many respects a weak man, was nevertheless astute and calculating. Throughout his career as head of the S.S. he surrounded himself with men who in one way or another compensated for whatever was lacking in his own nature, while at the same time ensuring that they remained his servants. He used their strength, their brutality, or their intelligence to fulfil his purpose for him in whatever portion of his total plan it suited him to place them. Since, unlike Göring or Goebbels, he preferred to hover in the background out of the public eye, except on those formal occasions when it was necessary for him to be seen alongside the other leaders, he was not averse to letting his subordinates act as his agents while he kept out of sight, the spider silently operating at the centre of his web. But in Heydrich Himmler met a man who became his match. Heydrich was quick to realize the intentions of the Reichsführer S.S. and to exploit them for his own purposes, while carefully posing in his presence and that of others as a dutiful subordinate. Yet a kind of dubious, mutual respect existed between the two men which amounted in Himmler's case to a form of affection; they shared the same negative ideals, though in nature and temperament they could not have been more diverse. For the next ten years, however, they were to be bound together, each man the other's evil genius, until Heydrich's assassination in 1942 suddenly removed him at a time when, in the estimation of many who knew him well, he was preparing to supersede Himmler and even outbid Hitler for power during this final period, for the Führer's leadership was undermined by his own obsessions and threatened by the intrigues of his subordinates.

In June 1931, at the age of twenty-seven, Heydrich gladly accepted this minor post in the S.S. in which an increasing number of men of officer rank and even of aristocratic background were enlisting. He took up his duties in Munich officially on 10 August, and by Christmas had been promoted to the rank of a major in the S.S. At the same time, on 26 December, he married his resolute fiancée Lina von Osten, who was then only twenty years old. Major Heydrich's salary was RM 180 a month, or about £15,[6] and from the start he began the patient and methodical compilation of secret information on the private lives of men and women inside and, when it was likely to prove useful, outside the Party as well. By the end of the year he had assembled a small staff of helpers, and in 1932 (during a period of which, April to July, the S.A. and S.S. organizations were, officially at least, disbanded by the German government), Himmler used Heydrich's skill and experience to help him reorganize the whole movement. In the summer Heydrich was promoted a colonel and given the title of Chief of the *Sicherheitsdienst*, but by then his influence was spread throughout the service, and he founded for Himmler an S.S. *Junkerschule*,[7] an *élite* leadership school at Bad-Toelz in Upper Bavaria.

By now the S.S. was a substantial force. Although the original 280 men whom Himmler found under him in January 1929 had increased by January 1931 to only 400 enlisted members, supplemented by some 1,500 part-time recruits, there were by the time the Brüning government disbanded the S.A. and the S.S. in April 1932 as many as 30,000 S.S. men. The organization, however, still remained nominally a part of the S.A.

With the rapid growth of the S.S., a more comprehensive form of para-military organization had to be devised. In this Himmler sought the advice of Heydrich who, in addition to his organization of the S.D., became in effect Himmler's Chief of Staff in the development of the S.S. as a whole, which was spread in units throughout Germany. Officers in certain centres such as Berlin, where Daluege controlled the S.S., acted with complete independence, and paid little or no attention to headquarters in Munich. The S.S. was now subjected to specialist departments for administration, training and discipline; among them was Heydrich's unit which, while claiming to be the intelligence section, was in fact a highly organized spy-ring with an increasing network of carefully graded agents and informers. A filing system was devised so that every useful detail about the public and private lives of every individual working for or against the Party, whether he was inside or outside it, was recorded, more especially if the information was of such a nature that it could at any time in the future be extracted and used as a weapon against him. The ultimate strength of Himmler and Heydrich came very much to depend on the fear the existence of these files generated once it became known that they were the closely-guarded possession of the S.D. Heydrich modelled his department on what he regarded as the British spy system, which he held to be the most efficient in the world.

The year 1932 was a period of difficulty and dissension for the

Party. Hitler's instinctive sense of caution and self-protection led him to counterbalance the growing powers of his subordinates by creating for them overlapping functions, so that they expended their excess energies in the exercise of mutual distrust, and were to a considerable extent neutralized through their own intrigue. He encouraged the development of the S.S. not only because it provided the movement with a superior, class-conscious force that encouraged former officers and men of the upper class to join its ranks, but also because the rapid increase of its numbers helped to counterbalance the unruly private army of the S.A. This numbered by 1930 some 100,000 men, drawn mostly from the unemployed, and it was giving Hitler considerable trouble at the very time when he needed the support of the right-wing politicians and industrialists.

The 'left' and 'right' wings of the Party were in a state of open dissension, and in September 1930, the month of the elections in which the Party hoped to win many more seats in the Reichstag, the S.A. went so far as to storm the Party offices in Berlin so as to give an open demonstration of their anger when Otto Strasser, the man they regarded as their champion, was dismissed from the Party. He and Stennes were embarrassing Hitler's attempts to win support from the Right. Only firm action by Hitler had stopped a catastrophe: to placate these unruly men he made himself Commander of the S.A. Exploiting the crisis of the unemployed, the Nazis won a substantial victory at the polls which entitled them to 107 seats in the Reichstag. It was then, in January 1931, that Hitler called on his old supporter Roehm, who had been working as a military instructor in Bolivia, to return to Germany and become Chief of Staff of the S.A. This appointment introduced a new, intrusive figure into the private world of Himmler and Heydrich. Roehm, a professional soldier, able and ambitious, imposed a new discipline on the S.A., of which the S.S. remained a part, while at the same time he entered into the round of political intrigue of which Göring was the principal agent and Goebbels the propagandist. The fact that Roehm was a notorious homosexual was to prove invaluable for Heydrich's files, but in the meantime it became obvious that Himmler's position in the Party and his relationship to Hitler and the other leaders must be more clearly worked out.[8]

Himmler never became a member of Hitler's more intimate social circle, certainly never in the sense that Goebbels or Göring rivalled each other in entertaining the leader, taking meals with him or accompanying him as confidential adviser on his missions. Hitler never stayed at Himmler's house in Gmund, though he made occasional brief visits. Himmler, hiding his ambitions under a kind of obsequious devotion to service, accepted a lower level of influence during this crucial period in Hitler's formidable onslaught on the succession of weak and crumbling governments in the Reichstag. It is true that he had become a Party deputy in the Reichstag in 1930,[9] but unlike Göring or Goebbels, he took no prominent part in the acrimonious and violent exchanges which Göring largely engineered in order to bring discredit to the Reichstag as a machine of government. His part in the Reichstag was that of the supporter of policies determined by others, and a revealing glimpse of him has been recorded on the day when Göring, as President of the Reichstag, outmanoeuvred von Papen's government and secured the dissolution of the Chamber. It was Himmler, resplendent in his black uniform, his pince-nez secure, who hurried from the Reichstag during the recess to fetch Hitler to a conference at Göring's presidential palace. He beamed, he clicked his heels, he Heil-Hitlered, and he urged the Führer to hurry as they had Papen at a disadvantage.[10]

A tenuous, but none the less important, link between Himmler and the Führer at this time lay in the financier Wilhelm Keppler, described by Papen at the Nuremberg Trial as 'a man who was always in Hitler's entourage'. By 1932 Keppler had become one of Hitler's closest economic advisers; he had been introduced to Hitler by Himmler, and his gratitude expressed itself later in his financial patronage of Himmler's racial researches.[11] Keppler became one of the principal men responsible for maintaining relations between the Party and a widening circle of industrialists, and it was through him that the notorious meeting between Hitler and Papen took place at the house of the banker Kurt von Schroeder in Cologne, on 4 January 1933, when certain plans to bring down Schleicher's government were discussed which were to result in Hitler becoming Chancellor at the end of the month. Himmler was a shadowy supporter on the occasion of this meeting, and later assisted in promoting the next stage of the negotiations through a newcomer to the political stage, Joachim von Ribbentrop, at whose villa in Dahlem the uneasy conferences were continued between Hitler and Papen with Keppler and Himmler still present.

Roehm, meanwhile, was taking an arbitrary line with the S.S. in Berlin, which under Daluege still managed to remain independent

Himmler's father, Gebhard Himmler

Himmler as a schoolboy in Munich (second row from the front, second from the right)

of Himmler in Munich. Roehm appointed his own director of training for the S.S. in his area, Friedrich Krueger, but on public occasions Roehm and Himmler appeared together in apparent harmony. Himmler was in no position to press openly for power; he was forced to play the part of the subordinate, while at the same time he studied the opportunities which the work of Heydrich and his S.D. agents were so diligently compiling. He was well satisfied with the rapid growth of the S.S. directly under his control, and with the carefully planned organization and training which had been achieved.

A description of the S.S. formations during the period 1933–4 was given before the International Military Tribunal at Nuremberg by von Eberstein, the man who had introduced Heydrich to Himmler; Eberstein was an ex-officer and civil servant who had joined the S.S. in 1928 and was typical of its aristocratic leanings. 'Before 1933', he said at Nuremberg, 'a great number of aristocrats and members of German princely houses joined the S.S.'[12] He mentioned, for example, the Prince von Waldeck, and the Prince von Mecklenburg, and after 1932, the Prince Lippe-Biesterfeld, General Graf von Schulenburg, Archbishop Groeber of Freiburg, the Archbishop of Brunswick and the Prince of Hohenzollern-Sigmaringen. When Himmler took over in 1929, there had been, according to Eberstein, only about fifty S.S. men in the district of Thuringia, where he was acting for the S.S. in Weimar, but after the seizure of power he had charge of some 15,000 S.S. men in the area covering Saxony and Thuringia. The elegant S.S. uniform attracted recruits and added to their social prestige. As Eberstein said at Nuremberg:

'The increase can be explained first by the fact that the National Socialist government had come to power, and a large number of people wanted to show their loyalty to the new State. Secondly, after the Party in May 1933 ordered that no more members should be taken, many wanted to become members of the semi-military formations such as the S.S. and S.A., and through them to become members of the Party later. But then again there were also others who sought the pleasures of sport and the comradeship of young men and were less politically interested . . . From about February or March 1934, Himmler ordered an investigation of all those S.S. members who had joined in 1933, a thorough re-investigation which lasted until 1935, and at that time about fifty to sixty thousand members throughout the entire Reich were

released from the S.S. . . . The selection standards required a
certificate of good conduct from the police. It was required that
people be able to prove that they led a decent life and performed
their duty in their profession. No unemployed persons or people
who were unwilling to work were accepted.'

For Heydrich, the S.S. already represented the nucleus of a secret
police once the Party came to power. As Reitlinger has pointed out,
an official political police already existed in both Berlin and Munich,
and when the great police purge came after 30 January many men
in this secret service remained to serve the Nazis; among them for
example was Heinrich Mueller, who later became head of the
Gestapo before he had in fact become a Party member. Affidavits
read at the Nuremberg Trial make it clear that the S.D. was well
prepared with its screenings of the members of the Political Police
in Munich, which was known as Department VI of the Police
Organization. Most of them were immediately absorbed into the
service of Himmler when he was appointed President of Police in
Munich by Hitler, a very minor office compared with that given to
Göring who, in addition to his Cabinet rank and Presidency of the
Reichstag, became also Minister of the Interior for the state of
Prussia. This appointment gave Göring charge of the police in
what was by far the largest and most influential state administration
in Germany. Göring immediately used his authority to place the
Berlin S.S. leader, Kurt Daluege, at the head of the Prussian police,
and appointed Rudolf Diels, a police official married to his cousin,
Ilse Göring, as head of the section of political police that he created,
the Berlin Police Bureau 1A, which was later to be renamed the
Gestapo. Daluege at this stage was wholly under the influence of
Göring and refused even to receive Heydrich, who went to Berlin
to see him on Himmler's behalf on 15 March. Daluege, young, bland
and opportunist without either intelligence or conscience, had
reached the rank of an S.S. general by the age of twenty-nine. Before
joining the S.S., he had been in charge of refuse disposal for the City
Engineer. Now he had to use his wits to steer his way through the
conflicting currents of his superiors' struggle for power.[13]

In the months immediately following Hitler's Chancellorship, it
was Göring, not Himmler, who was the principal activator of police
control. He poured his prodigious energy into the defeat of the
remnants of democracy in Germany and into the rout of the Com-

munists, the Party's chosen enemy in the Reichstag and in the streets. Speed was what mattered, and the use of violence and terror to break up the forces of resistance before they could realize what was happening and oppose this sudden, savage onslaught by rallying themselves to out-vote Hitler in the elections due on 5 March. Within a week the Prussian Parliament was dissolved; within a month unreliable police chiefs and civil servants alike were dismissed and replaced, and the police, both new and old, were armed; 'a bullet fired from the barrel of a police pistol is my bullet', cried Göring. To stop disorders, either real or imagined, Göring commandeered 25,000 men from the S.A. and 10,000 from the S.S. and armed them to supplement the activities of the police; the Communist leaders were arrested and their party virtually put out of action before the elections could be fought. In February, the night of the Reichstag fire, both Hitler and Göring declared that a Communist *putsch* had been imminent and that the fire was a beacon from heaven with which to blaze the trail of the Communist traitors. On 28 February the clauses of the constitution guaranteeing civil liberties were suspended, and anyone could be placed without trial under 'protective custody'. At the polls the Nazis secured only a bare majority along with their allies the Nationalists, but with the Reichstag stripped of its Communist deputies Hitler was able to put through an Enabling Bill on 23 March which gave him power to govern by means of emergency decrees.

Action of this order was scarcely in Himmler's nature. When it was decided that the Catholic Conservative government in Munich should be removed, it was the S.A. under the Ritter von Epp, the friend of Roehm, who dismissed them on 8 March. Himmler, the Bavarian President of Police, was by-passed. In the same month, Göring set up his first concentration camps in Prussia under the supervision of Diels, and in April segregated his political police in their own headquarters in the Prinz Albrechtstrasse in Berlin. In January they became known officially as the *Geheime Staatspolizei*, the Secret State Police, or Gestapo for short. This was a first significant move towards centralization in the police control of the state, and it was a warning to Himmler, whose autonomy still lay only in Bavaria.

Between April 1933 and April of the following year, Himmler took his own devious but independent line of action. Heydrich had become head of the Bavarian secret police and of the S.S. Security

Office. Himmler established his own model concentration camp at Dachau, parallel with those created by Göring and others which were set up elsewhere, both semi-officially and unofficially by the S.S., the S.A. and the Nazi Gauleiters, who had been hurried into office in the various *Gaue*, or regions, into which Germany was divided for Nazi administration. At Nuremberg Göring claimed that he closed those unauthorized camps that came to his notice and where, he gathered, brutalities were practised. A camp founded by the S.S. near Osnabrück led to active friction between Himmler and Göring, whose investigators, led by Diels, claimed they were fired upon by the S.S. guards when they were sent to find out what was happening. Himmler was forced to close the camp on direct orders from Hitler. Göring's intervention was largely dictated by his desire at this time to become the co-ordinator of police activities throughout Germany. That he failed was due to the persistent ambition of Himmler to improve his personal position and the desire of Roehm to merge the large forces of the S.A. into those of the regular army with himself as Supreme Commander, a situation which neither Göring nor Hitler would tolerate.

To control his camp at Dachau, Himmler established a volunteer formation of S.S. men willing to undertake long-term service as camp guards. This central formation was called the Death's Head (*Totenkopf*) unit and granted the special insignia of the skull and crossbones; the officer put in command of this and other Death's Head units was Theodor Eicke, a former Army officer and veteran of the First World War, who was one of Himmler's most trusted adherents on racial matters. One of Eicke's guards at Dachau was an Austrian, Adolf Eichmann; another in 1934 was Rudolf Hoess, later to take charge of extermination of the Jews at Auschwitz.

Hoess – another man, like Goebbels and Heydrich, at one time intended for the Catholic priesthood – had been a soldier during the 1914–18 war, and later joined the Free Corps.[14] He had been involved in a brutal political murder and imprisoned for six years before becoming a Nazi after his release and joining the S.S. This extraordinary man, so dutiful and even intelligently moralizing in his attitude, wrote his memoirs in confinement after the Hitler war and explained in great detail his relations with Himmler. He had belonged to the idealistic agricultural organization called the *Artamanen*, a nationalist youth movement which was dedicated to the cultivation of the soil and the avoidance of city life. It was through this that he claims he first came to know Himmler, who, in June 1934 at an S.S. review in Stettin, invited him to join the staff in Dachau, where in December he held the rank of corporal in the Death's Head Guards.

Dachau, Himmler's experimental concentration camp, was established by an order signed by him as Police President of Munich on 21 March, and authorized by the Catholic supporter of the Nazis, Heinrich Held, the Prime Minister of Bavaria, a few days before his forcible expulsion by the S.A. The order, which appeared in the Munich *Neueste Nachrichten* on the day it was signed, read:

'On Wednesday 22 March, the first concentration camp will be opened near Dachau. It will accommodate 5,000 prisoners. Planning on such a scale, we refused to be influenced by any petty objection, since we are convinced this will reassure all those who have regard for the nation and serve their interests.

Heinrich Himmler
Acting Police President of the City of Munich'

Dachau, which was situated about twelve miles north-west of Munich, became a permanent centre of sanction by the Nazis against the German people and all those whom Hitler was later to subject. In the first unbridled period of power, the seizure of men and women for interrogation, often under torture, by the S.S. and the S.A. grew out of hand, and by Christmas 1933 Hitler found it necessary to announce an amnesty for 27,000 prisoners. No one now knows how many were in fact freed, and Himmler was later to boast that he succeeded in persuading Hitler to omit any prisoners in Dachau from the amnesty.

The order for protective custody was as brief as the order establishing Dachau; it read: 'Based on Article I of the Decree of the Reich President for the Protection of People and State of February 28 1933, you are taken into protective custody in the interest of public security and order. Reason: suspicion of activities inimical to the State.'

Göring was quite open about the reason for establishing the camps: 'We had to deal ruthlessly with these enemies of the State . . . Thus the Concentration Camps were created to which we had to send first thousands of functionaries of the Communist and Social Democratic parties.' Frick was later to define protective custody as 'a coercive measure of the Secret State Police . . . in order to counter all aspirations of enemies of the people and the State.'[15]

Göring's barbarous vigour was one aspect of Nazi cruelty; Himmler's attention to the details of brutality was another. Almost twenty years separate us from the full exposure of what happened in the concentration camps, and no documentation could be more complete, ranging from the testimony given by thousands of persecuted men and women who managed to survive, to the detailed witness of such men as Hoess and Eichmann, Himmler's agents in the most fearful record of torture, destruction and despair that human history has ever compiled in such thorough and horrifying detail. While Göring as a man was no more brutal than many other oppressors in the evolutionary struggle of modern Europe, the coldly punitive administration of sadism by Himmler challenges comprehension. Yet it is necessary to understand him, not least because there will always exist human beings who, once they are given a similar power over others and have similar convictions of superiority, may be tempted to act as he did.

Himmler had learned to live and work by regulations, and on 1 November 1933, the rules governing life and death in Dachau were completed by Eicke under Himmler's exacting direction. The legalistic phrasing, the comfortable work of men sitting at desks as Himmler so often sat, covers with a bureaucratic gloss the acts of terrorism which the careful rules incite. For example:

'The term commitment to a concentration camp is to be openly announced as "until further notice" . . . In certain cases the Reichs-führer S.S. and Chief of the German Police will order flogging in addition to detention in a concentration camp . . . In this case, too, there is no objection to spreading the rumour of this increased punishment . . . to add to the deterrent effect. Naturally, particularly suitable and reliable people are to be chosen for spreading of such news.

'The following offenders, considered as agitators will be hanged: anyone who . . . makes inciting speeches and holds meetings, forms cliques, loiters around with others; who for the purpose of supplying the propaganda of the opposition with atrocity stories, collects true or false information about the concentration camp . . .'[16]

Himmler's secret pursuit of power began outside Prussia, where he realized Göring was omnipotent. Roehm, watchful of the situation, realized that Himmler and Heydrich formed a powerful team and would not be content with the minor place in the Nazi state which had been allotted to them; he decided it might be wise not to alienate the leaders of the S.S. By the summer Göring's initial energy was spent, and his pleasure-loving nature, combined with the desire to accumulate other positions of importance under Hitler, led him to slacken his control over his subordinates, who were more directly involved in the struggle for supremacy developing between the S.A., the S.S. and the Gestapo. Daluege, Göring's Chief of Police, had by now decided to keep in touch with Munich.

Artur Nebe was the principal S.S. man among the many working in the Gestapo; Diels claims Nebe was spying on him for Heydrich, and that Karl Ernst, Roehm's Chief of Staff of the Berlin S.A., was actually threatening his life until Roehm ordered him to desist and suggested to Diels he had better join the S.S. for his own self-protection. The opportunity to do so came after an S.S. raid on Diels's flat had led to an open breach between Göring and Himmler, which they had the good sense to heal at a meeting in Berlin. Diels was placated with an honorary commission in the S.S. But this did not save him from having to escape in October from threatened arrest by the S.S. on an order, he claimed, issued by Göring himself. This happened after Göring had been shown evidence prepared by Heydrich of Diels's anti-Nazi activities before his adoption by Göring.

Whether Diels was telling the truth or not, his story is important because it reveals the gradual growth in stature of Heydrich and Himmler in the eyes of the men in Berlin. Germany consisted of many semi-autonomous states both large and small, of which Bavaria, where Hitler's Nazi faction had originated, was now second only to Prussia in importance. Himmler knew as well as Göring that Hitler wanted to unify the control of Germany, and as a reward for his supreme efficiency in Bavaria he asked the Führer to extend his powers in the remaining states of Germany. In the race to build single police-states, Göring had made a powerful initial spurt, but he lacked the staying-power to win. From October, Himmler began to gather for himself the offices of Chief of the Political Police in the remaining states of Germany, completing the process by March in the following year.[17]

This assimilation of special powers in the German states through acquiring the office of Commander of Political Police was illegal because Frick, the Nazi Minister of the Interior, was never consulted, in spite of the fact that the provincial governments were responsible to the Ministry of the Interior for their police administration. To cover his activities, Himmler always declared himself the servant of the provincial governments when, after parading the local S.S. formations in order to intimidate the officials, he assumed his new command on their behalf. Frick, in the face of Hitler's policy of the gradual centralization of power, was all but helpless to defend his own rights as Minister against these obvious encroachments by Himmler into his area of responsibility. According to the anti-Nazi Gisevius, he roused himself to forbid the states to create further offices without his direct consent, but Himmler circumvented this by forcing the finance ministers of the provincial governments to subsidize his S.S. formations and the concentration camps in their area. In one way or another, Himmler built up the network of his powers until the web spread over the whole of Germany with the exception of Göring's Prussia.

At the same time, during the autumn of 1933, Heydrich had established in Berlin, in open defiance of Göring, a section of the S.D. at premises in Eichen-Allee, and in November Gregor Strasser, who had once been Himmler's employer, made his celebrated pun in a note sent to Hans Frank: 'Hitler seems to be entirely in the hands of his Himmlers and *Anhimmlers* (adorers).' Nevertheless, it was Roehm who received official promotion to Hitler's Cabinet in December 1933, a step which so alarmed Göring that it made him carefully reconsider his future relationship with Himmler.

Gisevius, at that time still an official in the Gestapo, has described how he became involved in the intrigues between Daluege, Diels and Heydrich. In February 1934 he was invited, to use a polite term, to attend a conference at the barracks of the S.S. *Leibstandarte* in Lichterfelde along with Nebe. They went, thinking their last hour had come; to their surprise, they were greeted by Dietrich, Commandant of the *Leibstandarte*, with flattering messages from Himmler and Heydrich. Their stand against corruption in the Gestapo was specially commended, and they were invited to sit down there and then and write a report of their 'grievances', as Dietrich put it. They did so, recording many instances of 'extortion, torture and killing'. As Gisevius puts it: 'It was always a favourite S.S. tactic to appear in the guise of respectable citizens and to condemn vigorously all excesses, lies or infringements of the law. Himmler, when talking to a small group, sounded like the stoutest crusader for decency, cleanliness, and justice.' Undoubtedly Himmler believed in his mission, like a strict schoolmaster, while Heydrich went on filling his files for the final assault on the citadel of Prussia.

To emphasize the need for the co-ordination of the political police under a single authority, Heydrich made use of a report from one of his agents that a Communist plot was forming, quite unknown to Göring's Gestapo, to murder Göring. Arrests were made before either Göring or Hitler was informed, and Himmler used the plot to press the Führer to place the whole police force of Germany under the control of the S.S. After some hesitation, Hitler agreed, and with Göring's consent the Prussian Ministry of the Interior was merged with the Reich Ministry of the Interior, and its political police, including the Gestapo, placed under Himmler as the new head of the national secret police force. To soften the transfer of power, Göring as Prime Minister of Prussia remained nominally responsible, but on 10 April he addressed the assembled Gestapo in the presence of Himmler and Heydrich, explaining to them that Himmler would in future take charge of their work as his deputy. He ordered them to support Himmler in the struggle against the enemies of the State, while Himmler in his turn protested his loyalty and gratitude in an excess of delighted subservience. 'I shall forever remain loyal to you. Never will you have anything to fear from me', he declared. On 20 April 1934 Himmler formally took over the Gestapo, with Heydrich as his deputy. The links in the chain of office were now complete.

# III

# *The Élite*

During the period he was gradually increasing the range of his power and influence, Himmler had realized it was no longer either proper or practical for him to continue as a farmer. The small-holding in Waldtrudering had been sold, and he had removed his wife and family, who now included an adopted boy called Gerhard as well as his five-year-old daughter Gudrun, to Lindenfycht at Gmund at the head of the beautiful lake of Tegernsee, some twenty-five miles from Munich.[1] When he took control of the Gestapo in April 1934, he moved his official residence to Berlin and settled in a villa at Dahlem, a fashionable suburb where Ribbentrop also lived. His headquarters in Berlin were at the Prinz Albrechtstrasse, where Göring had established the Gestapo; Heydrich's headquarters were set up near-by in the Wilhelmstrasse.

Himmler's domestic life was meagre. He had no strong feeling for the woman he had married; his passionate devotion was to his work in Berlin, and this led to a gradual separation which, although it was never made formal, was none the less real.[2] Marga stayed in Gmund, and this remained to the end of Himmler's life his solidly bourgeois family home. Marga's frequent letters, no longer senti-mental as they once were, are full of domestic chatter about the weather, her husband's clothes, the losses and gains in the vegetable and fruit garden and complaints of his infrequent visits: 'We look forward to your visit . . . Don't bring along so many files and other things to read. We want a bit of your attention too.' From as early as 1931, she began to address him in her letters as '*Mein Lieber Guter*', and when he is away she seldom fails to remind him, as always, that the housekeeping money is due. Marga was undoubtedly a good and frugal housewife, scraping the last penny of value out of the money her husband gave her, but her husband's long absences hardened her. Her social station in life did not rise with his, since she could not come to town and share it with him. As early as October 1931 she writes naïvely about the good news for the Nazis, adding, 'How I'd like to be present at all these great events.' But Himmler kept her as firmly as possible in the background. She was, nevertheless, very conscious of being the Herr Reichsführer's wife, and dealt with the local tradespeople on those terms, driving as hard a bargain as she could in the process. They much preferred to deal with Himmler, who, when they encountered him during one of his visits, seemed to them far more human and less socially pretentious. He loved his daughter Gudrun, and it was to see her rather than Marga that he came to Gmund.

Marga had two sisters, Lydia and Bertha; Bertha on 19 April 1936 received an official letter from her brother-in-law which began:

> 'I am told that you've been in our office again making tactless and bloody silly (*saudumne*) remarks. I herewith forbid you (i) to enter my office; (ii) to telephone anyone in my office except myself or S.S. Brigadeführer Wolff . . . Henceforth you are to refrain from any remarks about S.S. matters and personalities. All departmental chiefs have been acquainted with this letter. Heil Hitler!'

He accused Bertha of making adverse remarks about Heydrich and saying that when he, Himmler, was absent from Berlin she had to run the office for him.

Himmler's relations with his parents during their final years were friendly and correct. He set his father the task of research into the family ancestry, and a letter about this, sent by the old man from Munich in February 1935, begins: 'My dear Heinrich, this time your father does not come to you with a request but to give you something', while his mother scribbles a postscript saying how proud she feels to see her son's name and picture so often in the papers. But, she adds, he should not work too hard; he must look after himself, and come and see them soon in Munich.

Himmler called to see his parents whenever he could and sent them for drives in his official car, carefully noting that the cost of the fuel should be deducted from his salary.

Himmler's removal to Berlin preceded by barely a month Hitler's sudden and savage assault on Roehm and his associates at the head of the S.A. We know that the decision to undertake this purge was not taken lightly, for Roehm, in spite of his threatening ambitions and his moral corruption, was a man towards whom Hitler still felt loyalty and even friendship. It is possible that he was afraid of him. At this early stage in his career as dictator he disliked taking any violent, widespread and public action which might lead to consequences he could not wholly foresee and which he feared he might be unable to control. But Himmler and Göring were determined to be rid of Roehm and break the influence of the S.A., and they joined together in the common cause to persuade Hitler that the commander of the S.A. and his dissatisfied forces were planning a *coup d'état.*

Roehm had made difficulties for himself by using the place he had won in Hitler's Cabinet to urge that the S.A. (which now numbered 3 million men) and the regular Army should be merged under a single command that he clearly wanted to assume himself. Hitler, who had his own eye fixed on Hindenburg's Presidency now that the old man was within a few months of his death, had struck a secret bargain with the High Command of the Army and Navy, agreeing that he would disband the S.A. if they would acquiesce to his becoming President. The S.A., in fact, was no longer of use to him, and its unruly presence in the state was a constant embarrassment now that the campaigns in the streets were won and the sureties of power lay in gaining final control of the armed forces themselves. He had in any case promised Sir John Simon and Anthony Eden, when they had visited Germany on 21 February as Ministers of State, that he would demobilize two-thirds of the S.A. and permit an Allied inspection of the rest.

Heydrich's files were gutted for evidence that would blacken Roehm and the commanders of the S.A. in the eyes of Hitler, and prove they were conspiring with other acknowledged dissidents, such as the subtle and devious Schleicher, whom Hitler had displaced as Chancellor, and Gregor Strasser, who had in 1932 attempted to draw a radical section of the Nazi party away from Hitler's authority and was now living in retirement. According to an affidavit made by Frick, Hitler's Minister of the Interior, and filed at the time of the Nuremberg Trial, it was Himmler rather than Göring who finally determined Hitler to take action.[3]

Himmler had spent the first weeks of the new phase in his command touring the principal centres where his S.S. detachments were stationed and addressing them on the subject of loyalty to the Führer. In Berlin, Heydrich was preparing for Göring the lists of those members of the S.A. who should be seized. On 6 June, Heydrich's S.D. was proclaimed by Hitler the official Intelligence office of the Party, from whom no information they required should be withheld. S.A. leaders in Berlin and the south were kept under constant watch.

The pace of events that led to the bloody climax of 30 June began to quicken. Hitler ordered Roehm to give all his storm-troopers a month's leave from July 1st, and Roehm himself, with Hitler's agreement, went on a nominal sick-leave to Bavaria on 7 June. He maintained a formal contact with Hitler, who even promised to visit him for further discussions on 30 June. After a conference with Hitler in Berlin on 20 June, Himmler claimed he was shot at while driving in his car to the interment of the body of Carin, Göring's first wife, in the mausoleum Göring had built at his great country estate of Carinhall, named after her.[4]

At the Nuremberg Trial, Eberstein described how 'about eight days before 30 June' he was summoned and told that Roehm was planning a *coup d'état*. Himmler ordered him to hold his S.S. men 'in a state of quiet readiness' in their barracks. Eberstein also gave an account of how the local executions were conducted under orders from Heydrich:

'In the course of that day, 30 June, a certain S.S. Colonel Beutel came to me from the S.S. with a special order which he had received from Heydrich. He was a young man, this Beutel, and he did not know what he should do; he came to obtain advice from me, an older man. He had an order in which there were approximately twenty-eight names and a postscript, from which it appeared that some of these men were to be arrested and others were to be executed. This document had no signature on it and therefore I advised this S.S. Colonel to get positive clarification as to what should take place, and warned him emphatically against any rash action.

'Then, as far as I know, a courier was sent to Berlin and brought back eight orders of execution which came from Heydrich. The order read somewhat as follows: "By order of the Führer and Reich Chancellor . . ." then followed the name of the person concerned, "so-and-so is condemned to death by shooting for high treason".

'These documents were signed by Heydrich . . . On the basis of these documents eight members of the S.A. and the Party too

were shot by the political police of Saxony in Dresden . . . That's
what I know about it, at least in my area.'[5]

Himmler during the period immediately preceding the purge kept
in touch with the War Office, and in particular with Walter von
Reichenau, a general in Army Administration who was prepared to
work with the Nazis.

Between 21 and 29 June, Hitler toured restlessly from place to
place on a variety of official duties, while in Berlin Himmler held
a conference of the S.S. High Command on 24 June, while the Army
was put on an alert on 25 June. On the same day Heydrich began,
with the help of a few chosen officers of the S.D., to prepare the final
lists of marked men both in the S.A. and outside it. In the middle
of the wedding-feast of Gauleiter Terboven of Essen, for whom
both Hitler and Göring acted as witnesses, Himmler arrived from
Berlin with urgent news that action must be taken with as little delay
as possible. This was no doubt part of Göring's and Himmler's
scheme to keep Hitler in a state of alarm; after further conference,
they left Hitler and returned to Berlin to carry out the final preparations for the purge.

Hitler was finally goaded into action during the small hours of
30 June, when he flew to Munich before dawn and drove by car to
the sanitorium at the Tegernsee, where he roused Roehm from sleep,
accused him of treachery and had him arrested. Himmler's special
detachment of guards commanded by Sepp Dietrich, the *Leibstandarte*, whose duty it was to protect Hitler, had been sent south
to give all necessary aid, but Hitler, unable or unwilling to face the
summary executions that were due to follow, retired to the Brown
House, the Party headquarters in Munich. Confusion followed, for
Hans Frank, the Bavarian Minister of Justice, was unwilling to
execute men in the mass without trial merely because their names
were on a typed list provided by Göring and Himmler and under-
lined in pencil by Hitler. Roehm himself was not finally shot until
2 July.

In Berlin, Göring and Himmler had neither time nor desire to
observe the formalities of justice. They had their lists, they had
their prisoners, and the executioners, squads of Göring's private
police, stood waiting to shoot their victims at Gross-Lichterfelde.
The scene in Göring's private residence at Leipzigerplatz, where he
and Himmler identified the prisoners as they were brought in,

accused them of treason and summarily ordered them to be shot as soon as their names had been ticked on the lists, has been described by eye-witnesses – in particular by Papen who, as Hitler's Vice-Chancellor, Göring thought it wise to protect. He sent his adjutant, Bodenschatz, to bring him to the Leipzigerplatz, where he could be placed under guard. As soon as Papen arrived, Himmler gave the signal by telephone that the Vice-Chancellery could be raided. Bose, Papen's press counsellor, was shot and his personal staff arrested. When Papen was finally given permission to leave, he found his office occupied by S.S. men and a state of violent confusion existing between them and Göring's own police. Finally Papen was put under house arrest with an S.S. guard, whose captain said he was responsible to Göring for the Vice-Chancellor's safety. Without doubt Himmler and Heydrich, new to the exercise of such absolute power, would have had him shot. Göring was more diplomatic.[6]

The orgy of killing that spread throughout Germany during the weekend started from Göring's headquarters. When they learned that Hitler accompanied by Goebbels was flying to Berlin from Munich, Göring and Himmler gathered their typed sheets together and drove with Frick to the Tempelhof airport to deliver an account of their stewardship. The sky was blood-red as the plane landed, and Hitler, sleepless for forty-eight hours, silently shook hands with the men, who clicked their heels as he greeted them, and then inspected a guard of honour lined up on the tarmac. The scene, unforgettably described by Gisevius who was present, had its own Wagnerian melodrama. Himmler, obsequious but officious, pressed his list of names under Hitler's bloodshot eyes. While the others stood around at a discreet distance, the Führer ran his finger down the record of the dead or those about to die, while Göring and Himmler whispered to him. Then, with Hitler in the lead, the executioners moved off to the waiting cars, moving silently like a funeral procession in order of precedence.

Goebbels hastened to suppress reports of the mounting deaths in the German press, which was by now under his complete control. Only representatives of the foreign press, who had been hastily convened earlier that afternoon by Göring, were given a bare outline of Roehm's alleged conspiracy by the man who had invented it. The assassinations did not stop until the following day, which was Sunday, when Frick, unburdening himself to Gisevius, finally expressed his horror at the behaviour of Himmler and Göring. He then went to warn Hitler, who had by now had some sleep, that the S.S. might well offer an even more sinister threat to his security than the S.A. But the Führer only wanted to relax at a tea-party he was giving in the garden of the Chancellery.

For Himmler and Heydrich, the provincials from the south, the massacre of 30 June was a rapid initiation into the ways of Hitler's court. Heydrich was created a lieutenant-general of the S.S. with effect from the date the men he had listed had begun to face the firing-squad. Göring received the personal congratulations of Hindenburg, sent from his deathbed. On 26 July the S.S. was formally given its independence by Hitler. When Hindenburg eventually died on 2 August, Hitler merged the offices of President and Chancellor and made himself *Der Führer*, Supreme Head of the State, and also Commander-in-Chief of the Armed Forces of the Reich. The Army was immediately required to take the oath of allegiance to Hitler in person.

On the day before Hitler's proclamation of the independence of the S.S., their associates in Vienna murdered the Austrian Federal Chancellor, Dr Dollfuss, as part of an abortive attempt to seize Vienna for the Austrian Nazis. Hitler at once disowned any part in this plot that had failed, not because he disapproved of what had been attempted but because it had been both ill-timed and unsuccessful. As would be expected, there is no exact record that either Himmler or Heydrich were directly involved in the instructions given to the S.S. in Austria. It must at least have shaken Hitler's confidence in the discretion of his S.S. commanders. Although they remained strictly silent at this stage, when Hitler chose to dissociate himself from the assassination, they were at a later and more favourable time after the *Anschluss* to hear the Austrian S.S. men who died during the course of the *putsch* proclaimed as martyrs by Rudolf Hess. In July 1934, however, when Hitler was still involved in the aftermath of the Roehm purge, this bloody act by his adherents in Austria compromised still further the heroic reputation he was attempting to build up in the world outside Germany. It is not known whether he reprimanded the men he had so recently promoted into the select ranks of the Nazi leadership, but at the very least, Himmler must have carried some responsibility for the indiscreet murder of the Chancellor, since the Austrian S.S. obtained their arms from the S.S. in Germany. Among the men arrested in Austria was Ernst Kaltenbrunner, a lawyer whom Heydrich had employed as

Himmler as a senior schoolboy at Landshut (front row, second from the right)

Landshut: the town where Himmler spent much of his youth. Himmler's house is shown prominently at centre right

The apartment in Amalienstrasse where Himmler lived from 1904 to 1913

his agent. After Heydrich's assassination in 1942, Kaltenbrunner was to take over the responsibilities Heydrich had exercised in Berlin.

Now that the S.S. was an entirely independent force, responsible through Himmler only to Hitler himself, Himmler became absorbed in consolidating its membership and carrying still further his growing obsession with their racial purity and their loyalty to his idea of establishing them as a special Order in the Party and the State. His concern was more for the quality of the S.S. than for their numbers. As we have seen, he had already begun, before 30 June, to remove those men who had been too hurriedly recruited after the seizure of power and who failed to pass his stringent tests. According to Eberstein at Nuremberg, during the period 1934–5 some 60,000 men were released from the S.S. Nevertheless, the S.S. was kept at a strength in the region of 200,000 men and represented a formidable force which made the Army, already divided in its attitude to Hitler, increasingly anxious. But Himmler's natural caution always made him wary of stirring up trouble. He preferred to work in secret, though he was always prepared to make public statements about the high standards he exacted from the S.S. and its undying dedication to Hitler.

From 1934 the S.S. was forbidden to take part in any troop manoeuvres with the Army, although some of its members were Army reservists, nor did its members openly receive a specifically military training. Nevertheless they were armed with small-calibre rifles and were trained to shoot. They were now vigorously selected for their Nordic excellence. As Himmler put it, the S.S. was to be 'a National Socialist Soldier Order of Nordic Men'.

As Gisevius said when giving evidence at Nuremberg,[7] 'The members had to be so-called Nordic types . . . if I am not mistaken, the distinguishing characteristics of men and women went as far as underarm perspiration.' The moral deception involved in recruitment was, Gisevius claimed, often irreparable; men joined frequently out of an honest desire to assist a force dedicated, as it seemed, to order and decency in contrast to the degenerate hooliganism of the S.A., only to find themselves later involved in the criminal practices imposed on them by Heydrich and Himmler. Large numbers of the S.S. were part-time men who pursued their normal activities, except for special occasions and national emergencies, giving only spare time to their S.S. duties. The oath taken by every man on entering the S.S. was: 'I swear to you, Adolf Hitler, as Führer and Reich

Chancellor, loyalty and bravery. I vow to you, and to those you have named to command me, obedience unto death, so help me God.'[8]

Heydrich had in 1932 founded a leadership school at Bad-Toelz in Bavaria, a centre for training which was to be maintained, with considerable variation in its curriculum, until well into the years of the war. Heydrich was as much concerned with the intelligence as he was with the physique of the S.S. leader. Sport, gymnastics and other activities that imposed the meaning of discipline on the students were the basis of their education, together with the Nazi version of history, geography, militarism and racial consciousness.

Himmler was determined to establish a centre for the S.S. leadership which would be worthy of the racial purification they represented. Though Himmler's mind had moved far from the Catholicism in which he had been brought up, the self-dedication of the Catholic monastic orders influenced him in devising his plans for this centre. Even Hitler compared him with Ignatius Loyola. Walter Schellenberg, who had studied both medicine and law at the University of Bonn and was one of the bright young intellectuals who joined Heydrich's S.D., was later to become one of the inner circle of men who made a study of Himmler and learned how to control him. In his *Memoirs* he writes: 'The S.S. organization had been built up by Himmler on the principles of the Order of the Jesuits. The service statutes and spiritual exercises presented by Ignatius Loyola formed a pattern which Himmler assiduously tried to copy.'[9] The Jesuitical ideal in Himmler's mind merged with his medieval vision of the Teutonic knights, whose combination of religious observance and brutalized chivalry inspired him to found a similar S.S. Order of Knights in a Germanic castle of their own.

The Order of Teutonic Knights founded at the close of the twelfth century with the combined aim of conquest and conversion, had its centre in the castle of Marienburg, which became the residence of the Grand Master of the Order. The Teutonic Knights boasted alike of their valour and their statesmanship, their self-denial and their skill as administrators, and at the height of their power in the fourteenth century they stretched their conquests through Poland as far as the Baltic States. The image of the Grand Master became a part of Himmler's obsession, but his mind, incapable of largeness of thought or inspiration, could only absorb simplified concepts from past history out of which he attempted to create dogmas for the present. He began to see himself as Grand Master of a modern

Teutonic order designed to rid Nordic German society of degenerate infiltration by Jewish blood. Like the medieval Teutonic Knights, he also looked east towards that other great threat to German purity, the inferior Slav races with their evil communist doctrines. As he put it himself in 1936: 'We shall take care that never again in Germany, the heart of Europe, will the Jewish-Bolshevistic revolution of sub-humans be kindled either from within or through emissaries from without.'[10]

For inspiration he founded the new Teutonic castle of Wewelsburg in the forests near Paderborn, an ancient town in Westphalia with historic associations that went back to Charlemagne. Wewelsburg was built on the foundations of a medieval burgh; it was designed for him by an architect called Bartels and took a year to construct, at a cost of some 11 million marks.

According to Schellenberg, the castle was run like a monastery and a hierarchic order of leadership after the pattern of the Catholic Church was imposed on those members of the S.S. privileged to visit Wewelsburg for the regular retreats organized by Himmler, who was, in Jesuitical terms, General of the Order. Each member of the secret Chapter had his own chair with a silver name-plate, and 'each had to devote himself to a ritual of spiritual exercises aimed mainly at concentration', the equivalent of prayer, before discussing the higher policy of the S.S.[11]

Wewelsburg was Himmler's only indulgence in the kind of luxury with which most of the Nazi leaders were surrounded. The castle was as magnificently appointed in the medieval manner as Carinhall, Göring's vast residence north of Berlin which he was extending and reconstructing at the same time as Himmler was building Wewelsburg. The design and association of the rooms were supposed to conjure the spirit of Germany's greatness; each was named after an historic figure such as Frederick the Great, and a collection of relics of the past was assembled in the castle's museum. Himmler's own room was named after Heinrich I, Henry the Fowler, the king who a thousand years before had been the founder of the German Reich.

The S.S. leaders, whether they were intellectuals or not, had to submit to these historical charades in order to please Himmler, who gave more and more of his time to the detailed study of such useless history as his power increased. Himmler had in him the makings of a recluse, a ruthless anchorite devoted to his studies and determined to remake mankind in the particular image conjured up by his eccentric scholarship. The great tragedy of our time is that for several years he possessed the power to experiment in Europe at the cost of millions of lives.

He had become by now violently anti-Catholic and anti-Christian, substituting for the faith in which he had been reared a facile acceptance of those particular superstitions, such as astrology, that suited his Germanic prejudice.[12] The Catholic Church came under attack in *Das Schwarze Korps* (*The Black Guards*), the illustrated weekly journal of the S.S. which began publication in April 1935 with the S.S. chronicler Gunter d'Alquen acting as editor under the special direction of Heydrich.

Himmler founded at the same time an institution known as the *Ahnenerbe* (Ancestral Heritage) for research into Germanic racial origins.[13] Himmler made himself President of this Society, and its director was Professor Dr Walther Wuest, whom Himmler made an honorary captain in the S.S. The institute had a special task to link the present with the past by investigating the claims of the Nordic peoples of belonging to Indo-Germanic stock and to revive the spiritual and cultural heritage of this, the noblest race on earth. *Ahnenerbe* undertook, for example, extensive archaeological excavations of Germanic remains at Nauen and Altkristenberg, and even sent an expedition to Tibet. To pay for these researches Himmler turned once more to his friend Keppler, Hitler's economic adviser, who founded a society of industrialists called the Friends of the Reichsführer S.S. which subscribed large sums to support Himmler in this work.

The supervision of the concentration camps passed to Himmler and the S.S. after the Roehm purge. Heydrich took charge of this work and made Eicke, now a brigadier-general of the S.S., his Inspector of Camps. The Death's Head Unit, which Eicke had trained for Himmler, took charge of those camps which had been established on a permanent basis, such as Dachau, the so-called model camp in the south, Buchenwald, founded centrally near Weimar in 1937, and the northern camp of Sachsenhausen, near Berlin-Oranienburg. The base camps and their subsidiaries multiplied with the development of tyranny until their establishment reached nearly a hundred centres before the war, and afterwards extended over the whole of occupied Europe with the spread of Hitler's conquests.

The record of these camps, in which between five and six million

Jewish victims alone are estimated to have died by the end of the war, became the ultimate indictment of the Nazi system. Their continued existence over a period of twelve years makes our century, which should have been the most civilized, one of the worst in human history. A pathological fear of the camps and what was done in them to helpless people spread all over Germany and occupied Europe; even to admit knowledge of them at the time they were in operation became a lasting inhibition in the minds of most German people. Open recognition of detailed facts which were first made known at the International Military Tribunal in Nuremberg after the war and have been elaborated at subsequent trials is still avoided by the majority of people both inside and outside Germany.

The principal author of this extended act of human degradation was Himmler, who believed his task to be a necessary duty in which human feeling had no proper place. Suffering was inevitable when a mass-deterrent on this scale had to be created, and he believed the guardians in the camps were more the victims of necessity than those whom they oppressed. It would be quite wrong to think that Himmler had no conscience and no pity; but his real pity was given to the men and women of his Death's Head units who had to have this fearful burden placed upon them. It became a constant anxiety that preyed upon him and eventually destroyed his health. His feelings about this, the worst of all his tasks, he was eventually to let loose on Kersten, the man who relieved his pain and became as a result the confidant of his most secret thoughts.

During this early phase, however, Himmler took great pride in the concentration camps. In October 1935, after receiving birthday congratulations from Hitler, he conducted Hess and other distinguished guests round the show places of Dachau, where the following month a unit of the S.S. additional to the Death's Head specialists were to be housed in cheerful barracks built for them by the prisoners. This new unit shared some garrison duty with the camp guards, but their main purpose was to undergo military training. The base camps had married quarters attached to them, and even in the worst phases of the history of the camps during the war the wives and families of the S.S. guards had to accustom themselves to the experience of living near these centres of torture and death.[14]

After the Roehm purge, the para-military nature of the S.S. was soon to be developed. Hitler had to watch not only those who were critical of his régime abroad and might have been prepared to take action against him, but also the High Command of the German Army, which still had the remnants of power to depose him if the will could be turned into the deed. The period of his gradual open defiance of the Allies and of the terms imposed by them in the Treaty of Versailles was about to begin, and the pattern of training for the S.S. changed in accordance with the stages through which Hitler's successful defiance of the Allies and his subjection of the High Command were to pass. In January 1935, he regained the Saar by plebiscite; in March he announced conscription for the Army and the open establishment of an Air Force, Göring's Luftwaffe; in June Ribbentrop, then Ambassador in Britain, succeeded in bringing off the Naval Pact which permitted Germany to develop a limited naval fleet; while in December came the shady dealings over Ethiopia which were in the end to leave Mussolini free to proceed with its conquest.

Hitler decided the S.S. should provide a full division of men trained for war, and he induced the Army to accept this anomalous position by making it part of the plan for conscription. In November 1934 a lieutenant-general in the Army, Paul Hauser, was selected to take charge of this aspect of S.S. training. Hauser took over Heydrich's leadership school at Bad-Toelz and turned it into the first of a number of highly disciplined establishments for training officer cadets. According to Reitlinger, Hauser after the war regarded his S.S. school at Bad-Toelz as an ideal model for the training of NATO officers. His school represented the beginning of Himmler's Waffen S.S., the military section of the S.S. corps which was later to become an international force when the S.S. spread its recruitment among the more 'suitable' races in the conquered territories.

Himmler's relations with Hitler, with Göring, Frick, and Schacht, the banker who became Hitler's Minister of Economics in 1934, with the Army High Command, and above all, with his principal officer, Heydrich, were governed by the opportunism which controlled the actions of all the Nazis, whatever the level of the position they held in the Party or the leadership. Opportunism is the peculiar vice of politicians, and the Nazi mentality, with its complete rejection of any kind of political morality, forced the pace of the intrigues by means of which they tried to outwit each other. Hitler was quite prepared to squander the limited talents of his commandants, ministers and advisers by allowing them to undermine each other's powers while leaving him supreme as the final arbiter of what after all should be done.

Himmler's place in this strange and ugly administration was still circumscribed on the one hand by Frick, the weak but obstinate bureaucrat who was Minister of the Interior, and on the other by the High Command of the Army, who disliked the continued existence outside their control of a quarter of a million men in S.S. uniform just as they had disliked the larger, but far less well disciplined forces of Roehm. As far as the bureaucrats were concerned, now that Göring's attention was diverted from the political police in his pursuit of other interests, Himmler and Heydrich made short work of Frick and of Guertner, the Minister of Justice, both of whom sought during 1934–5 to restrain them and their agents in the S.S. and the Gestapo from seizing any person they wished and holding them in 'protective custody'. Frick even attempted to draft a law, initially limited to Prussia, giving prisoners in the camps a right of access to the courts. When this draft was put on the agenda of the Prussian Ministerial Council by Göring, Himmler was invited to attend the meeting, though he was not a member of the Council, and he saw to it that the draft was rejected. His victory over Frick was complete, when on 2 May 1935, the Prussian court of Administration accepted that the activities of the Gestapo were outside their jurisdiction.

It was not, however, until 10 February 1936 that Hitler finally decreed that the Gestapo was a special police organization with powers that extended to the whole of Germany. The following June Himmler was made Chief of the German Police in the Ministry of the Interior, so confirming by right of decree what had been the practice for a considerable period owing to the absence of any effective opposition. Frick, though technically Himmler's superior in police matters, gave up the hopeless task of attempting to interfere with him.[15]

Another open critic of Himmler was Schacht, the banker, who was a ruthless and ambitious autocrat. Having been made Minister of Economics by Hitler, he was determined to conduct his affairs in his own way, though he was eventually to be superseded by Göring. Gisevius states that he went to Schacht's residence and at his request searched it with an engineer for hidden microphones when the Minister suspected that Heydrich's agents were spying on him and

recording his sharp-tongued remarks; they found a microphone
built into the telephone. Schacht in his memoirs, *My First 76 Years*,
claims that Himmler had threatened him at the time he had accepted
office, and had even gone so far as to tell him to resign; Schacht
sent a curt message back that he would resign only when the Führer
told him to do so and that the S.S. should keep out of his way.

The strategy adopted by Himmler and Heydrich against the High
Command of the Wehrmacht was even more insidious and led up
to the notorious cases against Blomberg and Fritsch early in 1938.
Werner von Blomberg, Hitler's Minister of Defence until he was
dismissed in 1938 for marrying a prostitute without knowing of her
police record, was ostensibly an enthusiastic supporter of Hitler.
Blomberg was tall, white-haired and smooth-faced, a man with
insufficient intelligence or guile to match the cunning of those
determined to be rid of him. His effective opposition to the extensive
militarization of the S.S. when conscription was introduced by
Hitler in 1935 was sufficient to make Himmler his enemy.

Werner von Fritsch had been appointed Commander-in-Chief of
the Wehrmacht in 1934 without Blomberg's approval; indeed Fritsch
and Beck, his Chief of Staff, who was later to be closely involved
in the Army plot against Hitler's life, were rumoured to be un-co-
operative, and opposed to the introduction of conscription, though
Hitler continued to have confidence in them. The rumours were
instigated by Himmler, and Göring, who by 1935 wanted Command
of the Army for himself, was by now prepared to take any suitable
opportunity to denigrate both Blomberg and Fritsch. The atmosphere in Berlin vibrated with gossip about *putsch* and counter-*putsch*.

On 19 January 1935, Blomberg, as part of an attempt to restore
friendly relations, invited both Göring and Himmler to address the
High Command in the Kaiser Wilhelm Academy, but they used the
occasion to make it clear to the Army that a military *putsch* would be
illegal. Nevertheless Blomberg went even further in his efforts to
appease Himmler; he invited him in the following month to address
a gathering of Army officers in the Hotel Vierjahreszeiten in Hamburg. Conscription, though still unannounced, was already agreed
and Himmler took his revenge on Blomberg by announcing that the
S.S. in time of war would have to be increased in numbers to fight
the enemy inside the frontiers of Germany while the Army fought
abroad; in this event the S.S. could resist any treacherous stab in the
back on the home front such as happened in 1918. As he spoke of

the ideal men he had enlisted in the S.S., he seemed to be challenging the racial purity of the officers in his audience.

In January 1935 Blomberg had appointed Canaris as the Chief of Military Intelligence, the *Abwehr*, an office which Heydrich, who had carefully informed on Canaris's predecessor, would have liked to absorb into the S.D., though this was hardly possible at the time. Thus began the uneasy relationship between Heydrich and his old naval instructor which covered the divergent political exploitation of their two Intelligence services. An initial working agreement, known as the Ten Commandments, limited Canaris's operations to military and not political espionage. A superficially friendly social atmosphere was re-established, and Heydrich was able to relieve the tension once more by playing his violin in Canaris's family circle. But the Admiral soon grew to fear Heydrich and his ultimate influence on Hitler and was prepared to receive secret information from such men as Helldorf, the Chief of Police in Berlin, about the activities of both Himmler and Heydrich.

Himmler's interest was by now no longer limited to Germany. He thought of those Germans who lived abroad, and in 1936 came to terms with Ernst Bohle, head of the foreign organization of the Nazi Party, which was concerned with spreading Nazism among Germans outside the Reich and establishing whatever proved possible in the way of espionage by setting up agents for Heydrich's S.D. abroad. Out of this intrusion into fields which, if they belonged properly to any department, were the concern of Canaris for Military Intelligence or of the Foreign Office, arose the curious incident of the Tukhachewski plot against the Stalin régime and the forged documents which Heydrich supplied to the Soviet government.

Marshal Mikhail Tukhachewski was at this time Deputy Defence Commissar of the Soviet Union, and had been in 1926 the principal Russian signatory of the protocols which had introduced German military experts into Russia. The story, as it has been reconstructed subsequently from statements and admissions by various men involved,[16] seems to have been that Heydrich heard late in 1936 that Marshal Tukhachewski and other generals in the Russian High Command were planning a military *putsch* against Stalin. Two lines of action were possible to make use of this information; the first was to support the *putsch*, the other to see that knowledge of it reached Stalin in such a form that the largest possible number of Russian generals should be arrested and tried for treason. Canaris,

who also knew of the plot, favoured the first line until a more oppor-
tune time came to use the second; Himmler and Heydrich wanted to
exploit the second line of action immediately. Later Heydrich
claimed that Hitler authorized the forging of documents by Behrens
of the S.D. and a Russian political agent who was in the pay of the
Germans. The 'documents' which were actually used as evidence
in the subsequent secret treason trial in Moscow in 1937, bore the
forged signatures not only of the Russian generals, but of the
German officers with whom they were represented as being in touch.
These papers were sold by Heydrich to Stalin through Russian agents.
Stalin is said to have paid 3 million gold roubles for the evidence
of his generals' treason; but he marked the money, since he rightly
assumed that it would be used by the Germans to pay their agents
in Russia, and that this would enable the police to trace a number of
S.D. spies. Later it also emerged that Stalin may well have planned
the whole operation and made use of the S.D. to provide him with
the evidence he needed to convict Tukhachewski and his associates.

The final stage in the modification of Himmler's power did not
come until the summer of 1936. This was preceded by the legal
recognition of the Gestapo in a Prussian statute of 10 February in
which a clause was inserted that no judicial appeal could be instituted against any decision made by the Gestapo; its activities were
absolute. By a succession of decrees starting on 17 June, Himmler
was, as we have seen, made Chief of the German Police, an office
still separate from that of the Reichsführer S.S.[17]

Himmler celebrated his new appointment with an odd ceremonial
on 2 July at which he commemorated the thousandth anniversary
of the death of Heinrich I, the protagonist of German expansion
in the East. This took place at Quedlinburg, a town in the region
of the Harz mountains which had been founded by Heinrich.

In his speech about one of the 'greatest Germans ever', as Gunther
d'Alquen called him in a glowing description of the event, Himmler
praised the 'clever, cautious, tenacious politician' in terms he felt
also suited himself. He used the occasion to attack the influence of
the Church in German history; Heinrich, he said, had refused to
allow the Church to interfere in State affairs. According to Himmler,
this Saxon Duke known as Henry the Fowler, who became the
founder of the German state, 'never forgot that the strength of the
German people lies in the purity of their blood'.[18]

In an article published in the same year, Himmler impressed once

again on readers, whom he addressed as fellow peasants, that the
precious heritage of blood in the German race must be maintained
by force:

'I, as Reichsführer S.S., who am myself a peasant according to
ancestry, blood and being, would like to state this second fact
to you, the German peasants: the idea of blood, advocated by the
S.S. from the beginning, would be condemned if it were not etern-
ally bound to the value and the holiness of the soil.'

The S.S. themselves, he wrote, stood side by side with the German
peasant stock, and were ceaselessly vigilant to protect the noble
German blood:

'I know that there are some people in Germany who become
sick when they see these black uniforms; we understand the reason
for this and do not expect we shall be loved by all that number of
people; those who come to fear us, in any way or at any time,
must have a bad conscience toward the Führer and the nation.
For these persons we have established an organisation called the
Security Service . . . Without pity we shall wield a merciless sword
of justice . . .

'Each one of us knows he does not stand alone, but that this
tremendous force of 200,000 men, who are bound together by
oath, gives him immeasurable strength . . . We assemble and
march according to unalterable laws as a National Socialist
military order of prominently Nordic men, and as a sworn
community on our way into a far future, . . . ancestors of later
generations, and necessary for the eternal life of the Germanic
people.'

Himmler's immersion in the past did not limit his interest in the
future. He always urged his S.S. men to procreate in order to increase
the number of pure-blooded German stock in Europe. This advice
culminated in Himmler's celebrated edict published in October 1939,
in which he exhorted the S.S. to conceive children before going into
battle. He watched the S.S. birthrate most carefully, but statistics
for August 1936 which have been preserved show that the average
size for S.S. families at that time was only between one and two
children. At the same time, Himmler was determined to take care
of the mothers of illegitimate children provided both they and their
babies met the required racial standards.

In 1936 the S.S. became the sponsor of the *Lebensborn* (Fount of Life) maternity homes, in which Himmler took great pride and which, as innumerable surviving records show, he supervised personally down to the last detail. In taking responsibility for the welfare of these young Germans, the S.S. ensured that they were suitably indoctrinated from the very start of their education, and every man had to contribute to the maintenance of these homes with deductions from his pay, the main burden being borne by bachelors.[19]

Himmler was true to his own teaching. Conscious, no doubt, that many people thought his own appearance remarkably 'un-Aryan', he ordered elaborate researches to be undertaken into his ancestry. The files of memoranda on this subject still exist, and they continue well into the period of the war; the centre for this research was at Wewelsburg, from which statements supplemented by elaborate genealogical forms would arrive as each stage of the investigation back to the eighteenth century was gradually completed. Similar research was undertaken into the ancestry of Marga Himmler. As soon as Himmler's interest became known, namesakes would write to him begging to be acknowledged as kinsmen of the Reichsführer S.S.

Himmler, an addict to detail, spent time in his office poring over letters and memoranda all concerned with proving the purity of his blood and that of his family, his staff and the men under his command. The surviving documentation on all this research, which represented years of painstaking work by large numbers of genealogists and clerks, and in many cases bitter heart-searching by those unable to prove their ancestry to be free of defilement, amounted to thousands of items in the bursting files of undestroyed Nazi history. After the war had already begun, Himmler intervened personally to reprimand an S.S. man who had accepted refreshments from the father of a Jew he was escorting from a concentration camp, and in April 1940 he sent a long letter of sympathy to another S.S. man at the front who had put on paper the terrible shock he received when he had discovered he possessed Jewish blood. He wrote antedating ancestral purity by a further century:

'I can so well imagine your position and your feelings. So far as our blood is concerned, I have stipulated that the end of the Thirty Years War (1648) is to be the day to which each of us is obliged to make sure of his ancestry. Should there be some

Jewish blood after that date a man must leave the S.S. . . . In telling you all this I hope that you will understand the great sacrifice I have to impose on you . . . In your heart of hearts you still belong to us, you can still feel you are an S.S. man.'

Himmler softens the blow he so sympathetically deals by adding that if the man were to die at the front, the S.S. will look after his wife and children.

During the war Himmler formed a permanent association with a girl called Hedwig who was his personal secretary and by whom in 1942 and 1944 he had two further children, Helge, a son, and Nanette Dorothea, a daughter. Hedwig was the daughter of a regular soldier, who had been at the time of her birth in 1912 a sergeant-major in the German Army. In 1936 she was awarded the standard sports certificate, the *Deutsches Sportabzeichen*, for her achievements in swimming, running and jumping. Nevertheless, researches into her 'Aryan' ancestry were initiated and continued into the years of the war.[20]

In spite of the fact that in 1937 Himmler solemnly went through the routine of qualifying for his own S.S. sports badge, forcing his inadequate body to run and to jump until he was persuaded by his adjutants that he had reached the necessary standards, his health was far from good.[21] He had been suffering from acute headaches for some years, and his congenitally weak constitution produced stomach-cramps, the intensity of which was increased by nervous tension resulting from continued worry over his responsibilities. He feared he might be developing cancer, the disease from which his father died.[22] It was Wolff who, knowing his suspicion of orthodox treatment, persuaded him in 1934 to undergo massage, and Franz Setzkorn, a nature healer, was called in to soothe away the pain. It was not until 1939 that a man was found who was able to bring more lasting relief to the strained nerves which made Himmler's stomach twist with cramp and his head feel like a ball of fire. This was Felix Kersten, the cosmopolitan Finnish masseur whose second home before the war was in Holland. Kersten's reputation for alleviating nervous pains had enabled him to maintain a lucrative practice in Berlin, near to which he had bought a country estate in 1934 called Hartzwalde. At this stage, however, they had not met.

In the middle of January 1937 Himmler was once more invited to address officers of the Wehrmacht during a course of political instruction designed to prepare them for the war which Hitler had decided was inevitable.[23] He did not spare them the detailed explanation of his views. He began by tracing the history of the S.S. from its original formation in 1923 as shock troops to support Hitler, and its reformation in 1925 in squadrons set up in various cities to patrol meetings. But from these small beginnings, said Himmler, the noble ideal of an *élite* corps had sprung. 'I am a strong believer in the doctrine that, in the end, only good blood can achieve the greatest, most enduring things in the world', said Himmler. In recruiting his S.S. men:

> 'only good blood, Nordic blood, can be considered. I said to myself that should I succeed in selecting as many men as possible from the German people, a majority of whom possess this valued blood, and teach them military discipline and, in time, the understanding of the value of blood and the entire ideology that results from it, then it will be possible actually to create such an *élite* organization which would successfully hold its own in all cases of emergency.'

For this reason, Himmler continued, very exacting standards were set for the recruiting of the S.S., including a minimum height, 1·7 metres, and the careful examination of portrait photographs by Himmler himself, who was determined to detect 'traits of foreign blood, excessive cheek-bones'. Special burdens were placed on those selected – 'valuable personnel is never trained by means of easy service' – and in spite of the economic hardships of the time, the S.S. men were expected to provide their own uniforms. Now, in 1937, the ranks of the S.S. stood at 210,000; only one in ten of those who applied to join were accepted. When a young man of, say, eighteen years wanted to become an S.S. man, 'we ask for the political reputation of his parents, brothers and sisters, the record of his ancestry as far back as 1750 .... We ask for a record of hereditary health,' and for 'a certificate from the race commission', which was made up of S.S. leaders, anthropologists and physicians, who conducted a full examination of the candidate. If he was only eighteen, the minimum age for consideration, he spent three months as an applicant, then after taking the oath to the Führer he became a recognized candidate for the S.S., spending a year obtaining his sports diploma and a further two years of military service in the regular Army. He then returned to the S.S. and was 'with special thoroughness instructed in ideology', learning among other things about the S.S. marriage law. Then, but only then, according to Himmler, was he finally accepted into the S.S.

Himmler did not refrain from putting himself on exhibition. 'The Reichsführer of the S.S.,' he said, 'is just as much an S.S. man in the sense of the S.S. organization as the common man of the front. On this 9th of November he is being awarded the dagger, and this is the occasion when he promises to abide by the marriage law and the disciplinary laws of the S.S.'

Himmler then laid stress on the importance of good health. City life with its rush made men 'grow pale and fat . . . which is never good for the State. If we desire to remain young we have to be sportsmen.' He went on to describe how he expected men to practise in using both left and right hands equally in learning to fire pistols and rifles, or in putting the shot; everyone from eighteen to fifty years of age must train to keep fit.

Ideological training went along with physical training. 'Weekly periods of instruction are held during which pages from Hitler's *Mein Kampf* are read. The older a person, the more steadfast must he be in his ideology.'

He then described the various divisions into which the S.S. were divided, including the S.D.: 'the great ideological Intelligence service of the Party and, in the long run, of the state,' and the Death's Head units, which 'originated from the guard units of the concentration camps'. The prisoners in the camps he described as 'the offal of criminals and freaks, for the most part, slave-like souls'. To attempt to indoctrinate such people was a waste of time; just to train them to keep themselves clean was as much as need be done. 'The people are taught to wash themselves twice daily, and to use the tooth brush, with which most of them have been unfamiliar. Hardly another nation would be as humane as we are.'

After dealing with the objective of the Security Service, he turned to the S.S. marriage laws. 'No S.S. man can get married without the approval of the Reichsführer S.S. A physical examination of the bride and guarantees for the bride's ideological and human character are required. In addition, a genealogical table up to 1750 is required; this results in tremendous work. It is our concern that our men get married.'

He went on to describe how he was at that moment in process of unifying the German police system – 'We now have for the first time in German history a Reich Police.' The importance of the police in time of war was paramount, fighting in 'a fourth theatre of war, internal Germany,' against the insidious forces of 'Jewish-Marxist-Bolshevist influence . . . It is the obligation of the S.S., and the police to solve positively the problem of internal security.'

He ended the speech with further references to the supreme racial struggle in which Germany was engaged:

'We are more valuable than the others who do now, and always will, surpass us in numbers. We are more valuable because our blood enables us to invent more than others, to lead our people better than others. Let us clearly realize, the next decades signify a struggle leading to the extermination of the subhuman opponents in the whole world who fight Germany, the basic people of the Northern race, bearer of the culture of mankind.'

This speech, as the generals present must have realized, was a direct challenge to the Army and must have reminded them of Roehm's assaults on their authority, though coming now from a source which was far more powerful, secret and sinister than anything Roehm had represented. The speech had the support of Hitler and was circulated, in a shortened form, as an official document, while the full text, taken down in shorthand, was smuggled abroad and published later in the year in an anti-Nazi journal. By that time, Hitler had favoured Himmler still further by announcing on 15 May that decisions issued from his office should have the same validity as ministerial decrees.

By the summer Berlin was seething with rumours that the S.S. were planning a *putsch* against the High Command. Fritsch, the Chief of Staff, was under surveillance by Heydrich's agents, while Blomberg was about to cause his own downfall. When Hitler held his notorious staff conference on 5 November, neither the field-marshal nor the general was enthusiastic in response to his extraordinary outburst about the necessity for war with the Western Powers and the annexation of Austria and Czechoslovakia. When Blomberg, after consultations with Göring, approached Hitler with the request that he might marry a typist with whom, at the age of sixty, he had become infatuated, Hitler consented with good grace and, along with Göring, even acted as a witness of the wedding on 12 January 1938.

The main facts of the disgraceful sequel to this marriage are well known, though accounts differ considerably about the nature of the complicity of Göring, Himmler and Heydrich in Blomberg's downfall. The dossier proving that the bride's mother kept a brothel and revealing that Frau Blomberg had herself a police record for prostitution emerged immediately after the wedding from the office of Count Helldorf, the Police President of Berlin. When Helldorf saw it he decided not to give it to Heydrich; he tactfully took the papers first of all to General Keitel, Blomberg's counsellor at the Ministry, whose son had recently married Blomberg's daughter. Keitel refused point-blank to handle the matter, and it was decided the papers should be sent next to Göring. According to Gisevius, Göring had some knowledge of the matter from the start, though there is other evidence that contradicts this. Josef Meisinger of the Gestapo, before his execution in Poland in 1947, claimed that he had faked the evidence against Blomberg's young wife, using her mother's record for the purpose, and that only Heydrich knew the forgery was on file waiting to be used once the wedding was over. If this were so, it seems most unlikely that Himmler was unaware of it. Whatever machination was used, the result was the same; Blomberg was disgraced and forced to retire.

This isolated Fritsch, about whom Heydrich also held damaging evidence implying that the general was a homosexual. Meisinger had also been in charge of this work. A professional blackmailer called Schmidt had been interrogated about Fritsch in 1935 and had claimed that he was blackmailing him for homosexuality. Schmidt was produced once again by Heydrich, Himmler and Göring to disgrace their second victim. Fritsch was directly charged with homosexual practices by Himmler in the presence of Hitler on 26 January; Schmidt was called in to identify Fritsch. Hitler did not want to act too hastily; he put Fritsch on indefinite leave pending some form of enquiry into the charges, while Himmler attempted to blacken him still further in the sight of the Führer by suggesting he would be the cause of a military demonstration against the régime when Hitler addressed the Reichstag on 31 January.

Meanwhile, during further interrogations of Schmidt, their principal witness, the Gestapo officials made a terrible discovery. It appeared that he had made a mistake in his deposition of 1935; the military gentleman from whom he had been exacting payments had been a retired cavalry officer called Captain von Frisch. Gestapo officials went at once to interrogate this officer at his house on 15 January, and found this new testimony was only too true. The Gestapo's primary case against Fritsch was now destroyed.

At a meeting with Beck and Rundstedt of the General Staff, Hitler finally agreed to allow official enquiries to be made jointly by the Army and the Ministry of Justice into the evidence against Fritsch. He insisted, however, that the enquiries were to be conducted in association with the Gestapo. This enquiry placed both Himmler and Heydrich in a most difficult position. The assessors now had the legal right to interrogate Schmidt, who was in the hands of the Gestapo. Himmler, naturally enough, had been opposed to any further enquiries from the start of the campaign by the Army to initiate them. Nebe, who appears to have been in touch with both sides in the struggle over Fritsch, had already given Gisevius a hint of the truth about the Gestapo's dilemma. The assessors were therefore encouraged to insist that the Gestapo hand their witness over. In the end, after close questioning, Schmidt unwillingly gave the assessors the address of the house where, he claimed, Fritsch had retired to fetch the money his blackmailer was demanding from him. The assessors visited the address, and found in a neighbouring house the Captain von Frisch who was the cause of the Gestapo's embarrassment. He was in bed seriously ill. During the visit the Captain's housekeeper admitted that the Gestapo had been there the previous month; she even remembered the date, 15 January. As soon as the Gestapo were informed of this visit, they took the Captain from his bed and placed him under arrest.

Hitler had by now announced the major changes in the High Command and in certain posts. He abolished the Ministry of War and assumed control himself of the organization, the O.K.W. or Supreme Command of the Armed Forces, which replaced it. These changes had been made public by him in a broadcast on 3 February, and in the course of a meeting of the principal officers of the new High Command the following day he went into great detail about both the Blomberg and the Fritsch cases. Ultimately he agreed to a special Court of Honour being convened on 11 March under the presidency of Göring, as the most senior officer in the armed forces.

Everyone was aware that the Fritsch case had broader implications than the reputation of a senior officer who had been wrongly used. According to Gisevius, the determination to turn the occasion into an exposure of the Gestapo was spreading to a wide circle of in-

fluential men, ranging from Admiral Raeder and Brauchitsch, whom
Hitler had made his new Commander-in-Chief, to Guertner, the
Minister of Justice, and Schacht, who had finally resigned from his
Ministry the previous November because he could no longer tolerate
Göring's interference in economic affairs. If, as Jodl noted in his
diary on 26 February, both Raeder and Guertner believed Fritsch
to be guilty, their sole interest in the case would be to expose the
Gestapo. Blomberg, in one of his final interviews with Hitler, had
gone so far as to say that Fritsch was not 'a man for the women'.

Fritsch, who was a Prussian nobleman as well as an officer who
believed in strict military formality and etiquette, behaved ill-
advisedly during the intervening weeks before the Court of Honour.
He therefore to some extent played into the hands of his enemies. If,
as Gisevius claims, he was 'an absolutely honourable man', he should
have formally denied the charges and then left the dispute entirely
in the hands of his lawyers and later of his defence counsel, once he
knew the Army was on his side and that a judicial enquiry followed
by a Court of Honour was to take place. However, after Himmler's
vicious denunciations he did not wait even to be retired; he insisted
on resigning, which not only made him appear guilty but created
legal difficulties when the Army proposed to set up a Court of
Honour in which the details of the evidence against him could be
subject to official examination. He further jeopardized his position
by admitting he had once taken 'a needy *Hitlerjunge*' into his household, and then, as an ill-considered demonstration of his innocence,
went on his own initiative to Gestapo headquarters for interrogation.
In February he decided to challenge Himmler, whom he regarded as
his principal enemy, to a duel at pistol-point.[24] Rundstedt, to whom
he entrusted his formal challenge for delivery to Himmler, considered the whole situation impossible, and never delivered it. He
eventually gave it to Hossbach, Hitler's adjutant, who kept it as a
curiosity. It would be interesting to know what Himmler's reaction
might have been had he received it.

Faced with Schmidt's admission to the assessors, Heydrich
decided the Gestapo had better lie its way out of the difficulties. He
had been directly responsible for the accusations levelled at Fritsch
in Hitler's presence on 26 January, ten days after the discovery by
his investigators that Schmidt was in error over the two similar
names. Heydrich categorically denied that any Gestapo official had
been to Frisch's house on 15 January, and he then had Schmidt

brow-beaten into a further admission that he had taken money from both men, and that therefore both Frisch and Fritsch were guilty. The unfortunate Frisch was prised out of the Gestapo's grip and placed at the disposal of the Minister of Justice. He admitted his guilt and confirmed that he had been a victim of Schmidt's blackmail. The final ordeal proved too much for him; he collapsed and died.

Himmler and Heydrich were now dependent on Schmidt and the Gestapo witnesses keeping to the lies they had been ordered to tell while giving their evidence before the Court of Honour on 11 March. Brauchitsch, Raeder and two Senate Presidents of the Supreme Court in Leipzig were to sit in judgment; Göring, as President of the Court of Honour, would, according to custom in such tribunals, conduct the examination.

Everything was set for what promised to be an extraordinary scene. The judges, except for Göring, were opposed to the Gestapo, but Göring had power to conduct the proceedings in his own way. A great deal depended on Fritsch; he was obstinately convinced that his name would be cleared, but would he develop the occasion into an assault on the Gestapo now that he had been denied the satisfaction of shooting Himmler? Would the Gestapo witnesses be able to sustain their latest story? Would Schmidt break down, or would Göring protect him? Would Heydrich and Himmler be called as witnesses? Nebe told Gisevius that Heydrich was certain the Court of Honour would mean the end of his career. The situation was so tense that this case to determine whether or not a man was a homosexual became one of those rarer moments in the history of the Nazi régime when the pressures of resistance to Hitler might well have erupted on a scale sufficient to shatter the foundations on which his tyranny was based.

No one, however, had reckoned on what actually did happen. On 10 March, the day before the Court of Honour, after a month of growing political crisis in Vienna, Hitler gave orders for the Army to be prepared to invade Austria two days later. At the very moment the Court began its session Hitler was using Seyss-Inquart and other Nazi leaders in Austria to force Schuschnigg, the Austrian Chancellor, into an impossible position so that the Army should have an excuse to invade. Schuschnigg was proving intractable, and before noon Hitler ordered Göring, Brauchitsch and Raeder to abandon their proceedings and come at once to the Chancellery. Himmler, Heydrich and the Gestapo had won a temporary reprieve. That afternoon Göring began his celebrated conquest of Austria by telephone, and by the following day Austria was in Nazi hands and Himmler was in Linz supervising security arrangements for Hitler's arrival that afternoon. Fritsch was forgotten in this hour of national triumph.

When the Court was reconvened a week later on 17 March, the whole political atmosphere had changed. Hitler was once more the hero, the great leader, and there was no longer any heart in the military opposition to make a stand against him. It is unlikely, in any event, that Fritsch would have had either the stamina or the effrontery to press his attack home until the Gestapo witnesses were discredited; all he was concerned about was the formal recognition of his innocence. In the end it was Göring himself who decided on the tactics to adopt to protect the Gestapo. He determined to sacrifice Schmidt, whom nobody was concerned to protect, and, by using his authority to bully and threaten him, forced admissions from him which, had they been used to charge the Gestapo with dishonourable treatment of its witness, could have put the case in its proper perspective. But having at least achieved, on the second day of the examination, an admission from Schmidt that he had been lying about Fritsch, Göring hastily called on Fritsch to make a closing statement in his defence, following which he was acquitted.

Both Himmler and Heydrich were far too preoccupied establishing a reign of terror in Austria with the aid of their allies, the Austrian Nazis, to be in attendance at the Court during 17 and 18 March. They left their Gestapo agents to survive as best they could. But both of them had been deeply concerned during January and February; Heydrich's wife has testified to her husband's tension during this time, and Schellenberg has told the story of how Heydrich, in a fit of nerves, asked him to dine at his office and came armed because he expected the Army to 'start marching from Potsdam'. Himmler's reactions were even more extraordinary. Describing Himmler during the earlier stages of the enquiry, Schellenberg wrote:

'I witnessed for the first time some of the rather strange practices resorted to by Himmler through his inclination towards mysticism. He assembled twelve of his most trusted S.S. leaders in a room next to the one in which von Fritsch was being questioned and ordered them all to concentrate their minds on exerting a suggestive influence over the general that would induce him to tell the truth. I happened to come into the room by accident, and to see these twelve S.S. leaders sitting in a circle, all sunk in deep and silent contemplation, was indeed a remarkable sight.'[25]

Himmler was sufficiently prepared for the Austrian *putsch* to have ready a new and special uniform of field grey in which to invade Austria. Accompanied by his staff and S.S. bodyguards, all heavily armed, he flew south to Aspern aerodrome, near Vienna. With him was his adjutant Wolff, Walter Schellenberg, who had been in charge of co-ordinating intelligence reports from Austria, and the Austrian official in the S.D., Adolf Eichmann, now a specialist in Jewish affairs, who had prepared lists of the large number of Austrian Jews Himmler was determined should be given no chance to cause trouble.[26]

The weather was bad and made the flight to Vienna in the over-loaded plane unpleasant, and Schellenberg records that Himmler discussed with him the administration of the new state of Ostmark, as Austria was now to be called. They were standing in the rear of the plane when Schellenberg noticed Himmler was leaning against the aircraft door and that the safety-catch was undone. He grasped him by his coat and flung him aside. When Himmler had recovered from the shock, he thanked Schellenberg and said he would be happy to do the same and protect his life for him some day.

Himmler and his entourage arrived at Aspern aerodrome before daybreak. They were uncertain of their reception in Vienna, but by the time they had arrived the struggle for Austria was already over. Hitler's troops had crossed the frontier overnight and on behalf of the provisional government orders had been given by Seyss-Inquart to the Austrian Army that they were to offer no resistance to the invaders. Himmler, who was Hitler's most senior representative in Austria, was met by the Austrian Chief of Police, Michael Skubl, whose feelings at having this duty to perform must have been bitter, since he had been appointed by Dollfuss on the very day of his murder by the Nazis. Himmler hurried by car to the Chancellery in Vienna to confer with Kaltenbrunner, the head of the Austrian S.S. Following exactly the procedure he had originated for himself in Germany, Himmler dismissed Skubl and put the police in the charge of Kaltenbrunner. Leaving the immediate control of Vienna in this man's hands, Himmler left by air for Linz to supervise the reception to be given Hitler that afternoon in the town where he had lived as a child. With him went Seyss-Inquart, now the new Nazi Chancellor of Austria. On the same day Heydrich joined Kaltenbrunner in Vienna, and the Austrian capital began to experience the savagery of Nazi control.

The hysteria of Hitler's reception in Austria – he had arrived on Saturday, and on Sunday with tears in his eyes had become President of Austria, which was created 'a province of the German Reich' by a legal enactment hurriedly put together – did not stop Himmler from warning the Führer against entering Vienna until every security precaution had been taken. He had himself returned there from Linz and set up his headquarters in the Imperial Hotel, while Heydrich commandeered the Metropole for the S.S. and S.D. headquarters. Together the unholy team went to work, Himmler and Heydrich of Germany, Kaltenbrunner and his colleague Odilo Globocnik of Austria.

Kaltenbrunner, who was in 1943 to be appointed successor to Heydrich by Himmler and who after the war was to stand trial at Nuremberg, was a lawyer who had turned to political intrigue. He was a huge man, coarse and tough, with small, penetrating eyes set in a wooden, expressionless face. He was excitable, and would slap the table with his hard, clumsy hands, which were discoloured with nicotine and reminded Schellenberg of the hands of a gorilla. He had joined the S.S. in 1932 and had been imprisoned by the Dollfuss Government for his activities. His associate Globocnik came from Trieste; he had been involved in robbery with violence and he continued to mix his criminal activities with politics even after Hitler had appointed him Gauleiter of Vienna.

The campaign of terror launched by these two men and the Austrian S.S. on behalf of Heydrich and Himmler was more fearful than anything that had yet happened in Germany; Seyss-Inquart himself was to admit after the war that 79,000 arrests took place in Vienna within a matter of weeks. Jews were evicted, humiliated and forced to scrub the streets. Many men of distinction among those opposed to the Nazis, both Jews and non-Jews, were to be sent to Dachau and other camps in Germany; the freight trains transporting prisoners crushed together in wagons became a regular service from Austria.

Schuschnigg and Baron Louis de Rothschild, the two most eminent men held in custody, were temporarily confined by Kaltenbrunner in the servants' quarters on the fifth floor of the Metropole Hotel, and they were inspected there by Himmler. Baron Rothschild, who realized that Himmler was planning to ransom him, spoke with ironic reserve when the Reichsführer S.S. enquired after his welfare, while Himmler showed off his authority by taking Schuschnigg with him to inspect the attic lavatories and command in his presence that the ancient fitments should be replaced by something more modern and hygienic for his distinguished prisoners. Nevertheless, he refused to let Schuschnigg, who like himself was short-sighted, have the use of his spectacles, which had been confiscated.

This oppression was the immediate outcome of Hitler's annexation of Austria. The Führer had come eventually from Linz to Vienna on Monday 14 March, staying one night only at the Imperial Hotel, where Himmler was also lodged; those Austrians prepared to be ecstatic were so: 'never . . . have I seen such tremendous, enthusiastic and joyous crowds', wrote Schellenberg. Nevertheless, he had to rush ahead of Hitler's procession of cars touring the city in order to supervise the dismantling of explosive charges attached to a bridge on the route. Himmler had been right to be cautious.

The Jewish population of Austria was about 200,000, and their organized persecution and removal became a major undertaking. Himmler went in person to search for a site for a local prison camp, and found a suitable place near Mauthausen on the Danube, where a camp was built on the wooded slopes above a quarry by slave-labour brought from Dachau. Himmler decorated the wooden guard-house set on the granite walls with curling roofs in imitation of the guard-houses on the Great Wall of China.

The importance of Adolf Eichmann as the agent of Himmler and Heydrich in the organization of Jewish affairs dates from the *Anschluss*. This man was lifted out of the obscurity to which he had almost always clung when he was abducted from the Argentine in 1960 and put on trial in Israel. He had escaped from an American internment camp after the war. When he stood under the glare of the lights in his bullet-proof box, he was revealed as a small-minded, if able and energetic, administrator and he shared a bureaucratic urge for tidiness in his fulfilment of the orders he had been given to organize the extermination of the Jews in his power; an overriding sense of duty compelled him to carry out whatever he was required to do. He had begun his S.S. career in the Death's Head Unit at Dachau, so he had few qualms about the spectacle of suffering in the camps, and it has been suggested that he was not averse to accompanying Heydrich on his frequent excusions into the city's brothels. He travelled all over Europe to threaten, to harry or to cajole the inefficient or the reluctant agents of the S.S. to get their Jews destroyed. His concern was with the transport of the victims and the statistics of death, which in his enthusiasm he was prepared to exaggerate in his reports to his superiors. Only when hard-pressed at his trial did he admit that he hated the work he had been given to do.

At Eichmann's own suggestion Himmler established the Office of Jewish Emigration in Vienna and put him in charge of it. As a result of Eichmann's work more than 100,000 Jews left Austria between mid-1938 and the outbreak of the war. All but a few departed destitute, their wealth and property in Austria seized by the Nazis. Baron Louis de Rothschild was only permitted to leave after a year's detention; the price of his freedom included the sacrifice of his steel rolling-mills to Göring, while the Palais Rothschild in Vienna became Eichmann's headquarters. The Jews were encouraged to emigrate, but the price exacted for exit permits, stamped *Jude*, was the loss not only of money and possessions but the fulfilment of orders to leave the country for ever, disowned and stateless. It was Germany over again.

This was the period when Himmler first conceived the idea of commercializing concentration camps. It was the *Anschluss* with its enormous influx of prisoners that made it evident to him that so many idle hands were a scandalous waste of potential labour for the Reich. Up to the time of the *Anschluss*, the population of Himmler's camps has been estimated by Reitlinger at an average of 20,000, and the prisoners' principal tasks had been the construction and extension of the camps themselves, with barracks and other amenities for the S.S. By April 1939, the prison-camp population had grown to some 280,000.

While Eichmann was extracting the wealth of the Jews, Himmler was forming companies on behalf of the S.S. to exploit the new labour resources of the camps in quarrying stone and providing bricks and cement for the vast building projects which Albert Speer, Hitler's young architectural adviser and future Minister of War Production, was encouraging the Führer to undertake.[27] The head of this business undertaking was Oswald Pohl, a man of working-class origin who in looks resembled Mussolini and whose sadistic greed in driving the human flesh under his control to the last flicker of productive energy made him one of the worst of Himmler's scourges.

Hitler's policy of divide and rule was extended now by Himmler to the administration of the camps. He had been careful in 1936 not to give Heydrich the entire control; both Eicke's inspectorate office and Pohl's business administration, the *Verwaltungsamt*, were from Heydrich's point of view intrusive elements which directly interfered with his own free hand in the management of the prisoners. Since the destruction of 'sub-human' racial elements and of the enemies of the State was Heydrich's aim, it conflicted with any interest, however low in character, which would lengthen the lives of the prisoners and give them any kind of encouragement through the provision of extra food. The attempt to commercialize the camps, which until the middle years of the war was to be a failure, was sabotaged from the start as a result of various rivalries that developed between those administering the camps. The supervision of their victims' labour gave the *Kapos*, the habitual criminals placed by the S.S. in the camps and employed as bullies and watch-dogs, new opportunities for exploiting and torturing the prisoners.

At the notorious conference over which Göring presided after the November pogrom in 1938, Göring's interest lay solely in preventing further loss to the Reich economy by the looting of property which, though occupied by Jews, was not always actually owned by them and was in any case insured against damage and theft. Heydrich's interest lay solely in the statistics of destruction and in the avoidance of paying any compensation. He boasted that already in a few months 50,000 Jews had left Austria, while only 19,000 had left Germany. He wanted the Jews segregated and expelled from the German community as soon as possible. Heydrich had in fact done what he could in advance to make the pogrom effective; after consulting Himmler, who was in Munich, he had issued detailed instructions to the Chiefs of State Police on how their men should control the anti-Jewish demonstrations so as to prevent damage to German-owned property, and he followed the pogrom with further arrests of Jews whose presence in Germany offended his sense of decency and order.

Hoess, who by 1938 had been promoted adjutant to the commander of Sachsenhausen, recalls an inspection of the camp by Himmler during the summer of 1938. He brought with him Frick, the Minister of the Interior, who was paying his first visit to a concentration camp. Himmler was 'in the best of humour and obviously pleased that he was at last able to show the Minister of the Interior and his officials one of the secret and notorious concentration camps'. He answered questions 'calmly and amiably although often sarcastically'. Afterwards his colleagues were entertained to dinner.

His successful intrusion into Austria had given Himmler a taste for foreign affairs, and like Göring Himmler was to be used by Hitler, though in a minor capacity, to carry out his less formal diplomacy alongside the formal negotiations of the Foreign Office, which Ribbentrop had taken over early in 1938. Himmler had become one of Hitler's close and more trusted subordinates. Though their relations remained punctilious, Himmler became to some extent a recognized companion who, unlike the generals who were doing their best to edge Hitler away from grandiose schemes for war, always supported Hitler's policy without question and, when asked to do so, gave advice on how best to carry this policy out. It was Himmler who had led the delegation that received the Führer at Linz, and a few weeks later, in May, he was among those chosen to accompany Hitler on his state visit to Italy, where he had to stay along with the Führer in the Quirinal, the Palace of the King. 'Here one breathes the air of the catacombs', Himmler was heard to remark, and his observation was passed on to the King.

Nevertheless, Hitler felt Himmler was worth cultivating as a diplomat; he had been sent to Italy before in both 1936 and 1937 on goodwill visits, and had on each occasion taken Heydrich with him. Friendly relations had been established with Bocchini, Mussolini's Minister of Police, and with Mussolini himself, who granted Heydrich a personal interview when Himmler fell ill during their first visit.

From 1938 Himmler used against both the Foreign Office and the High Command exactly the same secret strategy he had used to undermine Göring's initial authority over the police. He maintained his friendly relations with Ribbentrop while at the same time he encroached on the duties of the Foreign Office, or duplicated them through the S.D. spy-ring abroad. Following talks with Hitler, in which the possibility that the Western Powers might use North Africa to counter-attack Europe once Germany had overrun it, Schellenberg, the most intelligent agent on Heydrich's staff, was sent in the autumn of 1938 on an adventurous mission to West Africa to spy on the harbour facilities, while the following January

Himmler made a report for his staff on conversations he had had with the Japanese Ambassador about a treaty to consolidate the Tripartite Pact, and an attempt which the Japanese were making to send agents into Russia to assassinate Stalin. In May 1939, Ciano reports that Himmler advised him that the Italians should establish a protectorate in Croatia, a policy in opposition to that of Ribbentrop, who wanted Yugoslavia to remain untouched. The following month, Hitler assigned to Himmler the difficult task of negotiating with the Italian Ambassador, Bernardo Attolico, for the resettlement of the Tyrolean Germans in the Reich. This was the first of these wholesale movements of population on racial grounds which appealed so strongly to Himmler's sense of ethnology.

Meanwhile Himmler's ambition in Czechoslovakia led him during 1938 to set up with Heydrich an organization of S.D. commandos who were to follow the German Army into the country 'to secure the political life and national economy', while inside the frontiers he hoped to gain personal control of the Free Corps organized by the Sudeten Germans, which Brauchitsch naturally expected to be the concern of the Army. Four days before the Munich Agreement, when it seemed certain Czechoslovakia would be invaded, he informed Henlein, the leader of the Sudeten Germans, that he would come under his exclusive command, and he moved six battalions of his Death's Head guards, two of them from Dachau, up to the frontier without authority from the High Command, who cancelled his orders to Henlein and gave a general instruction that the Death's Head men were to be subject to military control. The order ended: 'It is requested that all further arrangements be made between the Commander-in-Chief of the Army and the Reichsführer S.S.'

The Munich Agreement of 30 September 1938 resolved this particular deadlock. Hitler, as usual, was not greatly upset to find Himmler trying to spike the Army's guns; it satisfied his intuitive sense of security. He had in fact as recently as 17 August decreed that Himmler's special armed forces, the future *Waffen* S.S., were to be regarded solely as a Party force under Himmler's command, and outside the control of either the Army or the Police; on 26 August Himmler was among the group that accompanied Hitler on an inspection of the Western fortifications. Perhaps these attentions led Himmler to exaggerate his authority. The part he had been expected to play, had the campaign against Czechoslovakia developed into invasion, was merely to provoke border incidents and to establish an immediate police control of the occupied territory in the wake of the Army. His plans, however, had now to be abandoned. According to Ciano, an acute if malicious observer, Himmler was 'in despair because an agreement had been reached and war seemed to be averted'. But Hitler was determined to keep the S.S. Command and the Army firmly separate. By September 1939, Himmler would have control of some 18,000 men trained for the field (the S.S. *Verfügungstruppen*, which were in 1940 to be re-named the *Waffen* S.S.) in addition to the men in his Death's Head units and the various branches of the S.S. and the Gestapo.

Himmler had caught the war-fever from Hitler, and joined with Ribbentrop in encouraging the Führer to go to any lengths to achieve the conquest of Europe. Göring and the High Command played the double game of appeasing Hitler by hastening the preparations for war, while at the same time doing everything in their power to postpone the outbreak of hostilities. In Göring's case, he conducted the negotiations for both war and peace alongside each other, knowing full well that Germany was ill-prepared for campaigns which might well spread to both the Eastern and Western fronts. For Himmler, whose military sense was as small as his knowledge of strategy, war was merely an assertion of racial superiority, about which he had no doubts at all of the outcome. Sir Nevile Henderson, the British Ambassador in Berlin at this period, wrote: 'In September 1938, as well as in August 1939, Ribbentrop and Himmler were, in my opinion, his [Hitler's] principal lieutenants in the war party,'[28] and, according to Henderson, Hitler's actions often sprang from their fabrication of situations which were calculated to urge him to make war. Lord Halifax endorsed this opinion in a report written in January 1939 for submission to Roosevelt and the French Government. Goerdeler, one of the most prominent men in the German resistance, writing at the time of Munich, again coupled Ribbentrop and Himmler as the principal agents driving Hitler into war. It was fitting, therefore, that Himmler should accompany Hitler and Ribbentrop to Prague on 15 March after the fearful scene during the hours after midnight at the Chancellery in Berlin, when Hitler, Ribbentrop and Göring had forced the aged Czech President in the midst of a heart attack to capitulate and give up what was left of his country to the savage encroachment of Germany. Himmler made Karl Hermann Frank, a leader of the Sudeten German Free Corps and a State Secretary under the new German

Protector, von Neurath, Higher S.S. and Police Chief. Frank, though nominally responsible to Neurath, was in practice responsible only to Himmler. In this way the security administration of Czechoslovakia was directed from Berlin, and the arrests began again.

The following June, Himmler was present at an important meeting of the Reich Defence Council at which high-ranking members from the civil and military authorities were present. Göring presided, and the subject was preparation for imminent war. Himmler pledged the use of the prisoners in his camps for war work.

An operation that formed a part of Himmler's initial contribution to Hitler's plan for the attack on Poland was named after him. It is ironic that Operation Himmler should have been a cruel act of deception involving a revolting atrocity. The general plan to stage faked incidents along the Polish frontier in order to provide suitable provocation for the invading forces had already been in Himmler's mind when he had hoped to take part in an attack on Czechoslovakia, but in that case his deceits were not needed. Now in the case of Poland, they were to be developed on a considerable scale, and Heinrich Mueller, the head of the Gestapo, was put in charge of these operations. It was part of the plan that a number of prisoners from concentration camps should be dressed in Polish uniforms, given fatal injections by a doctor and at the right moment shot at until they were bordering on death. These victims were to be brought in under the code-words 'canned goods'. Their bodies were to be photographed for publication and shown to press representatives accompanying the German Army.

The story of these faked attacks and of their attendant atrocities was revealed at Nuremberg after the war in an affidavit sworn by the S.D. man who led the principal raid on 31 August against the German radio-station at Gleiwitz, close to the Polish border.[29] Having affirmed this story at Nuremberg, he escaped and was not heard of again until he re-appeared under his own name in 1964, and sold the story to *Der Stern*. At Nuremberg, he told how he raided the station, taking with him a Polish-speaking German who broadcast a provocative speech against the Reich, and how at the last minute he deposited a dying man on the scene whom the Poles were supposed to have killed. This was Operation Himmler, the first criminal act with which the Second World War began on 1 September 1939 with the invasion of Poland.

# IV

# *Secret Rivals*

The subtle balances of power between the Nazi leaders at the beginning of the war are not easy to measure. After his successes in Austria and Czechoslovakia, Hitler withdrew himself from the others, becoming more arbitrary and autocratic in his procedure and less susceptible to advice or pressures designed to change his line of action. If Ribbentrop and Himmler rather than Göring or Goebbels were said to be in favour of war during 1938–9, this was due solely to their more ready response to Hitler's will. They blindly supported and encouraged his advance towards war and had none of the reservations about Germany's readiness for full-scale hostilities which occupied Göring's mind. Goebbels after the summer of 1938 had been temporarily in disgrace with the Führer because he had asked to be relieved of his duties so that he might divorce his wife and marry the Czech actress, Lida Baarova. After his experiences with Roehm and Blomberg, and later with Brauchitsch, the Commander-in-Chief of the Army who had had a troublesome divorce and married a young girl, Hitler was tired of seeing the love affairs of his subordinates interfere with their concentration on the grand strategy that he now had in mind. Himmler's discreet liaison in Berlin with his secretary Hedwig was to be far less disruptive. According to Lina Heydrich, Himmler indeed became a different man as a result of his orderly love affair. Hedwig even led him to abandon the little chain which secured his pince-nez to his ear, and influenced him to wear his hair with a less severe cut.

Himmler's relationship with Heydrich during the first year of the war became deeply involved. When Himmler had first appointed Heydrich to the S.S., they had both been young men, Himmler thirty-one years old and Heydrich twenty-seven. Even now, at the beginning of the war, Himmler was still not yet forty and Heydrich thirty-five. The closer observers of these two very different men, such as Gisevius, Kersten and Höttl, differ very little in their assessment of Heydrich.[1] To Höttl, who worked for Heydrich and later for Schellenberg on the forgery of passports and banknotes, Himmler was a mediocrity in comparison with Heydrich, who had little use for his commander's obsessions, racial or otherwise, and rapidly learned how to exploit the power delegated to him. In the end, according to Höttl, he undermined Himmler's position to such an extent that he achieved direct access to Hitler and, had he lived, might well in 1943 have been appointed Minister of the Interior by the Führer in order to break, or counterbalance, the power accumulated by Himmler. However, Heydrich's position in relation to Himmler was weakened, not strengthened, when in September 1941 Hitler, without consulting Himmler, appointed him Deputy Reich Protector in Czechoslovakia. Heydrich was instructed to master that unhappy country, which was proving rebellious under the comparatively weak rule of Reich Protector Neurath, who had been Hitler's Foreign Minister before the appointment of Ribbentrop. Neurath was forced to leave matters entirely in the hands of Heydrich.

Heydrich's gradual movement towards comparative independence came during the first two years of the war. Himmler, who was never a man for immediate action, delegated to him an increasing number of the monstrous tasks required by Hitler, and even tolerated a situation in which Heydrich reported direct to the Führer or to Göring. Himmler, it must always be remembered, was a sick man who from 1939 to the end of his life could only find relief from his physical and psychological tensions through Kersten's expert massage.

It is a profound mistake to underestimate Himmler, the very mistake, in fact, which allows such apparently insignificant men as he to win extensive power in politics or industry. Behind the rimless pince-nez, the trim and correct moustache, the receding, obstinate chin, and the narrow, sloping shoulders there was a man of passionate beliefs, whose attitude to power was not to luxuriate in it like Göring, or to fulfil the ambitions of an orator and political demagogue like Goebbels, but to realize a self-conceived, Messianic mission on behalf of the Germanic race.

But with his particular temperament and poor physique, he never could become a man of action. There can be no doubt that he always wanted to prove himself in this way; he saw himself as a uniformed policeman and soldier, even as a commander in the field, but he lacked both the mental and physical stamina for these things, and in the end he only made himself ridiculous. But by that time Heydrich was dead. During the years preceding 1939, while the S.S. was being developed, and during the first two years of the war, it was Heydrich who was astute enough to supply Himmler with ideas and the means to carry them out, becoming his *alter ego* until the point was reached when he was able to break free and make his own bid for power, serving directly under Hitler.

According to his long-suffering wife, Lina Heydrich, who was as ardently Nazi as Magda Goebbels and like her enjoyed attending smart parties given for smart Nazi wives, her husband would come home cursing the stupidity and waste of time which Himmler's racial and other beliefs imposed on the administration of the S.S. Once he had seized power over Himmler, he did not fail to let him see the contempt he had for all this crazed mythology. For Heydrich it was not the theory but the practice that mattered; as he saw it, there was no need for elaborate theories on which to base the obvious necessity to persecute all those whose mere existence impeded 'Aryan' dominance. But whatever open differences there were between Heydrich and Himmler, Heydrich was always careful to keep their formal relationship unimpaired.

According to Gisevius, who for a brief period worked under him, Heydrich was 'diabolically clever', keeping himself always in the background and using roundabout ways to achieve his aims. His methods of terrorism were kept as secret as possible. He had a 'peculiarly murderous bent', teaching his men 'the by-laws of applied terror', one of which was, as Gisevius put it, to 'pass the buck'. He practised his oppression always in the name of discipline, justice, or the needs of being a good German, leaving it to Himmler to preach the more high-flown doctrines that in the end led to the same oppression of the same people. In all the Nazi leadership, as Gisevius points out, it was the experts in violence who rose to the top: 'The dominant trait of all of them was brutality. Göring, Goebbels, Himmler, Heydrich . . . thought and felt only in terms of violence.' Schellenberg, who served Heydrich and Himmler for twelve years, has left the best description there is of Heydrich:

'When I entered his office Heydrich was sitting behind his desk. He was a tall, impressive figure with a broad, unusually high forehead, small restless eyes as crafty as an animal's and of uncanny power, a long, predatory nose, and a wide, full-lipped mouth. His hands were slender and rather too long – they made one think of the legs of a spider. His splendid figure was marred by the breadth of his hips, a disturbing feminine effect which made him appear even more sinister. His voice was much too high for so large a man and his speech was nervous and staccato, and though he scarcely ever finished a sentence, he always managed to express his meaning quite clearly.'

According to Schellenberg, Heydrich became the 'hidden pivot around which the Nazi régime revolved', and his keen intelligence and forceful character guided the development of the whole nation:

'He was far superior to all his political colleagues and controlled them as he controlled the vast intelligence machine of the S.D. . . . Heydrich had an incredibly acute perception of the moral, human, professional and political weaknesses of others, and . . . his unusual intellect was matched by the ever-watchful instincts of a predatory animal . . . He operated on the principle of "divide and rule," and even applied this to his relations with Hitler and Himmler. The decisive thing for him was always to know more than others . . . and to use this knowledge and the weakness of others to render them completely dependent on him, from the highest to the lowest . . . Heydrich was in fact, the puppet-master of the Third Reich.'

His only failing, according to Schellenberg, who both admired and feared Heydrich, was his ungovernable sexual appetite, which he indulged without caution or restraint.

In 1940 he established his own high-class brothel, the notorious Salon Kitty, a mansion rented by the S.D. in the Giesebrechtstrasse, just off the Kurfürstendamm in the west end of Berlin.[2] Salon Kitty had nine bedrooms, in all of which concealed microphones were installed connected to a monitoring room in the basement. This was a pleasant means of spying, primarily on diplomatic visitors to Germany. Schellenberg is careful to point out that his responsibilities ended with supervision of the recordings, while Artur Nebe, the Chief of the Criminal Police, controlled the women, because in the past he had been connected with the vice squad. Important diplomats, such as Ciano, were early induced to visit Salon Kitty by

Heydrich and others who knew the establishment's secret uses, and their conversation while drunk or making love was recorded on tape. In February 1941, Heydrich invited Kersten to visit the house, remarking that it had been opened in agreement with Ribbentrop to save their foreign guests from becoming the victims of the worst type of prostitutes; although it had to be subsidised, he believed it would soon become self-supporting. He was, he said, even contemplating opening a similar establishment for homosexuals. According to Schellenberg, Salon Kitty was established without the knowledge of Ribbentrop, and the Foreign Minister had visited it himself before he learned who was in control of the management.

Kersten had the opportunity of seeing Heydrich primarily through Himmler's eyes; though he had some direct dealings with Heydrich, he avoided him because he knew that he was under suspicion because of his growing intimacy with Himmler. Although, like Schellenberg, Kersten praises Heydrich's striking Nordic appearance, the brilliance and polish of his speech 'in the concise military manner', and his remarkable ability to expound his arguments to Himmler in such a way as to force the decision he wanted from him, he also sees certain weaknesses of character that Schellenberg either overlooks or chooses to ignore. While Himmler treats Heydrich with 'open friendliness', Heydrich addresses his chief with 'quite inexplicable servility'. 'Yes, Reichsführer, certainly, Reichsführer, yes, yes, indeed,' is his response once Himmler raises objections. Although Heydrich is 'far more dynamic', and outclasses Himmler every time in the way he can present his arguments, 'Himmler seems to possess some sort of secret power over Heydrich, before which Heydrich submits unconditionally.' Himmler's adjutants, Wolff and Brandt, both themselves in a position to exercise influence over Himmler, seemed to Kersten to have a poor opinion of Heydrich, whom they saw as a man operating entirely in a selfish vacuum, without a friend or supporter, either man or woman. No one trusted him: everyone tried to avoid him.[3] Among his great weaknesses was his hatred of being beaten or unsuccessful in sport, and in order to prove his skill in action he joined the Luftwaffe and won the Iron Cross after making sixty operational flights.

Kersten observed that Himmler had his own methods of resisting the resolute personality of Heydrich. He records that he had seen Himmler 'quite overwhelmed' by Heydrich's powerful arguments, but nevertheless he had also seen him telephone Heydrich's office afterwards and leave instructions with the subordinates to hold up any measure to which he had been led to acquiesce in Heydrich's presence, using now the need to consult Hitler as his reason for delay. In this way Himmler preserved his superior position and postponed making decisions, a habit which was to increase with him during the war to such an extent that it helped destroy him.

It was not until after the death of Heydrich that Himmler, still carefully shielding himself behind Hitler, admitted to Kersten that the hold they had on Heydrich was knowledge that there was Jewish blood in his family; Hitler had decided that the knowledge and ability Heydrich possessed were best kept active in the service of the Party, while the need to atone in their eyes for the taint in his blood would make this Nordic officer a more valiant persecutor of the Jews than any so-called pure-blooded Aryan. It pleased both Hitler and Himmler to make Heydrich their principal agent against the race to which in some part they imagined he belonged. Read Machiavelli, said Himmler in conclusion. A few days later he added that Heydrich had always suffered from a sense of inferiority, that he had been 'an unhappy man, completely divided against himself, as often happened with those of mixed race'.

'He wanted to prove the Germanic elements in his blood were dominant', said Himmler. 'He never really found peace.'

Himmler lit a cigar, and gazed at the receding veils of smoke.

'In one respect he was irreplaceable,' he added. 'He possessed an infallible nose for men. Because he was divided himself, he was sure to sense such divisions in others. They were right to fear him. For the rest, he was a very good violinist. He once played a serenade in my honour. It was excellent.'

But Heydrich was dead, and it was easy, therefore, for Himmler to be either cynical or sentimental about him. There was no doubt about the tension and perhaps even the jealous possessiveness in their relationship; they had risen together as self-made men who had used their wits to gain advancement, and each had been and indeed still was dependent on the other. Those around them, trained to be watchful for weakness, were only too ready to dramatize what they observed in the behaviour of their superiors. To Schellenberg Himmler appeared, as to so many others, like an exacting headmaster, insisting on precision, industry and loyalty with a 'finicky exacti-tude', yet fearing to express an opinion of his own in case he should be proved wrong. He preferred others to take the responsibility off his shoulders, and receive the blame. 'This system', wrote Schellenberg, 'gave Himmler an air of aloofness, of being above ordinary conflicts. It made him the final arbiter.' But it also revealed a grave weakness of character in a man so prone to accumulating power.

This weakness was shown in his lifelong subservience to Hitler. 'Look at Heini – he'll crawl into the old man's ear in a minute', Schellenberg heard one of the adjutants whisper when Hitler was talking endlessly to Himmler, who listened with rapt attention. When Kersten asked him whether he would kill himself if Hitler ordered him to do so, Himmler replied, 'Yes, certainly! At once! For if the Führer orders anything like that, he has his reasons. And it's not for me as an obedient soldier to question those reasons. I only recognize unconditional obedience.' One of the characteristics of Himmler's nature was that, having gained power, he was most loath to use it except when he was certain no risk was involved. The death of Heydrich only intensified his isolation and his weakness of character in the face of Hitler.

Matters had been very different three years earlier, when Hitler's troops poured into Poland after the devastating raids inflicted by Göring's Luftwaffe. The S.S. fighting formations, some 18,000 men, took part in the war which was virtually over by 18 September. Himmler, travelling in his special armoured train known as Heinrich, left for the north on 13 September, taking Ribbentrop with him. They followed Hitler's own train and another housing the High Command up to the Danzig area. Himmler was for long to resent having no control over the use of the S.S. formations, and it seems that their casualties were heavy. All the Reichsführer S.S. was able to do was accompany Hitler on formal inspections of the battlefronts, and he followed him back to Berlin on 26 September.

Heydrich did not travel with Himmler in this vain pursuit of military command; the S.D. was represented on the train by Schellenberg, who was at first received rather coldly by both Himmler and Wolff, Himmler's Chief of Staff. Schellenberg seized the opportunity to gain Himmler's favour, and at the same time to study the atmosphere and character of the men at the top. On the way back from a flight over the burning city of Warsaw, Schellenberg's efforts to impress Himmler at length succeeded; he was invited to take supper with the Reichsführer S.S. and given confidential information about the secret agreement between Germany and Russia for the partition of Poland. They also decided to investigate Hitler's private physician, Dr Morrell, whose panic while accompanying the Führer to the battlefronts had not impressed the Reichsführer.

Walter Schellenberg was, as we have seen, one of the intellectuals of the S.S. He had been educated in a Jesuit school; his university training in law and medicine at Bonn was over by the time he was twenty-two. His alert intelligence and quickness of observation fitted him for the various missions of espionage which he describes with such zest and self-satisfaction in his memoirs. As he gained the confidence of Heydrich and Himmler, he advanced his position in their service, and his value to us includes not only his detailed accounts of the more entertaining activities he undertook for the S.D., but the descriptive analyses he has left of his colleagues and, in particular, of Heydrich and Himmler. In the various departments into which Heydrich divided the S.D., Schellenberg worked in A.M.T., or Department IV, specializing in counter-espionage inside Germany and the occupied countries. Later, in June 1941, he was to take over Department VI, which co-ordinated Foreign Intelligence, and when Canaris's Intelligence Service for the High Command was disbanded in 1944, Schellenberg's responsibilities were expanded to include this work as well. At the height of his career after Heydrich's death, he was to become one of the closest of Himmler's advisers, and he worked hard for some action independent of Hitler to end the war and to ease the situation in the concentration camps.

Schellenberg was soft-spoken, even ingratiating in his manner; he wanted his superiors to like him. He claims he was for a brief period attracted to Heydrich's neglected wife, Lina.[4] For him intrigue was a profession, and his pride in it survived the war and is present in every chapter of his fascinating and exciting autobiography. In the use of intrigue he was as guilty as any of his associates, but he remains a far more engaging rascal than they.

Meanwhile Heydrich had achieved his private ambition by flying sorties with the Luftwaffe. Later in September he visited Himmler in his train, and he took charge of security arrangements for the victory celebration in Warsaw. On 27 September, he was rewarded by being made head of the *Reichsicherheitshauptamt*, the Reich Chief Security Office (R.S.H.A.).[5] This was to give him a far greater measure of independence in his relations with Himmler, and opened up for him the means of direct access to Hitler. R.S.H.A. gave Heydrich control of Mueller's Gestapo, Nebe's Criminal Police or *Kripo*, the German C.I.D., and the S.D., which now became an official organization of the State as distinct from the Party. It was R.S.H.A., still nominally under Himmler, that moved into action in Poland, using special formations of S.S. men and police known as the *Einsatz*, or Action Groups, to carry out the duties assigned them.[6]

On 6 October, the day following his victory parade among the ruins of Warsaw, Hitler made the notorious speech in the Reichstag in which he attacked Poland and challenged her allies: 'The Poland of the Versailles Treaty will never rise again', he declared. The mass movement of population was forecast in order to knit the German peoples together and sever them from contamination by the Jews, of whom large numbers living in Poland were already at the mercy of Heydrich's raiding groups. On 7 October, Himmler's fortieth birthday, Hitler appointed him head of a new organization, the Reich Commissariat for the Consolidation of German Nationhood (R.K.F.D.V.), with the essential task of creating colonies of Germans in areas from which Jews and other alien and unwanted people had been expelled. Himmler's friends celebrated the day by dedicating to him a handsome volume published in his honour – *Festgabe zum* 40 *Geburtstage des Reichsführers S.S. (A Memorial Address to the Reichsführer S.S. on the Occasion of his Fortieth Birthday)* – in which he was singled out as the man primarily responsible for building a new order in Europe to meet the needs of German expansion.

Himmler was himself to describe what happened less than a year later, after the fall of France. Notes in Himmler's handwriting survive for a lecture given to the Supreme Army Commanders on 13 March 1940. In this speech he made his policy for Poland absolutely clear – that the Slavs were to be dominated by the Germanic leadership, that their living space was to be appropriated so that they might never again attack Germany in time of weakness, that their inferior blood meant there must be no mixing of the races. 'Executions of all potential leaders of resistance', scribbled Himmler in his angular, spidery hand. 'Very hard, but necessary. Have seen to it personally . . . No underhand cruelties . . . Severe penalties when necessary . . . Dirty linen to be washed at home . . . We must stay hard, our responsibility to God . . . A million workslaves and how to deal with them.'

The fearful winter of 1939–40 saw whole communities of men and women uprooted from their homes in order to fulfil a compulsory emigration plan for which no proper provision had been made. The chain of callous orders passed down the line from Himmler's and

Heydrich's offices until they reached the local Action Groups, who had been trained to carry out orders without consideration for the consequences to the human beings they evicted. Over 250,000 people of German origin living in Russian-occupied Poland and the Baltic States were by agreement to be transferred to German-occupied Poland, while as the result of an order made by Himmler on 9 October, double that number of Jews and rejected Slavs had to be moved away east to make room for them. Later, by 1943, the numbers exchanged were increased to 566,000 racial Germans brought in from the eastern and south-eastern areas and 1,500,000 Poles and Jews expelled.[7] In November Darré, Reich Minister of Agriculture, was given by Himmler at his own request the task of re-settling the German immigrants on confiscated Polish farms. He wanted to play his part in the great racial migrations which were the outcome of the theories he had taught Himmler ten years before. That he failed in this self-appointed task was perhaps inevitable in view of the vast, complex, overlapping and rival administrations imposed on the torn body of Poland by Hans Frank's cruel administration, and the mutually antagonistic organizations of the military and of Himmler's and Heydrich's police. The S.S. commanders were Friedrich Krueger, a former expert in street-fighting and gun-running, and the peculiar alcoholic sadist whom the S.S. had first enlisted in Austria, Odilo Globocnik, whom Himmler had finally to remove because of his persistent thieving.

Historians have been at pains to find some date for the original conception of genocide in the minds of the Nazi leadership. The casual massacre of Jewish people by the S.S. or the Action Groups began with the war itself, but by January the mass evacuation of Jews from the western provinces had reached proportions which made a high death rate inevitable in the chaos of overloaded and unheated wagons that were shunted around in railway sidings, until the bodies of adults and children alike fell frozen to the ground when the doors were finally thrust open. In December Eichmann was ordered by Heydrich to try to bring some order into the handling of the deportation. The migration of Jews from Germany itself was about to begin when Göring interposed, as President of the Reich Defence Council, to stop the movement because of the rumours of death and suffering which were circulating among the diplomatic corps in Berlin. Meanwhile, Hitler accepted a plan presented to him by Himmler to enslave those Poles in the west who could not be evacuated, depriving them of their property and their children of education, unless they were racially suitable for removal and integration into Germany through *Lebensborn*, which first tested them and then placed them with foster-parents.

The formal acceptance of genocide as Nazi policy did not happen until early in 1941, and was then directly linked in Himmler's mind with the coming invasion of Russia. But by that time his racial prejudice had found outlets which prepared both him and his agents for the supreme test with which they would be faced in 1941. In October 1939 he was required by Hitler to assist in a nation-wide euthanasia programme for the insane, which by 1941 had led to the 'mercy-killing' of some 60,000 German patients in mental institutions.[8] Though the idea was Hitler's, originating in a scribbled note to Philip Bouhler, the head of the Führer's Chancellery, the S.S. was responsible for supplying doctors to carry out the task, while Viktor Brack, a friend of the Himmler family and Bouhler's liaison officer with the Department of Health, was put in charge of the administration. The relatives of the people selected for destruction knew nothing of what was happening, and the notification of the cause of death was falsified. Extermination centres were set up under strict guard, and the S.S. doctors and their nursing and ambulance staff underwent their initial experience of selecting, transporting, gassing and cremating large numbers of helpless people.

The first extermination programme, which was under the medical direction of Karl Brandt, was therefore an arbitrary act by Hitler against the Germans themselves, and was only brought to an end by a telephone call in August 1941 from Hitler to Bouhler after public protests had been made, more particularly by the Churches.[9] For once the Führer had been made to think again as the result of public pressure. Himmler himself became increasingly uneasy about the reaction against the mercy-killings, and in December 1940 he expressed this view to Brack. But the euthanasia programme was not stopped until August 1941, when other work was planned for Himmler's selected medical teams. A much larger extermination programme was beginning by then in Russia. The euthanasia centres were not closed down, but used for the destruction of mental patients from the concentration camps or from among the large numbers of foreign workers brought into Germany. Brack was perfectly prepared to extend the work of euthanasia to extermination of prisoners who were listed as defectives when the point was reached at which there was no difference whatsoever between the operations.

Brandt, questioned in connection with his part in the extermination of the insane at the Doctors' Trial after the war, said:

'It may seem to have been inhuman . . . The underlying motive was the desire to help individuals who could not help themselves . . . Such considerations cannot be regarded as inhuman. Nor did I ever feel it to be in any degree unethical or immoral . . . I am convinced that if Hippocrates were alive today he would change the wording of his Oath . . . in which a doctor is forbidden to administer poison to an invalid even upon demand. He was not in favour of the preservation of life under any circumstances . . . I do not feel myself to blame. I have a perfectly clear conscience about the part I played in the affair.'[10]

A second form of experience for Himmler's doctors began in 1939 when the first recorded medical tests were made involving the use of men in the concentration camps. Liquid war gases, mustard and phosgene, were applied to the skin of selected prisoners and their symptoms were observed and photographed up to the time of death. Reports on their observations were sent by the doctors to Himmler, who ordered further experiments to be carried out on a larger scale. Later, in 1942, there was even to be argument as to whether or not payment should be made for prisoners used in these experiments. One doctor, insulted by this idea, wrote in a report: 'When I think of our military research work conducted at the concentration camp Dachau, I must praise and call special attention to the generous and understanding way in which our task was furthered there and the co-operation we were given. Payment for prisoners was never discussed. It seems as if at Natzweiler camp they are trying to make as much money as possible out of this matter.' According to one witness, the subjects suffered such appalling pain 'one could hardly bear to be near them'. Nevertheless to show their goodwill to the Reichsführer S.S., the prisoners at Buchenwald sent him a valuable Christmas present of a green marble desk set made in the camp sculpture shop, where *objets d'art* were produced by artist-prisoners for the S.S.

In Himmler's mind the preservation of life and the administration of death were indivisible. In the same month when the eviction of the Jews started in Poland and the S.S. doctors began killing the insane in

Germany, Himmler issued his *Lebensborn* decree of 28 October 1939, in which he said:

> 'Beyond the boundaries of bourgeois laws and customs which may in themselves be necessary, it will now become the great task, even outside the marriage bond, for German women and girls of good blood, not in frivolity but in deep moral earnestness, to become mothers of the children of soldiers going off to war . . . On the men and women whose place remains at home by order of the state, these times likewise impose more than ever the sacred obligation to become again fathers and mothers of children.'[11]

Himmler pledged himself and the S.S. to care for all children of pure blood, whether legitimate or not, whose fathers died fighting for Germany. However, he ordered the hanging of a Polish farm labourer for having had sexual relations with a German woman, while women who allowed Polish prisoners or workers sexual liberties were given severe prison sentences. This was race pollution.

Himmler watched over his S.S. organization during the war with all the care of a foster parent. The S.S. were still supposed to rank as an order of chivalry and the officers to behave like knights. In April 1942 Himmler signed an order exhorting his men not to seduce girls out of frivolity and so deprive the nation of potentially fruitful mothers. All seductions were to be reported to him personally. Later, in 1943, he was appalled when he learned there were no less than 244 cases of gonorrhoea in the *Leibstandarte* S.S. Sepp Dietrich hastened to inform him of other facts, and Himmler was able to write in July about the 'pleasingly large number of illegitimate children' in the *Leibstandarte*. 'I want the names of all those children as well as of their mothers,' he added. Pedantic regulations were also compiled to control the conduct of the women serving with the S.S. units; their spare time had to be kept occupied, according to Himmler's ideas, with healthy sport and cultural opportunities. As for homosexuality among S.S. men, this he regarded as equivalent to sabotage.

In return for loyal and deserving service, Himmler initiated a welfare scheme for his men, giving exactly the same personal attention to the details of individual cases in this field as in any other. Widows of S.S. men with children were pensioned; Himmler did not spare himself in sending numerous comforting letters and even small presents of chocolate to such women and their children. Similar pains were taken to look after men invalided out of the S.S.; details of their health, their diet, their needs poured through the S.S. type-writers; the surviving mass of letters and memoranda often bear the personal comments and initials of the Reichsführer S.S. himself. Like a good headmaster, Himmler gave every teacher on his staff and every boy in his school individual attention as far as was pos-sible, no matter how many hours of work it cost. For example, considerable correspondence passed between Himmler and a Secre-tary of State in the Ministry of Agriculture as to whether or not his monthly contribution to *Lebensborn* might be reduced to one mark or not.

Even in time of war, Himmler began to plan for the future. What kind of flats should be provided for a peace-time S.S., each man fathering not less than six children? When such men died, should not their graves be marked by a Teutonic cross, in contrast to the soft and sexless symbol of Christianity? S.S. leaders should possess their coats of arms as befits 'Teutonic brothers'.[12] Discipline must be self-administered; it was unthinkable that an S.S. man should endure the normal military or civil forms of justice. According to Himmler, an S.S. man should never get himself into difficulties by buying goods on an instalment plan. 'An S.S. man doesn't buy what he cannot afford,' Himmler boasted. 'An S.S. man is the most honest soul on earth.' He prided himself that there were no locks on the cupboards in S.S. barracks.

Mother Crosses were presented to S.S. wives who had given birth to seven or more children. The Reichsführer S.S. concerned himself deeply in all matters of maternity, carefully vetting the pedigree of girls who were said to be pregnant by S.S. men before he would grant them the necessary permit to marry. Himmler never ceased to be obsessed by the problems of fine breeding. Hours passed through-out the war while he sat poring over the individual pedigrees of girls with whom S.S. men were involved. What about reviving the old Teutonic myth that copulation conducted on the gravestones of one's ancestors was once said to endow any child so conceived with the brave Teutonic spirit of his forefathers? Special leave was to be given to married S.S. men to encourage procreation, though not necessarily on gravestones. If the men could not be sent back to their women, then the women were to be brought to their men. It is typical that a substantial file survives in which a case of adultery between an S.S. man and a soldier's wife is weighed most carefully; Himmler finally decided in favour of the young couple, and sent the woman who had informed on their activities to learn her lesson in a labour camp.

In his conduct of the *Lebensborn* movement, Himmler's racial obsessions combined with his genetic fantasies and reflected the strange humanitarianism that always lurked in Himmler's nature and which he satisfied through his relations with children, beginning with his own and extending to his nation-wide family of god-children. The parents of German children of pure race who shared his birthday were encouraged to invite Himmler to become a god-father. Special two-page forms were issued so that the stringent scrutiny that preceded the conferring of this honour could be conducted. But Himmler's desire to be the godfather of future generations of pure Germans was also developed through the *Lebensborn* movement. In Himmler's eyes children of sound racial background should be rescued from parents who for political or other reasons were undesirable, and placed in the rehabilitation centre of a *Lebensborn* home.

These homes were staffed by women leaders most carefully chosen for their disciplined and devoted nature; they combined the character of nurses, welfare officers and political educators for the mothers and children in their care. Mothers in the *Lebensborn* homes were not allowed to entertain men, though, wrote Himmler in an order dated 11 January 1941, on very special occasions they could entertain male guests who 'might be offered a cup of coffee, but be given no opportunity for intimacy'. All cases of extreme indiscipline had to be brought to Himmler's personal notice. The mothers were also required in 1941 to eat porridge and fruit for breakfast, and Himmler ordered statistics to be compiled about their resulting blood pressure. The consumption of porridge, said Himmler, was a status symbol in Britain. When the women complained that the porridge would make them fat, Himmler wrote on 12 December 1941:

'I want them to be told that Englishmen, and particularly English Lords and Ladies, are virtually brought up on this kind of food . . . To consume it is considered most correct. It is just these people, both men and women, who are conspicuous for their slender figures. For this reason the mothers in our homes should get used to porridge and be taught to feed their children on it. Heil Hitler!'

He instanced the slim figures of Lord Halifax and Sir Nevile

Henderson as proof that porridge did not fatten such men of breeding. The regular health statistics of both mothers and children became required reading at Himmler's office. 'Any racially good mother is sacred to us', wrote Himmler.

The *Lebensborn* movement which had begun to provide welfare centres for orphans and unmarried mothers with their children, was extended during the war. Himmler established special S.S. homes and institutions to take over young children in the occupied territories who had the right racial characteristics. Writing in June 1941, Himmler outlined his plan in a letter to one of his officers:

'I consider it right and proper to acquire racially desirable infants of Polish families with a view to educating them in special (and not too large) kindergartens and children's homes. The appropriation of these children could be explained on the grounds of health. Children not turning out too well would be returned to their parents.

'I suggest starting in a small way, perhaps with two or three homes at first to gather some practical experience. As for the children who turn out satisfactorily, we should get precise details about their ancestry after six months or so. After a year of successful education we might consider putting such children into the homes of racially good German families with no children of their own.

'Only exceptional men and women, particularly well versed in racial matters, should be considered as heads of institutions such as I envisage them.'[13]

Childless families worried Himmler. In a letter written in April 1942 he advocated the infertile partner in a childless marriage allowing the potentially fertile one to copulate outside the marriage for the sole purpose of begetting children. But these childless families became of increasing importance from 1942 as centres of adoption for the large numbers of children with Germanic characteristics stolen by the S.S. from the occupied territories.

In a later speech given on 14 October 1943, Himmler felt free to go much further. He said, speaking of the Slav nations: 'Obviously in such a mixture of peoples there will always be some racially good types. There I think it is our duty to take their children, to remove them from their environment, if necessary by stealing them . . . Either we win over any good blood that we can use for ourselves and give it a place in our people or . . . we destroy this blood.' The political purpose of this aggregation of German stock was quite clear:

> 'For us the end of this war will mean an open road to the East, the creation of the Germanic Reich in this way or that . . . the fetching home of 30 million human beings of our blood, so that still during our lifetime we shall become a people of 120 million Germanic souls. That means that we shall be the single decisive power in Europe. We shall expand the borders of our German race 500 kilometres further out to the East.'

The number of children up to the age of twelve who were removed in this way will never be known. Though most came from Poland, there were cases of adopted children from Yugoslavia, Czechoslovakia and Russia. This wholesale Germanic adoption was limited by the scale of the organization that could be set up in wartime to deal with it, but an affidavit sworn after the war by Dr Hans Hilmar Staudte, a lawyer attached to the *Lebensborn* movement, claimed that between two and three hundred children were adopted for Germanization in the Warthegau administrative district of Poland. After testing they were placed with German foster parents whose name they were given, their own first names being kept as far as possible in their German form. The children, of course, were taught to speak German, and in effect became Germans. The problem of tracing individual cases still continues to this day in the International Tracing Centre at Arolsen.

Early in 1943 Himmler's fancy was taken by two blond and blue-eyed Russian boys he saw in Minsk. These children were in effect adopted for a while by Himmler and his aides: after having been cleaned and schooled a little, they were sent by air to join Himmler on his train. They travelled for a while with him and there was much S.S. correspondence over the loss of one of their overcoats in Munich. Then they were placed in a school to be trained in the proper ways of the Reich.

The national reaction to *Lebensborn* was often critical. Because the homes were full of unmarried mothers many people thought they were brothels set up for the S.S. The Church in particular opposed the homes. In a speech given to an intimate circle of high officials much later in the war, during May 1944, Himmler spoke informally about the *Lebensborn* movement and the attacks that had been made upon it, and on himself for advising his S.S. men to procreate:

'. . . At first these *Lebensborn* homes, like every new idea, became the object of scandalmongers by the score. They called them breeding-grounds, human stud-farms and so on. In fact, in these homes we merely look after mothers and the children, some of them legitimate, some not. I would say the ratio is about fifty-fifty, more likely sixty-forty in favour of the legitimately born babies.

'In these homes every woman is addressed as Frau Marta, or Frau Elisabeth, or whatever her name happens to be. No one bothers whether their babies are legitimate or illegitimate. We look after mother and child, protect them, help them in their problems. There is only one thing unforgivable in these homes: if a mother fails to care for her child as a mother should.

'Towards the end of 1939, after the Polish campaign, as soon as we knew that the war would go on in the West – the British and French having turned down the Führer's peace offer after the Polish campaign – I issued an order which at that time caused quite a controversy and got the scandalmongers going again with further loads of abuse, directed largely at me. That order of mine simply said: every S.S. man before going to the front should procreate a child.

'It seemed to me a thoroughly simple and decent order, and by now, after many years of terrible losses sustained by the German people, those who failed to comprehend my order at the time will have come to see that it makes sense. After all, I gave these matters a great deal of careful thought. My consideration was simply this: it's a law of nature that the most valuable blood is lost for the nation so long as it cannot be procreated. It stands to reason that the man who is racially the most valuable will be the bravest soldier, and the one most likely to be killed in action. A nation which, in the course of twenty-five years has lost millions of its best sons, simply cannot afford such a loss of its blood; hence if the nation is to survive, and if the sacrifice of its best blood is not to be wasted, something had to be done about it.'

At the time he was making this speech about the procreation in the S.S., Hedwig, Himmler's recognized mistress, was in the last stages of pregnancy with her second child. She gave birth to a daughter, who was named Nanette Dorothea. Her son Helge had been born on 15 February 1942.[14]

The establishment of this second family placed a strain on Himmler's deliberately restricted income. Schellenberg throws some light on this situation. Himmler, during a period of truce with Bormann, with whom he was later to form a kind of tactical relationship, asked for a loan of 80,000 marks from Party funds, ostensibly to build a house. Bormann granted him the loan, but at a very high rate of interest which Himmler could scarcely afford to pay out of his official salary. Schellenberg was astonished at this extraordinary arrangement which he found 'incomprehensible', and made his own observation on Himmler's domestic problems:

'Himmler's first marriage had been unhappy, but for his daughter's sake he had not sought divorce. He now lived with a woman who was not his wife, and they had two very nice children to whom he was completely devoted. He did what he could for these children within the limits of his own income, but although, after Hitler, Himmler had more real power than anyone else in the Third Reich, and through the control of many economic organisations could have had millions at his disposal, he found it difficult to provide for their needs.'[15]

When Schellenberg suggested a mortgage would be cheaper than the loan, Himmler rejected the suggestion with an 'air of resignation'. It was, he said, 'a completely private matter and he wanted to act with meticulous rectitude; in no circumstances did he want to discuss it with the Führer'. Meanwhile, he supported his family at Gmund, and although his wife knew of his liaison with Hedwig, he maintained formal good relations with her for the sake of their daughter Gudrun.

In November 1939, Himmler had assigned a special mission to Schellenberg, who abducted from Venlo, a town just across the Dutch frontier, two British Intelligence officers with whom he had been in contact, posing as an anti-Nazi German officer. The British agents, Captain S. Payne Best and Major R. H. Stevens, were accused of being involved in an attempt on Hitler's life at Munich on 8 November. Though is is now widely assumed that the attempted assassination had been pre-arranged with Hitler's approval, seven men lost their lives in the explosion that occurred after the Führer and other leaders had left. Hitler needed this excuse for propaganda to stir the German people against the Allies and to show what desperate enemies Himmler's agents had to face. On 21 November Himmler announced that the British Intelligence service was behind the plot, and that prisoners had been taken.

The Venlo incident itself was to become one of the more entertaining spy stories of the war, both Schellenberg and Captain Payne Best giving their own detailed accounts of what happened. Both the British officers spent the next five years in concentration camps, and Schellenberg was promoted to S.S. Major-General for his efforts in having captured them. Schellenberg's specialization in foreign espionage led to the practice of placing S.D. and Gestapo men as attachés in various German legations and embassies abroad, which enabled Himmler once more to encroach on Ribbentrop's territory. In March 1940, as a follow-up to the Venlo incident, Schellenberg enabled Himmler to present a detailed report to Hitler establishing the close connection that existed between British and Dutch military Intelligence. Hitler was later to use this incident to help justify his attack on the Netherlands for violating their neutrality.

In the early months of 1940 Hitler was preparing for the assault on the West. The loss in February of the plans for the campaign against Holland and Belgium – when a special courier who was carrying them made a forced landing in Belgium owing to poor visibility – caused consternation among the Nazi leaders. While Göring raved at the carelessness of the Luftwaffe and dismissed the commander of the Air Fleet whose officer had done the damage, Himmler, according to Schellenberg, was so excited and confused he was quite unable to give clear instructions about the immediate necessity to draw up security regulations for the Army.

Himmler's military ambitions were still frustrated. The S.S. fighting forces acquired their official title of *Waffen* or Armed S.S. during the Western offensive, in which only two S.S. divisions served alongside some eighty-seven divisions of the Army. They were given favoured positions in which to display their ruthlessness in battle, while the special armoured S.S. regiment, the *Leibstandarte Adolf Hitler* under Sepp Dietrich, played as spectacular a part as possible in the fall of Rotterdam and Boulogne. Theodor Eicke's Death's Head division made up of German camp guards behaved with shameless ferocity, as the massacre of British troops at Le Paradis in May 1940 showed; the celebrated Private Pooley was one of only two survivors.

But in spite of this activity by the S.S., Himmler seems to have taken no direct part in the campaign, which lasted from April 1940, with the initial occupation of Denmark and Norway, to 21 June, when the conquest of Belgium, Holland and France was complete and the armistice was signed by Hitler in the Forest of Compiègne, a ceremony at which Himmler was not present.

While Heydrich had sprung once more into his Luftwaffe aircraft to enjoy aggression in the field – from which he sent Himmler a postcard on 5 May promising to be back at his desk within eight days – the Reichsführer S.S. trundled west in his armoured train, once more following in the wake of Hitler. He managed to send a letter to '*Mein lieber Heydrich*' on 15 May explaining that he had spent some days at the Führer's headquarters and adding, with an ironic reference to the Polish campaign, 'the only difference is that we are at a different place'. The close of the letter throws some light on his feelings for Heydrich. 'I think about you very much. I hope everything is going well. And I wish you renewed success, happiness – and everything good. Love from Wölfchen and Häschen. Yours, Heinrich Himmler.' Then he placed a formal order that Heydrich was to send a daily report by telephone stating what he had done and how he was. Heydrich was to fly with the Luftwaffe until the end of the campaign in June, and be present to enjoy all the fruits of victory in Montmartre. He spent July in the urgent preparation of plans for the control of Britain by the Gestapo and S.D. after the conquest in the autumn. On 27 September S.S. Colonel Professor Dr Franz Six, former head of the faculty of economics in the University of Berlin, was appointed to head the Action Group activities in Britain which would follow immediately upon the invasion.

Meanwhile Himmler was facing certain difficulties in extending his wartime powers. Hitler was determined to restrict the members of the *Waffen* S.S. to some four divisions (at most about 5 per cent of the armed forces), while Himmler himself was personally committed to such high standards of selection that the average recruit to the German Army fell far below his Nordic ideal. It was during 1940 that Himmler and his sport-and-nature-loving Chief of Staff for the *Waffen* S.S., Gottlieb Berger, decided that all men of Nordic race might qualify for admission to their forces, whether they were German or not. By the end of 1940 there was a so-called Viking Division in the *Waffen* S.S. under the German divisional Commander, Felix Steiner, and volunteers from Holland, Denmark, Norway and

Finland had begun to join. By the closing months of the war, in 1945, there were thirty-five *Waffen* S.S. divisions, most of them substantially recruited from the occupied countries. Himmler made his racial theories work in his favour, and they enabled him to fulfil his ambitions of commanding on his own account a substantial body of men separate from the regular Army, over which he exercised no influence except for a few disastrous months during 1944–5. In a private memorandum that survives, dated 13 April 1942, Himmler insists that all the German leaders and sub-leaders of these foreign S.S. units must receive special ideological training and report to him personally before taking up their duties. They must, he says, have 'a firm faith in our ideal'.

On 7 September 1940, Himmler went to France to address the officers of the S.S. *Leibstandarte Adolf Hitler* at Metz. Only a month before, on 6 August, Hitler had told the S.S. in a speech that their future role was to be that of a volunteer *élite* force whose duties would be strictly those of a political police, while three weeks before that, from the public platform of the Reichstag, the Führer had shown his favour to the victorious Army by creating twelve new field-marshals. Himmler felt aggrieved and made insidious remarks about the attitude of the Army to the S.S. during the course of a speech in September, the chief aim of which was to state in no uncertain terms the importance of the S.S. to the welfare and advacement of the State, and of the S.D. to its internal security. He knew that many men in the wartime S.S. did not understand the ideals for which he had struggled since 1929, and he realized that the forcible deportations, 'the very difficult task out there performed by the Security Police supported by your men', seemed distasteful to some of them. So he went on to tell them why this must be done:

'Exactly the same thing happened in Poland in weather forty degrees below zero, where we had to haul away thousands, tens of thousands, hundreds of thousands, where we had to have the toughness – you should hear this but also forget it again immediately – to shoot thousands of leading Poles, otherwise revenge would have been taken on us later, . . . all duties where the proud soldier says: "My God, why do I have to do that, this ridiculous job here!" – It is much easier to go into combat with a company than to suppress an obstructive population of low cultural level, or to carry out executions, or to haul away people, or to evict crying and hysterical women, or to return our German racial

brethren across the border from Russia and to take care of them
. . . You have to consider the work of the S.D. man or of the man
of the Security Police as a vital part of our whole work just like
the fact that you can carry arms. You are the men to be envied
because . . . if a unit achieves fame . . . it can be decorated. It is
much more difficult in other positions . . . in this silent com-
pulsion work, this silent activity.'[16]

Himmler talked next about the necessity to improve political
education in the *Waffen* S.S., so that the activities of the S.D. would
be better understood; they must realize, he said, that the duties of
the S.D. man were 'very, very difficult', and 'very, very valuable'.
Then he began to tell them of his vision of the future, his dreams of
S.S. garrisons 'safe-guarding the race' by establishing settlements
outside Germany and extending 'our *Lebensraum*' into colonies set
up, for example, in South Africa, in the Arctic, and in the West.
'The first two years of peace will be decisive for our future', he said.
'Peace begun with an iron hand . . . We must start an unheard-of
education of ourselves. It is necessary that obedience be granite-like.'
What is done after the war, 'during Adolf Hitler's life, will live on
for centuries to come . . . If we make a mistake, the mistake too will
live on for centuries.'

Even guard duty in the camps over 'the scum of mankind', said
Himmler, will form 'the best indoctrination on inferior beings and
the inferior races. This activity is necessary, as I said, to eliminate
these negative beings from the German people, to exploit them for the
great folk community by having them break stones and bake bricks
so that the Führer can erect his grand buildings. If the good blood
is not reproduced', he went on, 'we will not be able to rule the world
. . . A nation which has an average of four sons per family can venture
a war; if two of them die, two live to transplant the name.' Then he
concluded: 'The ultimate aim for these eleven years during which I
have been the Reichsführer S.S. has been invariably the same: to
create an order of good blood which is able to inspire Germany . . .
an order which will spread the idea of Nordic blood so far and
wide that we will attract all the Nordic strain in the world, and take
away that blood from our adversaries, absorb it so that never again
. . . will Nordic people fight against us.' This, he said, was the 'great
common goal' for which the S.S. was 'a means to an end – always
the Reich, the ideology, created by the Führer, the Reich, created
by him, the Reich of all Teutons.'

Himmler's absence from the victory celebrations in France was largely due to his continued ill-health. From the time of the first treatment he had been given by Felix Kersten, the masseur, he had experienced a relief that seemed magical to his strained nerves. Kersten was two years older than Himmler, and very different from him in temperament. After a hard life in his youth, he was determined to enjoy the wealth and position that his highly specialized and lucrative practice among the European aristocracy had brought him. According to his own account, he was born in the Baltic provinces, in Estonia, had studied agriculture in Holstein, managed a farm in Anhalt, served in the Finnish Army during the war against Russia in 1919, becoming as a result a Finnish citizen, and had then entered the Veteran Hospital of Helsinki suffering from rheumatic fever. It was here that his outstanding gift for massage had been discovered. He had determined to make healing through massage his career, labouring, he claimed, as a longshoreman and dishwasher in order to pay for his medical studies. He had first gone to Berlin in 1922; there he had studied at the University and then trained under the celebrated Chinese physician, Dr Ko. Kersten claimed that Dr Ko 'declared he had never met anyone with hands like mine. He said my sense of touch was nothing short of miraculous.' So great was the Chinese doctor's confidence in Kersten that he allowed him to take over his practice in Berlin when he returned to China in 1925.

Kersten delighted in attending the distinguished patients who sought him out, and had established himself at The Hague at the personal invitation of Prince Henry of the Netherlands, who had become one of his patients in 1928. In 1934 he had bought his German estate of Hartzwalde some forty miles north of Berlin, intending eventually to return and become a 'gentleman farmer'. In 1937 he had married a beautiful girl from Silesia who was barely half his age.

This was the man who on 10 March 1939 had first met Himmler, and had been more than surprised to find him a 'narrow-chested, weak-chinned, spectacled man with an ingratiating smile'. Left for a few minutes among Himmler's books, he had seen many volumes on German and medieval history, on Henry the Fowler and Genghis Khan, and on Mohammed and the Mohammedan faith. In his bedroom, he saw that Himmler was reading the Koran in a German translation, a book he kept constantly by him. Kersten, a man of the world, had thought him at the time 'a pedant, a mystic, and bookish'. Moreover, 'his hands were soft'.

At the first examination they discussed his symptoms, the immediate cause of which appeared to be ptomaine poisoning that had excited an old nervous complaint originating from severe typhoid fever contracted during the First World War. As a child, Kersten learned, Himmler had suffered from paratyphoid, and as a youth from dysentery and jaundice. Kersten turned back Himmler's shirt and felt the sensitive area round his stomach. His touch, Himmler said, was 'like balm', and he urged Kersten to treat him. Kersten realized he could bring Himmler temporary relief, but never cure him.

Kersten was a man who combined a profound dedication to his unique skill as a masseur with a desire for wealth and social success. He was a fortunate man, whose great gift of healing brought him the gratitude of many people who were in a position to give him the kind of life the more worldly side of his nature enjoyed. His successful treatment of Rosterg, a German potash magnate, had enabled him to acquire his estate of Hartzwalde when Rosterg had given him 100,000 marks. It was at Rosterg's earnest request that he had first agreed to examine Himmler in 1939.

Before the war began, Kersten had attended him both in Berlin and at Gmund and had grown familiar with the weak and opinionated nature of his patient. He knew that Himmler wanted war as much as Hitler, and he had already learnt how to argue with him on such subjects unscathed. Kersten was, however, notoriously without interest in politics; but he was, after all, not German, and therefore immune from German law and discipline. He could still have withdrawn from treating Himmler when war began, as his wife and friends begged him to do. But when he sought the advice of his contacts in the diplomatic corps at the Finnish Embassy in Berlin, they urged him to stay with Himmler, whose conversation after treatment, free from any sense of discretion, might well prove of the greatest value if what he revealed were passed on to the Embassy. Irmgard Kersten, who was German, liked best to live at Hartzwalde, and when Stalin overran Estonia, Kersten's native land, and declared war on Finland, the country whose nationality he had taken, it was to Hartzwalde that Kersten brought his father, who was approaching ninety, to live out his life in Germany.

Himmler was not in a position to force Kersten to attend him until the spring of 1940, when he confined him to Hartzwalde and refused him a visa to return to his patients in Holland. A few days later it was Himmler who broke the news to him that Germany had invaded Holland; he had been refused his visa to protect him from the consequences of the invasion. Again the officials at the Finnish Embassy urged him to stay with Himmler rather than leave Germany. This contact with Himmler, they said, was work that could be of the greatest national importance.

On 15 May 1940 Kersten had received his first order to join Himmler's armoured train and attend the Reichsführer as his official staff doctor. Here he had treated Brandt, Himmler's secretary, as well as Himmler, and begun another association at headquarters of which he was later to make full use. But from the summer of 1940 until the autumn of 1943, when he managed to persuade Himmler to let him live in Stockholm, he was in effect at the Reichsführer's complete disposal, though he treated such other patients as he could reach in Germany. Himmler demanded that he give up his home and contacts in The Hague. His services even became a point of barter between Ciano and Himmler, and Kersten won from Himmler the most unusual privilege of using the Reichsführer's own postal channel for private correspondence, an arrangement supposed to be connected with his love affairs. In fact he used it for keeping in touch with his underground contacts in Holland.

It was in August 1940 that he obtained his first release for a man in a concentration camp – one of Rosterg's servants who had been imprisoned solely for political reasons. Later, before leaving Holland, he had secured the release of one of his friends, an anti-quarian called Bignell, on the strength of a telephone call to Himmler, who was at the time in urgent need of treatment. Kersten soon learned the technique of flattering Himmler and appealing to the right side of his vanity in these moments when, through the relief he could bring, he had the upper hand. The requests gradually became habitual; as Himmler put it himself: 'Kersten massages a life out of me with every rub.' Heydrich and the leaders of the S.S. grew jealous of this alien influence in Himmler's private life. Only Kersten's special place in Himmler's favour spared him from interrogation and arrest by the Gestapo; Heydrich's suspicions of him never relaxed.

The concentration camps remained directly under Himmler's

control. At the beginning of the war, according to Kogon, there were more than a hundred camps with their numerous satellites, though Dachau remained the symbol for all. Other large camps included Buchenwald, Sachsenhausen, Gross-Rosen, Flossenbürg, Ravensbrück for women, and Mauthausen near Linz, in Austria. At the height of the war there were some thirty principal camps, some being nominally more rigorous than others. After the war had begun, new camps were set up in the occupied territories, such as Auschwitz and Lublin in Poland and Natzweiler in the Vosges, while others, such as Bergen-Belsen, were established in Germany. Kogon estimates that not less than a million people were held in the camps at any one time during the war, with an increasing flow both in and out as the exterminators developed the pace of their work.

Discipline was constantly tightened. Hoess was still at Sachsenhausen when Himmler paid a visit unannounced during January 1940. He complained bitterly that a working party of prisoners and their guards had failed either to recognize him or salute when he had passed them in his car, and as a result of this incident the Commandant was dismissed. Six months later, in June 1940, Hoess was to be promoted Commandant of Himmler's new camp at Auschwitz.

The fact that a million men and women existed in the camps at Himmler's mercy led in the first place to the organized medical experiments which, though practised on a relatively limited scale, seem more horrifying than the act of extermination itself. That some 350 qualified doctors (one doctor in every 300 then practising in Germany) should have been prepared to take active part in this fearful misuse of the bodies of helpless men and women seems a greater degradation of humanity than the spectacle of Hoess, the ex-criminal Commandant of Auschwitz, faithfully obeying his orders beside the gas-chambers.

At a trial known as the Doctors' Case and held before a Military Tribunal in Nuremberg from December 1946 to July 1947, twenty-three of these doctors were permitted to defend themselves before the court. The majority of the experiments undertaken by the doctors at the direct instigation of Himmler were in fact calculated murder under the guise of collecting medical data, and most of them meant the infliction of indescribable agonies on the patients. At their trial, the representative doctors who were accused of having done these things mustered their great excuse – the doctrine of obedience:

'At that time I was Rascher's subordinate. He was a staff surgeon of
the Luftwaffe' – and the doctrine of war, 'the absolute necessity of
victory in order to eliminate evil elements'. A professor who worked
on the typhus vaccine experiments at Natzweiler defended his
actions through which ninety-seven prisoners died by citing a single
loss of life that had occurred among a group of men under sentence
of death who had volunteered in America to assist in experiments to
trace the cause of beri-beri fever.

Himmler's direct participation in this most cruel work is proved
by surviving letters and memoranda.[17] The principal experiments
occurred during the period 1941–4. They began, as we have seen,
with Himmler giving his consent as early as 1939 for the use of
prisoners to test mustard gas and phosgene, tests which were later
to be conducted by a Professor of Anatomy who held an officer's
rank in the S.S. These experiments were directly associated with
Himmler's Institute for Research and Study of Heredity, the
*Ahnenerbe*, which was directed by Wolfram Sievers, a former
bookseller, who on Himmler's orders in July 1942 set up an Institute
for Practical Research in Military Science as a department of
*Ahnenerbe*. Sievers wrote to Hirt: 'The Reichsführer S.S. would
like to hear more details from you at an early date about your
mustard-gas experiments . . . Could you not some day write a brief,
secret report?' These tests involved the infliction of burns on the
victim's body which spread from day to day and often led to blindness and death. Post-mortem examination revealed that the intestines
and lungs were eaten away.

Dr Sigmund Rascher, a former staff surgeon of the Luftwaffe and
an officer in the S.S., had no difficulty in May 1941 in obtaining
from Himmler, who had sent him flowers on the birth of his second
son, the favour of having certain prisoners put at his disposal for his
low-pressure, high-altitude experiments which, as he warned the
Reichsführer S.S., would involve the risk of death. 'I can inform you
that prisoners will, of course, be gladly made available for the high-
flight researches', wrote Rudolf Brandt, Himmler's secretary.
There were additional reasons for Himmler's interest in the doctor.
Rascher's mistress, who was fifteen years older than her lover,
claimed she had given birth to three children after her forty-eighth
year; she was also a personal friend of Marga Himmler. There were,
it is true, certain racial difficulties in her ancestry which had prevented her marriage until Himmler intervened to clear the way for

her, and he willingly became the godfather of Rascher's remarkable offspring.

Rascher's experiments, nominally undertaken on behalf of the Luftwaffe, took place mainly during 1942 at Dachau, and Rascher sent reports on their outcome to Himmler; the reactions of the men placed in the Luftwaffe's low-pressure chambers loaned to Dachau were filmed. In all, nearly 200 men were submitted to these experiments, and over seventy died as a result. Both the reports and photographs survive and were used in evidence during the various trials at Nuremberg. Himmler's direct personal interest in the experiments is proved by his notorious letter to Rascher dated 13 April 1942:

'The latest discoveries made in your experiments have specially interested me . . . Experiments are to be repeated on other men condemned to death . . . Considering the long-continued action of the heart, the experiments should be specifically developed so as to determine whether these men can be revived. Should such an experiment succeed, then the person condemned to death shall of course be pardoned and sent to a concentration camp for life.'

Himmler's enthusiasm proved in the end, like Rascher's, to be that of an amateur. The experiments were considered useless in the eyes of doctors more expert than Rascher, including Himmler's own medical adviser, Professor Gebhardt, who considered the reports 'completely unscientific'. The low-pressure chamber was eventually withdrawn from Dachau in March 1942 in spite of Rascher's strenuous opposition. During the Doctors' Trial at Nuremberg, a doctor who was accused of assisting Rascher in his experiments but found not guilty, was asked whether he had any scruples about them. He replied: 'I had no scruples on legal grounds. For I knew that the man who had officially authorized these experiments was Himmler . . . Consequently, I had no scruples of any kind in that direction. In the sphere of what one may call medical ethics it was rather different. It was a wholly new experience for us all to be offered persons to experiment on . . . I had to get used to the idea.' He satisfied himself that experiments of this kind had happened abroad, and that sufficed. Rascher, on the other hand, wrote to Himmler: 'Your active interest in these experiments has a tremendous influence on one's working capacity and initiative.'

In August Rascher, under the supervision of a medical specialist began a second series of tests; these concerned the effects of freezing on the human body and they were considered useful because German pilots were often precipitated into the sea. The experiments were supposed to determine how men subjected to extreme cold could be revived. At the Doctors' Trial, another of the accused who was found not guilty, gave evidence of a conversation he had had with Himmler:

DEFENCE COUNSEL: Did Himmler say anything more about supercooling experiments at this meeting?

DEFENDANT: Yes. He began by saying that the experiments were of the greatest importance to the Army, Air Force and Fleet. He talked at great length about such tests and how they should be conducted . . . He added that country people often knew excellent remedies which had long proved their worth, such as teas brewed from medicinal herbs . . . Such popular remedies should by no means be overlooked. He said he could also well imagine that a fisherman's wife might take her half-frozen husband to bed with her after he had been rescued and warm him up that way . . . He told Rascher he must certainly experiment in that direction as well . . .

DEFENCE COUNSEL: Did Himmler add anything more at these discussions?

DEFENDANT: He said it certainly would not be asking too much to require concentration camp prisoners, who could not be sent on active service on account of the crimes they had committed, to take part in such experiments; . . . in that way they could rehabilitate themselves . . .

DEFENCE COUNSEL: What impression did you receive from these remarks?

DEFENDANT: They were of a kind you could not be wholly out of sympathy with in the grave emergency of those days.

Rascher's reports began to come in by October 1942, and a conference on the subject attended by nearly a hundred medical officers of the Luftwaffe followed in this same month. After this, one supervising specialist declined to take any further part in the experiments in which around 15 men out of the 50 or so used had already died. Rascher then continued the experiments on his own, and the deaths increased to between 80 and 90. The men, either dressed in flying uniform or stripped, were immersed for periods of up to one and a half hours in water kept a few degrees above freezing. Himmler, again taking a personal interest in the experiments, wrote to Rascher on 24 October: 'I am very anxious as to the experiments with body warmth' – though Rascher in a report from Dachau dated 15 August had suggested dispensing with these because the reaction of the frozen men was too slow. Himmler also showed his indignation with those who were criticizing Rascher's use of human beings. 'I regard as guilty of treason', he wrote, '. . . people who, even today, reject these experiments on humans and would instead let sturdy German soldiers die . . . I shall not hesitate to report these men.'

Four prostitutes were sent from the women's concentration camp at Ravensbrück to supply the animal warmth in which Himmler believed, but one of these girls unfortunately turned out to be German. Rascher remonstrated with her, but she said she had volunteered for six months' brothel duty in order to secure her future release from the camp. 'It hurts my racial feelings', wrote Rascher to Himmler on 5 November, 'to expose as a prostitute to racially inferior concentration camp elements a girl who has the appearance of a pure Nordic.' So the experiment went on without her, and Himmler came to see the results personally at Dachau on 13 November. In the same month, he wrote to a senior officer in the Luftwaffe, asking for Rascher's release from the Luftwaffe so that his work could be continued solely under the S.S. 'These researches', he wrote, '. . . can be performed by us with particular efficiency because I personally assumed the responsibility for supplying from concentration camps for these experiments anti-social elements and criminals who only deserve to die.' Now, he went on to complain, Christian medical circles were beginning to protest, and the experiments would best be conducted by the S.S. alone, with a 'non-Christian physician' acting as liaison officer between the Luftwaffe and the S.S. He singled out a Dr Holzlöhner as the principal troublemaker.

Rascher was eventually released from the Luftwaffe so that he could maintain his practices in secrecy. His experiments at Dachau continued, and he sent a detailed report dated 12 February 1943, pointing out how the prospects and fulfilment of sexual intercourse between the frozen men and the prostitutes substantially quickened the return of warmth. He then went on to ask Himmler for yet another favour: could he be removed to Auschwitz – 'the camp itself is so extensive that less attention will be attracted to the work.

For the subjects howl so when they freeze!' Himmler was conducting other experiments at Auschwitz, and Rascher stayed at Dachau until he was arrested with his wife in 1944 for child abduction: the three children whose birth had so impressed their godfather Himmler had all been misappropriated. According to evidence given at Nuremberg, Himmler prevented any investigation of Rascher's case; he remained under arrest and was shot at Dachau before the arrival of the Americans. According to Gebhardt, his wife was hanged at the same time 'at Himmler's suggestion'.

Although Rascher in the end proved to be a criminal sadist who took particular delight in causing intense suffering under the mask of science, he was only one of many who worked to satisfy Himmler's obsession with medical experiment. During 1942–4 the work went on in a number of camps. In addition to the experiments with mustard gas and phosgene, which as we have seen began as early as 1939, Professor Gebhardt, Himmler's personal physician and consultant surgeon of the *Waffen* S.S., took charge of the sulphonamide tests on women at Ravensbrück, which was only eight miles from his orthopaedic clinic at Hohenlychen. These tests were initiated by Himmler as a response to the Allied use of sulphonamides and penicillin, knowledge of which was reaching the German soldiers and affecting morale. In May 1942 Himmler held a conference at which Gebhardt and the Chief of the S.S. Medical Service were present, and undoubtedly Heydrich's death in Prague from gangrene influenced the decision taken by Hitler and Himmler to order the experimental infection of Polish women under sentence of death at Ravensbrück with gas-gangrenous wounds. This work was supervised by the chief of the S.S. Medical Service and Gebhardt, and various sulphonamide preparations were tested on these 'rabbit girls', as they were called. Dr Fritz Fischer, one of Gebhardt's assistants at Hohenlychen and a senior medical man working on these experiments, which inflicted the most fearful pain on the victims, said at the Doctors' Trial:

'Loyalty to the State appeared to me at that period, when some 1,500 soldiers were falling daily on active service and several hundred people were dying daily behind the lines as a result of war conditions, to be the supreme moral duty. I believed we were offering reasonable chances of survival to the subjects of our experiments, who were living under German law and could not otherwise escape the death penalty . . . I was not then a doctor in civil life, free to take his own decisions. I was ... a medical expert bound to act in exactly the same way as a soldier under discipline.'

From Himmler's point of view as expressed at his conference in May, the women were being granted 'an excellent chance of reprieve'.

Among the worst experiments in the camps were those that developed from the cruel, clumsy attempts to achieve methods of mass sterilization. These began as early as the autumn of 1941, when it became clear that the extermination of the races in the East could be effected most easily by such means. A scheme for sterilization by drugs was presented to Himmler in October 1941 by a specialist in venereal disease. 'The thought alone that the three million Bolsheviks at present German prisoners could be sterilized so that they could be used as labourers but be prevented from reproduction, open the most far-reaching perspectives', he wrote. Himmler was interested and authorized that 'sterilization experiments should in any case be carried out in the concentration camps'. All experiments in sterilization drugs proved abortive, but Viktor Brack had already, in March 1941, sent Himmler a report on 'experiments with Röntgen castration', recommending the use of 'high X-ray dosages' which 'destroy the internal secretion of the ovary, or of the testicles, respectively'. Exposure to the rays, Brack pointed out, would take only two minutes for men and three for women, and could be administered without their knowledge while, for example, they filled in forms at a counter. Severe burns would result, however, within a few days or weeks and 'other tissues of the body will be injured'. Brack presented his scheme again a year later, in June 1942, stating that 'castration by X-ray ... is not only relatively cheap but can also be performed on many thousands in the shortest time'.

The following year the experiments began in Auschwitz and its subsidiary camp at Birkenau, where young Polish Jews were operated upon by X-ray, which caused them great pain in spite of which they were forced to continue at work. Subsequently many of them were castrated by normal means so that their testicles could be examined. These experiments continued until the end of April 1944, when Brack's successor reported to Himmler that mass sterilization by X-ray could no longer be considered practicable.

Another experimenter, a professor from Upper Silesia, was given

the opportunity to attempt sterilization of women prisoners in
Ravensbrück, though Rudolf Brandt wrote to him on 10 July 1943:
'Before you start your job, the Reichsführer would be interested to
learn from you how long it would take to sterilize a thousand
Jewesses'. He envisaged checking results by 'locking up a Jewess
and Jew together for a certain period and then seeing what results
are achieved'. The professor's method was to inject inflammatory
liquid into the uterus, the results of which could be examined by X-
ray. It was administered without anaesthetics, and children were
among the victims. The numbers may now never be known who
suffered from these cruel and fearful tests. Evidence was given at the
Doctors' Trial by a few survivors.

In 1943 the experiments were extended to epidemic hepatitis
virus research at Sachsenhausen. 'I approve that eight criminals
condemned in Auschwitz [eight Jews of the Polish Resistance
Movement condemned to death] should be used for these experiments', wrote Himmler to a doctor on 16 June 1943. 'Casualties
must be expected', he had been warned a fortnight earlier. Phlegmon
was artificially induced by doctors at Dachau, the subjects chosen in
this case being Catholic priests; Gebhardt claimed that he had
protested to Himmler about this, but that the Reichsführer S.S.,
eager to 'dig up old popular remedies out of the rubbish heap' as a
challenge to the academic medicine which he despised, had refused
to have the work stopped.

Ravensbrück was so conveniently near to Gebhardt's clinic at
Hohenlychen, that he took advantage of experiments in bone
transplantation which had been developed in the camp, with the
'special approval' of Himmler, to steal the shoulder-blade of a
female prisoner and transfer it to one of his private patients.

In the autumn of 1943 Himmler personally intervened in a dispute
about the choice of subjects for the typhus vaccine experiments at the
special centre which had been set up in Buchenwald under Grawitz
in 1941. Himmler's instructions were that only persons under
sentence of at least ten years' penal servitude were to be used.
Similar experiments were undertaken at Natzweiler camp in 1943
under the initial supervision of a professor of hygiene. In July 1944,
Himmler authorized the use of gypsies for testing the possibility
of drinking sea-water; since he regarded the gypsies as scarcely
human, he added that 'for checking' three other, more normal
people, should be added to the subject-list.

Himmler as a standard-bearer at the barricades the November *putsch* in Munich

Himmler's house at Gmuud

The process of extermination that had begun with the insane in 1940 was continued in the case of many mentally defective and deformed children; Himmler's orders, as far as defective children in the camps were concerned, were quite explicit; they must be done away with along with other 'incurables'. In June 1942 Himmler gave consent to the 'special treatment' of tubercular Poles. Only in 1943, when the working capacity of all prisoners was regarded as important, was a special order from Himmler circulated to the Camp Commandants that 'in future only insane prisoners can be selected for Action 14f 13', the reference number for euthanasia. 'All other prisoners unfit for work (persons suffering from tuberculosis, bedridden invalids, etc.) are definitely to be excluded from this action. Bedridden prisoners were to be given suitable work which can be performed in bed.' There is evidence, however, that the extermination of sick and unwanted prisoners did in fact continue.

In July 1942, as we have seen, an Institute for Practical Research in Military Science was founded by Himmler inside his Ancestral Heritage Community, the *Ahnenerbe*. This Institute, working in close association with the Reich University of Strasbourg, began to assemble the collection of skeletons and skulls of Jews under the supervision of an expert on anatomy, who on 9 February 1942 had urged Himmler to help his researches by enabling him to procure 'the skulls of the Jewish-Bolshevik Commissars who personify a repulsive yet characteristic subhumanity'. Himmler formally agreed on 23 February, and by the autumn Sievers, the manager of *Ahnenerbe*, was able to report to Eichmann in a memorandum headed 'Assembling of a skeleton collection' that a consignment of 115 persons, including 30 Jewesses, was to be made available. They were gassed the following year at Oranienburg by Joseph Kramer, who subsequently described under examination, with the cold exactitude of a good technician, precisely how he and his men carried out their tasks. The gas was provided by Hirt, and the bodies were sent direct to the Institute for preservation in tanks. A witness at the Institute described the first delivery, the remains of the thirty murdered Jewesses: 'The bodies were still warm when they arrived. Their eyes were wide open and glazing. Their eyeballs were bloodshot, red and protuberant. There were also traces of blood about the noses and mouths . . . There was no sign of *rigor mortis*.' Consignments of male bodies followed at intervals.

Himmler was very proud of the research that he had instituted and his relationship to the *Ahnenerbe* organization. Giving his evasive evidence during the Doctors' Trial, Gebhardt said:

'He became, I am now told, President of *Ahnenerbe*, the Ancestral Heritage Community. He was the centre of . . . the so-called Friends of Himmler circle which he founded. It was a dangerous mixture of eccentric individuals and industrialists. From that quarter he obtained both the funds and the encouragement to undertake the thousand and one schemes which he put into operation. I have an idea that the extraordinary, newly-founded Institute where all these scientific friends of his met was in fact the Ancestral Heritage Community. Himmler, in a word, as I have often pointed out, was attached to a crazy, completely false notion of antiquity . . . The danger lay in the fact that it was always he who made the decisions.'

Thus Himmler, who was too reserved a man to extend his power over the surface of Germany in the flamboyant manner of Göring, sent his roots deep into the subterranean earth of the camps, creating there a life-in-death for a vast but hidden community that was to absorb and destroy millions of Europeans, and most of all the Jews. This was to become the secret empire of death rejected by the conscience of the German people who, though they were in varying degrees aware of its existence, did so little to oppose it. Himmler, armed with the executive savagery of Heydrich, largely severed himself and his activities from the attention of the other leaders, leaving them to exercise control over the life of Germany and its captured territories while he developed the processes of death in order to purify the race he believed he was born to make paramount. He sank himself deeper and deeper into his racial obsessions and their outward manifestations in the *Lebensborn* institutions, the researches of the Institute for the Study of Heredity, and the overwhelming task of eliminating the suffocating presence of the Jews and Slavs in Eastern Europe. From the West he was for some while largely excluded because of Hitler's desire to come to some sort of favourable terms with this area while he crushed opposition in the East through the invasion of Soviet Russia. Only later was Himmler permitted to extend the full measure of his persecution to the resistance movements in the West.

Himmler's differences with the other leaders, particularly with Göring and Ribbentrop, were caused by his encroachments on what they regarded as their privileged territory. Himmler's information services were in some ways superior to those of either Göring or Ribbentrop because the men he employed, such as Schellenberg, were often of superior skill and intelligence. At the time of the Battle of Britain, Himmler's assessment of British aircraft production was over double that of Göring, whose easy optimism that he could destroy the Royal Air Force in a matter of days was partly based on his estimate that the output of planes in Britain was only some 300 a month. Göring did not welcome the challenge of such contradicting figures, nor did Ribbentrop approve of Himmler's interference in foreign affairs. They differed in 1940 over policy in Rumania, and in October Himmler was sent by Hitler on a further mission to Spain to try to involve Franco in the war. During the same period he went to Norway to strengthen the campaign against the growing resistance movement; he introduced the fearful system of persecuting men and women opposed to Germany by arresting their dependent kinsfolk and children and holding them as hostages.

Ribbentrop equally resented the extension of Himmler's Intelligence services abroad under Schellenberg, and his attempts to influence German policy in the occupied countries. The breach in the relations between the two ministers came to a head in the winter of 1941–2, when, according to Frau von Ribbentrop, Himmler even 'tried to enlist my husband in his personal intrigues ... My husband considered it impossible from the point of view of foreign relations that Himmler should succeed Hitler'. Ribbentrop in his *Memoirs* summarized his points of difference with Himmler at the time, including among them Himmler's uncompromising attitude to freemasonry and the Church, his treatment of the Jews, and his evil influence in such countries as France, Denmark and Hungary. He complained that his ambassadors were kept under surveillance by the S.D., and that secret reports on them were sent direct to the Führer. Ribbentrop bitterly resented the fact that this was done behind his back, especially when these reports led Hitler to take decisions based on what he called 'false information'. He complains that in Rumania, for example, Himmler supported Horia Sima after he had decided in conference with Hitler that the man they should support was Antonescu.[18]

In an attempt to force Ribbentrop's hand, Schellenberg contrived one of those Machiavellian tricks in which he took such delight in order to discredit Ribbentrop's own secret service. He was, he claimed, under instruction from Himmler 'to do my best to destroy this organization.' He succeeded in feeding certain of Ribbentrop's agents with false information about the Polish Government in exile in London, and then sat back to count the days until the erroneous reports arrived on Ribbentrop's desk and were duly forwarded to the Führer. Such tactics were hardly calculated to bring Ribbentrop and Himmler closer in their personal relations.

In January 1941, Himmler made an effort to extend his power and that of Heydrich over the German Courts of Justice by asking Hitler to hand over their control from the Ministry of Justice to Frick's Ministry of the Interior, where the Secretary of State, Wilhelm Stuckart, was a member of the S.S. and under Himmler's influence. Hitler, wary as ever when asked to dispose of power, failed to respond, and the courts themselves remained outside the control of the Gestapo until the end of the war.

Himmler's control of criminals and political police affairs was, however, complete. Each *Gau*, or administrative province in Germany, had its Higher S.S. Leader, the counterpart of the Nazi Gauleiter himself but directly responsible to Himmler and Heydrich. As the rule of the Reich spread, these S.S. Leaders were appointed in places as far apart as Oslo and Athens, Warsaw and The Hague. In Russia they were attached to each of the Army Groups. These men were supreme in all matters which they were able to call criminal and political, and answerable only to their headquarters in Berlin.

More complicated by now were his relations with Heydrich, who, when he had left his desk in May 1940 to fly with the Luftwaffe over the stricken people of France, had only himself two years left to live. Of these the first fifteen months were to be spent in preparing the Action Groups for the war against Russia in the summer of 1941 and in perfecting the extermination system in the camps set aside for that purpose by Himmler, while the last nine months were spent in his duties as Reich Protector in Czechoslovakia, where he was to be assassinated in May 1942. During this time it is plain that he considered himself Hitler's favourite, ear-marked for promotion to a ministerial level, outflanking Himmler in the movement to the top of the hierarchy. Meanwhile Himmler was treated as an ally by his most powerful subordinate, and they worked closely together on the plans to take control of Russia.

On 13 March 1941 Hitler issued a directive signed by Keitel concerning the coming campaign in the East. This directive disturbed the High Command; it stated that 'in the area of operations the Reichsführer S.S. is entrusted, on behalf of the Führer, with special tasks for the preparation of the political administration, tasks which result from the struggle which has to be carried out between two opposing political systems. Within the scope of these tasks, the Reichsführer S.S. shall act independently and under his own responsibility.'[19] Not content with giving Himmler the task of purging Communism from Russia, and Göring, as plenipotentiary of the Four Year Economic Plan, responsibility for stripping individual territories of food and other products valuable to Germany, Hitler the following month suddenly salvaged Alfred Rosenberg, the old-time Party intellectual, and appointed him Minister for the future occupied territories of the East, an appointment so ludicrous that it can only be explained as a formal attempt to counter the combined and growing power of Himmler and Heydrich or the potential greed of Göring's agents.

During the period of intense preparations for the invasion of Russia, which were developed at the same time as those for the mass extermination of the unwanted peoples, Himmler and Heydrich had to establish plans for the Action Groups which would be acceptable on the one hand to the Army and, nominally at least, to Alfred Rosenberg. Rosenberg constantly tried to intervene in the plans that Heydrich was preparing, though Himmler contemptuously ignored his existence. These differences brought Heydrich and Martin Bormann, Hitler's powerful aide, closer together, for Bormann disapproved of Rosenberg, who had wild ideas of playing the part of a Baltic-German liberator of the Russian people from Soviet tyranny. As for the Army, Schellenberg was required in June to use his legal diplomacy in order to negotiate suitable terms with General Wagner, representing the High Command; the plan he devised and which was finally signed released the Security Police and the S.D. from Army control outside the immediate fighting area, leaving them free to conduct the campaign in their own way. The Army, in fact, was expected to assist them in carrying out their atrocities.

When the invasion, after much postponement, finally came on 22 June 1941, Heydrich once more disappeared in order to fly with the Luftwaffe, and his plane on one occasion was seriously damaged by Russian flak. He managed to bring the aircraft back near the German lines, and landed it, crawling to safety with his leg injured.

This exploit won him the Iron Cross, First Class, from Hitler, but Himmler must have been distraught at the news of the danger he had been in. While Heydrich flew on his missions over Soviet territory, his Action Groups began their fearful massacres, shooting, hanging and terrorizing prisoners, Communist officials and partisans, as well as whole Jewish and gypsy communities.

After the war, Otto Ohlendorf, one of Himmler's intellectuals and an officer in charge of an Action Group, made a sworn statement which reveals in terrible detail how these commando security squadrons went to work:

'In June 1941 I was appointed by Himmler to lead one of the special action groups which were then being formed to accompany the German armies in the Russian campaign . . . Himmler stated that an important part of our task consisted in the extermination of Jews – women, men and children – and of communist functionaries. I was informed of the attack on Russia about four weeks in advance . . . When the German army invaded Russia, I was leader of the Action Group D in the Southern Sector; . . . it liquidated approximately 90,000 men, women and children . . . in the implementation of this extermination programme . . . The unit selected . . . would enter a village or city and order the prominent Jewish citizens to call together all Jews for the purpose of resettlement. They were requested to hand over their valuables . . . and shortly before execution to surrender their outer clothing. The men, women and children were led to a place of execution which in most cases was located next to a more deeply excavated anti-tank ditch. Then they were shot, kneeling or standing, and the corpses thrown into the ditch . . . In the spring of 1942 we received gas vehicles from the Chief of the Security Police and the S.D. in Berlin . . . We had received orders to use the vans for the killing of women and children. Whenever a unit had collected a sufficient number of victims, a van was sent for their liquidation.'[20]

Later in his statement, Ohlendorf said that he was prepared to confirm the affidavit given by another Action Group commander that he had been responsible for the deaths of 135,000 Jews and Communists during 'the first four months of the programme'.

The ferocity with which Hitler, Göring and Himmler planned their assault on Russia is unique in history. Göring, in a directive to his agents dated 23 May 1941, the first of the series that were to make up the notorious Green File on the economic exploitation of

Russia, spoke of 'the famine which undoubtedly will take place', and accepted as inevitable that 'many tens of millions of people in this area will become redundant'. So enthusiastic was Himmler to equip his men for Russia that as early as February he had made a special journey to Norway, where he travelled to the northern areas to visit his police units and to survey the needs for campaigning during the Russian winter. When he came back, he ordered Pohl to obtain the currency to buy stoves and furs in Norway for his men.

In March, the following month, Himmler summoned Heydrich, Daluege, Berger and a number of senior officers to his retreat at Wewelsburg. Wolff was also present, and so was Erich von dem Bach-Zelewski, an expert on partisan warfare who was later to be called as a witness for the prosecution before the International Military Tribunal at Nuremberg. According to Bach-Zelewski, Himmler declared at this secret conference that one of the aims of the Russian campaign was 'to decimate the Slav population by thirty millions'.[21] Wolff prefers to remember this statement in another form, namely that Himmler considered war with Russia would result in millions of dead.

The decision to adopt genocide as an active and fully organized policy in the purification of Europe for the 'Aryan' race was undoubtedly reached in 1941. There is a fundamental distinction between the practice of genocide and the callous and deliberate cruelties that led to the deaths of tens of thousands of unwanted people from the time of the occupation of Poland and the exchanges of population that followed. Wolff declares that Himmler was deeply oppressed by the decision that he was to be ultimately responsible for this crime, the greatest that any one man has ever committed in recorded history against his fellows. Kersten confirms this.[22] The decision in favour of genocide was preceded by a vaguely conceived 'final solution' in the form of despatching millions of the European 'subhumans' to Madagascar, following an enforced agreement with the French to use the island for this purpose; this idea had sprung from the early policy of encouraging Jewish emigration from Germany during the middle 'thirties. The Madagascar project, first discussed openly in 1938, was kept alive (in theory, at least) until the end of 1940, since during that year Eichmann himself was detailed to prepare a plan to set up an autonomous Jewish reserve under a German police-governor on the island, to which some four million Jews should be sent. Both Heydrich and Himmler approved the plan, but according to the Dutch edition of Kersten's *Memoirs*, Hitler had already abandoned this idea shortly after the capitulation of France, and had told Himmler he would have to undertake the progressive extermination of European Jewry.[23] It was not, however, until February 1942 that what was by then the fiction of the Madagascar project was officially abandoned in a memorandum sent by Hitler to the Foreign Office.

The decision to practise organized mass extermination, a national policy of genocide, seems to have been arrived at only after secret discussions which were inevitably dominated by Hitler. According to both Wolff and Kersten, Himmler was often very disturbed during this period, as if absorbed in a problem he was unable to discuss with anyone around him.

During the summer a firm decision was reached. On 31 July 1941, Göring sent his carefully worded directive to Heydrich, who was entrusted with the administrative planning for the extermination.

> 'Supplementing the task that was assigned to you on 24 January 1939, to solve the Jewish problem by means of emigration and evacuation in the best possible way according to present conditions, I herewith instruct you to make all necessary preparations as regards organizational, financial and material matters for a total solution [*Gesamtlösung*] of the Jewish question within the area of German influence in Europe . . . I instruct you further to submit to me as soon as possible a general plan showing the measure for organization and for action necessary to carry out the desired final solution [*Endlösung*] of the Jewish question.'[24]

According to Lammers, Head of the Reich Chancellery, while giving evidence at the Nuremberg Trial, the nature of the *final* as distinct from the *total* solution was made known to Heydrich by Göring verbally. There can be little doubt that Heydrich knew it in any case, and he appointed Adolf Eichmann his principal deputy in the matter. Eichmann was also responsible to Himmler, who had retained his direct control over the concentration camps, some of which were to be set aside as centres for extermination. Giving evidence at his trial in Israel in 1961, Eichmann claimed that even as late as November 1941 he 'did not know any details of the plan', but that he 'knew one was being drawn'.[25]

Heydrich's assistant, Wisliceny, gave evidence at Nuremberg in January 1946 which implied that Eichmann received definite orders from Himmler during the spring of 1942. At a meeting in Eichmann's office at the 'end of July or the beginning of August', the killing of Jews in Poland was discussed:

'Eichmann told me he could show me this order in writing if it would soothe my conscience. He took a small volume of documents from his safe, turned over the pages and showed me a letter from Himmler to the Chief of the Security Police and the S.D. The gist of the letter was something as follows: the Führer had ordered the "final solution" of the Jewish question; the Chief of the Security Police and the S.D., and the Inspector of the Concentration Camps were entrusted with carrying out this so-called "final solution". All Jewish men and women who were able to work were to be temporarily exempted from the so-called "final solution" and used for work in the concentration camps. This letter was signed by Himmler in person. I could not possibly be mistaken, since Himmler's signature was well known to me.'[26]

This order, said Wisliceny, was sent by Himmler to Heydrich and to the Inspector of the Concentration Camps; it was classified top secret and dated April 1942. Eichmann went on to explain that 'the planned biological destruction of the Jewish race in the Eastern territories was disguised by the wording "final solution" . . .' and that he personally 'was entrusted with the execution of this order'.

Long after the final decision had been taken, Himmler remained deeply oppressed. During a period of treatment by Kersten in Berlin, he admitted on 11 November after considerable pressure that the destruction of the Jews was being planned. When Kersten expressed his horror, Himmler became defensive – the Jews had to be finally eradicated, he said, since they had been and would always be the cause of intolerable strife in Europe. Just as the Americans had exterminated the Indians, so the Germans must wipe out the Jews. But in spite of his arguments, Himmler could not hide the disturbance of his conscience, and a few days later he admitted that 'the extermination of people is unGermanic'.

Auschwitz, near Cracow in Poland, became the principal centre for Himmler's extermination plan. It had once been the site of an Austrian military encampment built on marshy ground, where winter fog rose from the damp earth. Himmler transformed this military establishment into a concentration camp for the Poles, and it was officially opened on 14 June 1940, with Lieutenant Rudolf

Hoess as its first Commandant. Joseph Kramer, who later had charge of Belsen, was his adjutant.

Hoess, who became one of Himmler's most closely trusted agents, was to survive the collapse of Germany. Although held prisoner in May 1945, his true identity was not suspected until some months after his initial release. When he was once more taken into custody, he admitted his identity and signed a statement on 16 March in which he declared: 'I personally arranged on orders received from Himmler in May 1941 the gassing of 2 million persons between June-July 1941 and the end of 1943, during which time I was Commandant of Auschwitz.' He was very frank and co-operative, giving his lethal evidence at Nuremberg with all the impersonal self-confidence of a good and modest steward. Later he was handed over to the Polish authorities and while waiting his trial wrote in longhand his autobiography, perhaps the most incredible document to come from any Nazi agent. While, for example, Schellenberg relishes his intricate acts of espionage for Heydrich and Himmler, writing his story as if it were a thriller, Hoess is perpetually modest, melancholy and moralizing. The spirit of his Catholic upbringing taught him the supreme virtue of obedience.

Hoess represents himself as a simple, virtuous man who liked hard work and soldiering, and felt oppressed by the criminal underworld with which he was forced to associate.[27] At Dachau he disliked the methods used by Eicke, and while confessing that his 'sympathies lay too much with the prisoner', he admits that he 'had become too fond of the black uniform' to admit his inadequacy and relinquish the work. 'I wished to appear hard', he writes, 'lest I should appear weak.' When he went to Sachsenhausen as an adjutant, he took charge of the execution of an S.S. officer who by an act of humanity had let a prisoner escape. 'I was so agitated', he recalls, 'that I could hardly hold the pistol to his head when giving him the *coup de grâce*.' But executions became a matter of routine, and Hoess learned to hide his head in the sands of obedience. His exemplary conduct led to his promotion as Commandant of Auschwitz. Here, he says, 'I lived only for my work . . . I was absorbed, I might say obsessed . . . Every fresh difficulty only increased my zeal.' But this idealism was betrayed by the 'general untrustworthiness that surrounded me'. His staff, he claimed, let him down, and he became powerless against the corruption and ill-will of his subordinates. He took discreetly to drink; his wife tried to help him by building up a social life in their home at the camp, but 'all human emotions were forced into the background'.

In November 1940 Hoess reported his plans for Auschwitz to Himmler, who brushed aside his Commandant's fears and grievances, and only became interested when the discussion turned on making Auschwitz into an agricultural research station, with laboratories, plant nurseries and facilities for stock breeding. As for the prisoners and their welfare, Hoess was left to 'improvise' as best he could. It was not until March the following year that Himmler paid a visit to the camp, accompanied by his officials and some 'high executives of I.G. Farben Industrie'. Glücks, the Inspector of Concentration Camps, arrived in advance and 'constantly warned me against reporting anything disagreeable to the Reichsführer S.S.' When Hoess tried to impress on him the desperate overcrowding and lack of drainage or water supply, Himmler merely replied that the camp was to be enlarged to take 100,000 prisoners, so as to supply labour contingents to I.G. Farben Industrie. As to Hoess, he must continue to improvise.

This was the man to whom Himmler entrusted his special confidence in June 1941 when, as Hoess put it, he 'gave me the order to prepare installations at Auschwitz where mass exterminations could take place . . . By the will of the Reichsführer S.S., Auschwitz became the greatest human extermination centre of all time.'

According to Hoess's detailed account of this meeting, Himmler explained to him that he had chosen Auschwitz 'because of its good position as regards communications and because the area can be easily isolated and camouflaged'. He told him that Eichmann would come to Auschwitz and give him secret instructions about the equipment that would have to be installed. Hoess has left a full and frank account of the experiments for which he and Eichmann were responsible and which had led to the construction of the gas-chambers during the following winter. By the spring of 1942 the organized killings were to begin as a routine operation at Auschwitz; Russian prisoners-of-war were used during the test period. 'The killing . . . did not cause me much concern at the time', wrote Hoess. 'I must even admit that this gassing set my mind at rest.' Hoess did not relish the violence of the blood-bath caused by other forms of killing, and Himmler had warned him that trainloads of deported Jews would soon be on their way.

It has been suggested that Himmler deliberately chose a camp in Poland as the principal centre for genocide in order that German soil should not be contaminated by the destruction of so much impure flesh.[28] Other subsidiary centres of mass extermination were also set up in Poland, such as Treblinka. Auschwitz, however, had the double task of providing forced labour for synthetic coal and rubber plants built in the district by I.G. Farben while at the same time preparing for human mass destruction. Hoess, far more anxious to fulfil his quota of death than to send slave labour to factories at some distance from the camp, went to visit the Commandant of Treblinka: 'He was principally concerned with liquidating all the Jews from the Warsaw Ghetto. He used monoxide gas and I did not think his methods were very efficient', wrote Hoess after the war.

A vast mass of documents – statements by innumerable witnesses, the endless records of the interrogations and the examinations conducted before and during the war crime trials – have become the basis for many studies of the extermination and concentration camps during the peak period of the war. What emerges from these terrible, pitiful stories, which few read except for scholars and research workers, is the sheer muddle in which this carnage was conducted. The administrators such as Eichmann and Hoess were in the end utterly unable to control the grafters and the sadists on whom they had to depend to carry out the work of the camps, the selection and destruction of the victims and the mass cremation of the bodies. The S.S. *élite*, living in their barracks or married quarters nearby, either took no part in the proceedings or remained as aloof as possible from the hell they had created and which it was their duty to maintain. The bodily control of the captives passed increasingly into the hands of the *Kapos*, who were hardened criminals or renegade prisoners; their conduct was in the end far more savage than that of the S.S., whose morale grew slack in the increasing chaos as the tide of the war turned against the Nazis. On top of this morass of suffering sat Himmler at his desk, doing what he conceived to be his duty in circumstances of increasing strain and difficulty.

From September 1941, Eichmann took full charge of the extermination schedules, drafting orders for Heydrich, controlling the transportation of the Jewish population and organizing a succession of conferences at which the detailed administration of death was determined. But on 27 September Heydrich achieved a major promotion. He was appointed Acting Reich Protector in Czechoslovakia, displacing von Neurath, who was weak and ailing. He was promoted S.S. General, and gained in one step the rank and privileges of a Minister. After the comparative poverty of his position in Germany under Himmler, he could now live in luxury in Prague.

It seems clear that Bormann, Heydrich's principal ally among Hitler's close advisers, had encouraged this appointment rather than Himmler who, according to Schellenberg, was 'not enthusiastic about it' but decided not to stand in the way because he did not want to offend Bormann. There could be no clearer indication than this of the ascendancy of Bormann at Hitler's court since Hess's sudden flight to Scotland the previous May; for Himmler himself was in high favour with the Führer, while Göring, owing to his growing self-indulgence and the failure of the Luftwaffe to maintain its aggressive reputation, was losing his former influence. In many respects Himmler was becoming the most powerful man in Germany under Hitler, though he never made a display of his position in public. Power for him was always a secret force.

His attitude to the new appointment of Heydrich was therefore a mixed one. He was no doubt pleased to have provided the Führer with a distinguished servant, and the affectionate feelings that he always had for his Nordic model were satisfied by his success; at the same time he regretted the measure of independence that Heydrich had now won, and the loss of his daily advice, on which Himmler had come absolutely to rely. Heydrich, however, had no intention of severing himself from his duties in Berlin, for he retained his office as head of R.S.H.A. and he travelled constantly between Prague and Germany. The register of phone-calls between Himmler's office in Berlin and Heydrich's in Prague is a further measure of the dependence of the Reichsführer S.S. on his energetic and decisive officer. There is no doubt, too, that Himmler felt some dismay at the progress of a man who he was intelligent enough to recognize was in certain respects his superior. Nevertheless, or perhaps because of this, he kept in the closest touch, and Heydrich's departure for Prague was preceded by several conferences with Himmler, mostly about the Eastern Front.

The departure of Heydrich for Prague was the cue for Schellenberg to change his allegiance. Schellenberg both admired and hated Heydrich, who he had reason to believe disliked him. Applying his professional subtlety to his master, he had climbed within seven years from a youthful apprentice attached to the S.S. to become, on

the day Russia was invaded, head of *Amt*. VI, the Foreign Intelligence Service of the S.D. A born intriguer, he saw that it would
now be wise to reorientate his services in the direction of Himmler;
he realized that in some respects he might perhaps be able to replace
Heydrich as Himmler's special confidant, in spite of the fact that he
was so different in character. As he put it himself: 'Many of my
opponents spread the libel that I was really Heydrich's "double" . . .
However, in time this malevolent propaganda faded away, and a
new myth was discovered in which Heydrich was replaced by
Himmler.' Schellenberg claims that he was given the responsibility
of drafting Hitler's proclamation to the German people about the
war on Russia, working against time through the night while Himmler
and Heydrich besieged him with 'phone calls. 'Himmler made me
nervous', wrote Schellenberg. 'As soon as Hitler asked him a question
or said something to him, he would run to the telephone and bom-
bard me with questions and advice.' Schellenberg was already beginning to enjoy the experience of Himmler's dependence upon him,
and his promotion followed rapidly.

Appointed Acting Head of the S.D. Foreign Intelligence Service
on 22 June, the day Russia was invaded, Schellenberg spent the next
two months in preparing a memorandum on the Political Secret
Service abroad which, when it was completed, apparently impressed
the Reichsführer S.S. sufficiently for him to impose it on the leadership of the S.S. and the Party in the form of an order, thus, as
Schellenberg puts it, 'acting as a propagandist for my ideas'. During
the next four years Schellenberg was to draw very close to Himmler
and, in the guise of his special adviser, try to make him adopt
policies and lines of action originating in his own devious brain.

He enjoyed the fruits of office in forms which might even seem
exaggerated for a secret agent in an American thriller. He describes
with glowing excitement the luxurious carpets in his executive suite,
the trolley-table holding his telephones and linking him direct to
Hitler's Chancellery, the microphones concealed at every point of
the compass, in the walls and lamps and under the desk, the alarms
controlled by photo-electric cells, the big mahogany desk with its
built-in automatic guns which could spray the room with bullets.
Guards could be summoned at the press of a button to surround the
building and block the exits, while his car was equipped with a
short-wave transmitter through which he could reach his office and
dictate to his secretary. Even his own body was equipped for sudden

death; when engaged on missions abroad, he wore an artificial tooth containing enough poison to kill him in thirty seconds.

Since July Himmler had spent a considerable time during the summer at the Russian front. He had set up his headquarters in the Soviet Military Academy at Zhitomir in the Ukraine, a hundred miles north of Hitler's headquarters known as Werwolf at Winnitsa. From Zhitomir, Himmler kept in touch with the work of the Action Groups and the Police and, to a lesser extent, with the *Waffen* S.S., whose four famous divisions, the Adolf Hitler (formerly the *Leibstandarte*), the *Das Reich*, the Death's Head and the Viking, fought brilliantly during the campaign until the reverses of the winter led to serious losses. But what Himmler was primarily concerned with was the work of the Action Groups behind the front, whose massacres of Jews, gypsies and political commissars began as soon as prisoners fell into the hands of the advancing Germans.

Heydrich, meanwhile, was dividing his attention between his duties in Berlin and in Prague, where, after initiating a brief, punitive reign of terror against the resistance movement immediately on his arrival in Czechoslovakia, he made it clear to the puppet government under President Hacha that he now expected maximum co-operation with Germany.[29] Heydrich's intentions in Czechoslovakia were in line with Himmler's policy for Eastern Europe: the extermination of undesirable racial elements and the Germanisation of the rest of the Czechs and their territory; this policy had been determined in 1940, a year before Heydrich's appointment, and approved by Hitler in full consultation with the Sudeten German Karl Hermann Frank, who was now S.S. commandant for Prague. On 2 October, Heydrich outlined his plans at a secret conference of Nazi administrators in Prague. Bohemia was by right German territory, and was to be re-settled by Germans; the Czech people of good race would be Germanized, the rest exterminated or sterilized. He then outlined the permanent racial plan for Europe, through which the Nordic races of Germanic origin would be federated under German control: 'It is clear that we must find an entirely different way in which to treat these peoples from that used for peoples of other races, the Slavs and so on. The Germanic race must be seized firmly but justly; they must be humanely led in a similar way to our own people, if we want to keep them permanently in the Reich and to merge them with us.'

In this, Heydrich was echoing the thoughts of Himmler. As the

Germans moved east, he said, they would turn the inferior races they did not destroy into helot armies, stretching from the Atlantic seaboard to the Ural mountains, to protect the Greater Reich from the peoples of Asia. The East, with its slave labour, would produce the food for the Aryan West.

In his dealings with the Czechs, Heydrich added, it would be wise to practise a certain tact now that the strong arm of the S.S. was being shown. 'I personally, for example,' he said, 'shall maintain pleasant social relations with these Czechs, but I will be careful not to cross certain barriers.' He then concluded with a careful reference to the Final Solution (*Endlösung*), warning his listeners to keep the matter to themselves; he would need, he said, a complete racial picture of the Czech people obtained by compiling under various guises a national register of the entire population:

> 'For those of good race and well intentioned the matter will be very simple – they will be Germanized. The others – those of inferior racial origin with hostile intentions – these people I must get rid of. There is plenty of space in the East for them . . . During the short time I shall probably be here I shall be able to lay many foundation stones in the affairs of the nation.'

Heydrich, less than a week after taking up his appointment, was already speaking like an established Nazi leader. Though the ideas he put forward were those familiar enough in Himmler's mythology, he spoke now in the first person. In the signal he had sent by tele-printer to Hitler's headquarters in Russia on 27 September notifying his arrival in Prague, he had ended by making it quite clear that 'all political reports and messages will reach you by the hand of Reichsführer Bormann'. There was no longer any question that he would communicate with the Führer through Himmler; according to Schellenberg, who had been invited by Heydrich to celebrate the news of his appointment over a bottle of champagne, Bormann had told Heydrich the Führer had greater responsibilities in store for him if he were successful in Czechoslovakia. He believed, therefore, as he had said at the secret conference in Prague, that he would not be in Czechoslovakia for long. He was, after all, still head of R.S.H.A., and he had no intention of cutting himself off from Berlin. A 'plane stood by constantly to carry him to and from Germany, but he took his wife and children to Prague and installed them in the beautiful and luxurious country seat assigned to the

Reinhard Heydrich

Walter Schellenberg

Protector at Panenske-Breschen, twelve miles from the capital. As a bribe for good conduct he increased the rations of Czech workers and adopted the pose, once the initial purge was over, of being Czechoslovakia's friend while attempting to increase the efficiency of her industry for the benefit of Germany. In spite of his ceaseless schedule of work, the regular journeys to Berlin, the frequent visits to Hitler in the Ukraine, he made a point of appearing to patronize the arts in Prague while subsidizing the performance of German opera.

Himmler was constantly in touch with him, and it was Heydrich, not Himmler, who controlled the lunch conference organized by Eichmann on 20 January 1942 at Wannsee, at which the various phases of the Final Solution were debated with the usual cynical circumlocution. The various claims of death by overwork, deportation to the East, sterilization and extermination were gone over for the 11 million Jews and part-Jews whom Heydrich estimated lived in Europe both within and beyond the territories under Nazi rule. The only Jews to be spared temporarily were those engaged in war work, at the urgent request of Göring's Ministry. Everyone present, leaders of the S.S. and government officials alike, pledged their assistance, and Thierack, the Minister of Justice, formally blessed the proposals and surrendered all jurisdiction over the Jews to the S.S. Cognac was served and the speakers grew loud and merry. Heydrich who, according to Eichmann when testifying in 1961 at Jerusalem, summoned the conference out of vanity and a desire to consolidate his power over the fate of the Jews, then left for Prague, where on 4 February he called another secret conference of his assistants in order to explain his long-term plan for Czechoslovakia; mass deportations of the millions who were not selected for Germanization. Under guise of a nation-wide check for tuberculosis conducted by racial specialists, the first steps in the national racial survey were begun.

With equal speed, Eichmann set about his work. On 6 March he held a conference to resolve the difficult transport problems connected with the evacuation of the Jews to the east and to debate the problem of organizing the sterilization of Jews involved in mixed marriages and their offspring. Heydrich, confined now for longer periods in Prague, left R.S.H.A. matters to Eichmann and his staff. In the spring, when Schellenberg was visiting him, he seemed more than ordinarily worried. Hitler, he said, 'was relying more and more on Himmler, who . . . could exploit his present influence with the Führer.' He no longer seemed willing to accept Heydrich's advice, and Bormann, he now felt, was jealous of him and hostile. 'Apparently there had been differences between him and Himmler, who had become jealous.' Both Bormann and Himmler resented the fact that Hitler had been prepared to confer with Heydrich alone, and Heydrich was certain by now that Bormann, his former supporter, was starting an intrigue against him.

This was the situation when Heydrich, who was very careless of his personal security, left his castle to be driven to the airport shortly after two o'clock on the afternoon of 27 May. Waiting for him near a sharp turn in the road were two Free Czech agents from Britain, who had been dropped by parachute the previous December to wait for final orders to attempt his assassination; one had a Sten-gun and the other a special grenade. At the crucial moment the Sten-gun jammed, and the second agent flung his grenade at the car. Heydrich, who seemed for the moment uninjured, got out of the car and pursued his assailants, firing his revolver while in their attempt to escape they dodged between two street cars that had drawn up. Then Heydrich suddenly collapsed; he had in fact suffered internal injuries at the base of his spine from the explosion of the grenade. The Czech police arrived and hustled Heydrich, who was in great pain, to hospital. The two agents both escaped at the time, but they died three weeks later resisting arrest.

Both Hitler and Himmler were at their separate headquarters in East Prussia when the news that Heydrich was seriously injured reached them from Frank. According to Wolff, who was with Himmler, the Reichsführer burst into tears, and then drove with Wolff to see Hitler at Rastenburg, some thirty miles distant. They decided at once to send their court physicians by air to Prague in a fervent attempt to keep Heydrich alive. None of them could save Heydrich from the gangrene set up by his wounds, and a week later he died, surrounded by doctors. Gebhardt described the frantic scene at the Doctors' Trial:

'I arrived by air too late. The operation had already been carried out by two leading Prague surgeons. All I could do was to supervize the subsequent treatment. In the extraordinary excitement and nervous tension which prevailed, and was not diminished by daily personal telephone calls from Hitler and

Himmler asking for information, very many suggestions were naturally made; I was practically ordered to call in . . . the Führer's own doctor, Morell, who wanted to intervene in his own fashion with his own remedies . . . The two gentlemen from Prague had already operated . . . they had made a first-rate job of the operation and also administered sulphonamide. I consider that if anything endangers a patient it is nervous tension at the bedside and the appearance of too many doctors. I refused, in reply to direct demands, to call in any other doctor, not even Morell . . . Heydrich died in fourteen days. Then I had to see to his family affairs.'

Meanwhile, a heavy vengeance was being taken on the Czechs by Frank at the order of Himmler. All life and movement was stopped in the city overnight on 27 May, and a million crowns reward was offered for news which would lead to the arrest of the assailants. Hostages were arrested in the tradition already well-established by the Nazis, who used the occasion as an excuse to rid themselves of people they knew to be hostile; hundreds were killed and thousands arrested. Himmler's teleprinter to Frank read: 'As the intellectuals are our main enemies shoot a hundred of them tonight.'

On 6 June the first in a succession of funeral ceremonies took place in the presence of Himmler, who was the principal mourner and personally took charge of Heydrich's two young boys who accompanied him. Frau Heydrich, who was pregnant, remained in her castle. Then the body was taken on a train under guard to Berlin, to lie in state at R.S.H.A. headquarters. At three o'clock on 8 June, Himmler led Hitler forward to open the obsequies over the coffin at the Chancellery, to which the body had been taken for its final display. Hitler laid a wreath of orchids beside the man he said 'was one of the greatest defenders of our greater German ideal, . . . the man with the iron heart'. Afterwards, he touched the heads of the two little boys whom Himmler was holding by the hand. The Berlin Philharmonic Orchestra played Wagner's Funeral March, and Himmler delivered the final lengthy oration on Heydrich's career before the body was taken to the Invaliden Cemetery for burial.

The following night, at the command of Hitler, the special vengeance of the Führer was visited on the Czech people at the village of Lidice, and upon their children. The Chief of the Security Police in Prague wrote the history of Lidice himself in the Gestapo order sent to the Resettlement Office in Lodz on 12 June:

'By supreme command, owing to the assassination of Gruppen-führer Heydrich, the village of Lidice in the Protectorate has been flattened. The entire male population was shot, the women assigned to concentration camp for life. The children were investigated with a view to their suitability for Germanization. Those not suitable are to go to you at Litzmannstadt for distribution in Polish camps. There are 90 children; they will go to Litzmannstadt in a coach attached to the train arriving Saturday 13.6.42 at 21.30. Will you please see to it that the children are met at the station and immediately distributed in suitable camps. The age groups are as follows: 1-2 years, 5; 2-4 years, 6; 4-6 years, 15; 6-8 years, 16; 8-10 years, 12; 10-16 years, 36.

The children to have nothing except what they stand up in.

*Special care or attention is not required.*'

Immediately after the death of Heydrich, Himmler himself, following an agreement with Hitler, took over temporary command of R.S.H.A., announcing this to the senior officers present while Heydrich's body still lay before them in state. According to Schellenberg, he used the occasion to make a severe criticism of each man in turn, except for Schellenberg himself, whom he referred to as 'the Benjamin of our leadership corps,' saying that Schellenberg would in future be required to work more closely with him. Schellenberg admits to blushing at the praise accorded him when the others, so much older than he, were blamed. By assuming Heydrich's command of the S.D., Himmler ensured that no one but himself had control of the secret safe in which so much damaging evidence existed about the Nazi leadership.

As for Himmler's attitude to Heydrich, we have his remarks to Kersten that have already been quoted. Perhaps, after all, it was a relief to be rid of so dangerous a man, who had shaken himself free from proper subordination. Two months after Heydrich's death, Himmler called Schellenberg to his office and stood beside him face-to-face with the death-mask of the dead man. Then he said, in a deeply serious voice, 'Yes, as the Führer said at the funeral, he was indeed a man with an iron heart. And at the height of his power fate purposefully took him away.' He nodded his head in approval of his own words and, says Schellenberg, his small, cold eyes glinted behind their pince-nez like the eyes of a basilisk.

# V

# *Final Solution*

Whatever doubts there may have been in Himmler's mind and conscience, there is no sign of them in the meticulous decrees and orders he despatched secretly to his officers. In these he weighed with a fearful exactitude how he might best dispose of the human raw material in his hands. After the Wannsee conference of January 1942, he made the parsimonious Oswald Pohl, who from 1939 had been in charge of the economic administration of the camps, head of a new department of the S.S. which gave him added incentives to develop the slave-labour programme. Pohl was told he must exploit the prisoners to the full as a means not only of helping Germany's war production, but of making profits for the exclusive benefit of the S.S.

Pohl, who had been a paymaster captain in the Navy, did his best to serve his masters in carrying out the impossible task of forcing efficient work out of dying men and women; indeed, he built himself a staff some 1,500 strong solely for this purpose. In the same month, on 20 February, Himmler issued a directive that 'special treatment' should be given to any prisoners who proved themselves undisciplined by refusing to work or by malingering. 'Special treatment is hanging', explained Himmler with a frankness unusual in such orders, but he added, 'It should not take place in the immediate vicinity of the camp. A certain number, however, should attend the special treatment.'

On 15 December 1942, Himmler wrote to Pohl on the problem of feeding the prisoners:

'Do try, in the New Year, to cope with the feeding of prisoners by acquiring raw vegetables and onions on the largest possible scale. At the appropriate periods give them carrots, cabbage,

white turnips, etc., in large measure. And during winter maintain
large stocks of vegetables, enough at any rate to provide a suffi-
ciency for each prisoner. That way, I think, we will appreciably
improve the state of health. Heil Hitler!'

In January 1943 Himmler issued personally very detailed instructions for executions in the concentration camps.[1] These
included the following clauses:

'The execution is not to be photographed or filmed. In exceptional cases my personal permission has to be obtained . . .
After every execution the S.S. men and officials who had anything
to do with it are to be addressed by the Camp Commandant or
the S.S. leader deputizing for him. The legality of the execution
is to be explained to the men, and they are to be influenced in
such a way as to suffer no ill effect in their character and mental
attitude. The need for rooting out elements such as the delinquent
for the common weal is to be stressed. Such explanations are to
be given in a truly comradely manner; they might be repeated
from time to time at social gatherings.

'After executions of Polish civilian workers as well as workers
from former Soviet territories [*Ostarbeiter*], their compatriots
working in the vicinity are to be led past the gallows with an
appropriate lecture on the penalties for disobeying our orders.
This is to be done as a regular routine unless there is a counter-
order necessitated by special reasons, such as the need to bring
in the harvest, or other reasons making it inopportune to encroach
on the working time available.

'Hanging is to be done by prisoners: in the case of foreign
workers preferably by their own compatriots. The prisoners are
to be issued a fee of three cigarettes for each hanging . . .

'The responsible S.S. leaders are to see to it that, while we have
to be hard and cannot tolerate softness, no brutality is to be
allowed either.'

In June 1944 he was forced to remind his S.S. men of the regulations
he had made against taking snapshots of these executions. 'In time
of war', he added to this reminder, 'executions are unfortunately
necessary. But to take snapshots of them only shows bad taste, apart
from being detrimental to the interests of our Fatherland. The enemy
might well abuse photographs of this kind in his propaganda.'

Himmler's concern with his own independence grew. In March he tried to establish munition works in certain camps, but Speer, the new Minister for Armaments, forestalled this; as Speer himself said when giving evidence before the International Military Tribunal at Nuremberg, 'uncontrolled arms production on the part of the S.S. had to be prevented . . . It was Himmler's intention to exercise his influence over these industries and in some way or other he would undoubtedly have succeeded in getting them under his control.'[2] Speer was only prepared to make use of prisoners on his own terms, and he saw to it that Hitler rejected Himmler's schemes. Those prisoners who were eventually used in the armaments works were made to fulfil a sixty-hour week. But the death-rate at the camps was so great and the number available for work diminished so rapidly that on 28 December Himmler was forced to send out another directive: 'The Reichsführer S.S. has ordered that the death-rate absolutely must be reduced.'[3]

During the first six months of the following year, Himmler replenished his diminished labour forces by taking into custody some 200,000 foreign conscripts who had committed petty offences, on the grounds that as a result they came properly under his jurisdiction. He was in a position to kidnap this large force of slave-workers from Speer as the result of a hard-fought agreement with Otto Thierack, Hitler's recently-appointed Minister of Justice, following a discussion between them at Himmler's Field Headquarters at Zhitomir on 18 September.

Thierack, a judge of the Nazi People's Court, had been made Reich Minister of Justice at the suggestion of Goebbels, and his instructions had been to create a system of law favourable to the Nazis. Among the points of agreement noted by Thierack's aide after the meeting with Himmler were:

'Correction by special treatment at the hands of the police in cases where judicial sentences are not severe enough.

'The delivery of anti-social elements from the execution of their sentence to the Reichsführer S.S. to be worked to death.'

(These 'anti-social elements' included persons under protective arrest – Jews, gypsies, Russians, Ukrainians, Poles with more than three-year sentences, Czechs and Germans with more than eight-year sentences.)

'It is agreed that, in consideration of the intended aims of the

Government for the cleaning up of the Eastern problem, in future
Jews, Poles, Gypsies, Russians and Ukrainians are no longer to
be judged by the ordinary courts, so far as punishable offences
are concerned, but are to be dealt with by the Reichsführer
himself.'[4]

As conditions in the camps became less and less controlled, the
opportunities for private, in the place of public, looting increased.
For example, by special orders from Himmler, the first dated as
early as 23 September 1940, gold teeth were to be removed from the
bodies of prisoners who had died, while the living had the dental
gold taken from their mouths if it seemed 'incapable of repair'.
The gold was supposed to be deposited along with all other
confiscated valuables in the Reichsbank in favour of an account held
by the S.S. under the cover-name of Max Heiliger; the Reichsbank
during the middle years of the war endeavoured to pawn the piles
of unwanted valuables for hard cash.[5] Speaking of this macabre
treasure-trove in the course of a speech made in October 1943,
Himmler said: 'We have taken from them what wealth they had. I
have issued strict orders which S.S. General Pohl has carried out,
that this wealth should, as a matter of course, be handed over to the
Reich without reserve. We have taken none of it for ourselves.' He
added that S.S. men who stole would be shot. It soon became
apparent, however, that this macabre treasure-trove was receiving
only a proportion of its rightful booty and that unscrupulous men in
every rank at the camps were stealing. Globocnik, for example,
amassed a fortune in Lublin during 1943, and Himmler was forced in
the autumn to send an official investigator to enquire into the
smuggling of gold, which was rife in Auschwitz. Prisoners were
often more valuable for the gold in their teeth than for the labour
of their hands.

With the development of his business sense, Himmler realized
that another source of money lay in the outright sale of Jewish
liberties. At the end of 1942 he was approached with the suggestion
that a whole S.S. division could be financed in Hungary by the sale of
emigration permits to Jews in Slovakia; Himmler was known to be
in favour of compromise with his policy of extermination in certain
cases where the financial gain to the Reich far exceeded the disadvantage of the survival of certain Jews. A memorandum written
in December 1942 and signed by Himmler reads: 'I have asked the

Führer about the absolving [*Loslösung*] of Jews against hard currency. He has authorized me to approve such cases, provided they bring in genuinely substantial sums from abroad.'

Eichmann, however, regarded such dealings as a sign of weakness, and opposed them. The attempt to bargain over Jewish life and liberty in this way eventually centred on the so-called Europa Plan, which Eichmann's representative Wisliceny first negotiated on behalf of the S.S. in the semi-independent state of Hungary, where Jewish refugees were congregating. At Eichmann's trial, Yoel Brand, a Zionist resident in Budapest, gave evidence of the many meetings he had had, some with Eichmann himself, in which the price of liberty for Jews was discussed. 'At one of these meetings,' said Brand, 'I was told that Himmler was very much in favour of Eichmann's proposal. Himmler, I was told, was in fact a good man and did not want the extermination of the Jews to continue.' Little was to come out of these negotiations; like the thirty pieces of silver, they proved in the end the price of betrayal. Only in the final losing stages of the war was Himmler, urged on by Kersten and Schellenberg, to give ground and conduct his own hard bargains with the Jews through their agent Masur.[6]

The policy from 1942–4 was extermination – extermination through work for those prescribed as medically fit for labour, immediate extermination for those who for reasons of age, ill-health or infirmity were held to be waste material. Himmler was to make his policy implacably clear in a speech he made at a meeting of his S.S. major-generals held at Posen on 4 October 1943,[7] speaking of the ravages and loss of life in Russia, he said:

'Thinking in terms of generations, it is not to be regretted; but in terms of here and now it is deplorable by reason of the loss of labour, that prisoners died in tens and hundreds of thousands from exhaustion and hunger ... We must be honest, decent, loyal and comradely to members of our own blood, but to nobody else. What happens to a Russian or to a Czech does not interest me in the slightest. What the nations can offer in the way of good blood of our type, we will take, if necessary by kidnapping their children and raising them here with us. Whether nations live in prosperity or starve to death interests me only in so far as we need them for slaves for our *Kultur*; otherwise, it is of no interest to me. Whether 10,000 Russian females fall down from exhaustion digging an anti-tank ditch interests me only in so far as the anti-tank ditch

for Germany is finished . . . It is a crime against our own blood to
worry about them and give them ideals, thus causing our sons and
grandsons to have a more difficult time with them. When somebody comes to me and says, "I cannot dig the anti-tank ditch
with women and children, it is inhuman because it will kill them",
then I must reply, "You are a murderer of your own blood,
because if the anti-tank ditch is not dug, German soldiers will die,
and they are the sons of German mothers. They are our own
blood." That is what I want to instill into the S.S. and what I
believe I have instilled into them as one of the most sacred laws
of the future . . . I want the S.S. to adopt this attitude to the
problem of all foreign, non-Germanic peoples, especially Russians.'

Later in the speech he made a statement which was to be the most
open expression of his determination to eliminate the European
Jews who lay in his power that he was ever to make at a formal
conference. The ambiguous terminology of genocide – the 'final
solution', the 'special treatment', the 'night and fog' symbolism[8] –
were for once set aside, and the fanatic exterminator was revealed
through Himmler's own words:

'Among ourselves it should be mentioned quite frankly – but we
will never speak of it publicly – just as we did not hesitate on
30 June 1934 to do the duty we were told to do and stand comrades
who had lapsed up against the wall and shoot them, so we have
never spoken about it and will never speak of this . . . I mean
cleaning out the Jews, the extermination of the Jewish race. It is
one of those things it's easy to talk about – "The Jewish race is
being exterminated . . . it's our programme, and we're doing it."
And then they come, eighty million worthy Germans, and each
one of them has his decent Jew. Of course the others are vermin,
but this particular Jew is a first-rate man . . . Most of *you* must
know what it means when a hundred corpses are lying side by
side, or five hundred or a thousand. To have stuck it out and at
the same time (apart from exceptions caused by human weakness)
to have remained decent fellows, that is what has made us so hard.
This is a page of glory in our history which has never been written
and will never be written.
    'We are a product of the law of selection. We have made our
choice from a cross-section of our people. This people came into
being aeons ago, through generations and centuries . . .
    'Alien peoples have swept over this people and left their heritage
behind them, . . . but it has . . . still has the strength in the very

essence of its blood to win through. This whole people is . . . held together by Nordic-Phalian-Germanic blood . . . The moment we forget the law which is the foundation of our race, and the law of selection and austerity towards ourselves, we shall have the germ of death in us . . . We must remember our principle: blood, selection, austerity.'

At another conference that took place earlier the same year, in April at the University of Khahov, Himmler addressed a similar audience made up of the commanding officers of the S.S. divisions serving in Russia. To them he spoke of 'the great fortress of Europe' they were privileged to defend and increase. 'It is here in the East that the decision lies; here must the Russian enemy, this people numbering two hundred million Russians, be destroyed on the battlefield, and one by one they must be made to bleed to death . . . Either they must be deported and used on labour in Germany for Germany, or they will just die in battle.'

Then he referred to the task of extermination which, he said, 'is exactly the same as de-lousing; getting rid of lice is not a question of ideology. It is a matter of cleanliness. We shall soon be de-loused.' The need of the future was to incorporate all the Nordic peoples into the Germanic Reich. 'I very soon formed a Germanic S.S. in the various countries', he said, referring particularly to Flanders and the Netherlands, Norway and Denmark. 'We very soon got Germanic volunteers from them', whether the leaders in these countries liked it or not. He asked his officers to tolerate the ignorance of the German language in those of German race whom he incorporated into the S.S.; they must assist the newcomers to learn the language. One day, he forecast, he would bring together the mass of German stock from all over the world, 'still more of those overseas, in America, whom one day we must fetch here by the million . . . We have only one task, to stand firm and carry on the racial struggle without mercy.'

At Posen, he also looked into the future; he spoke with the burning tongue of the prophet to men who listened uneasily to dreams in which few of them had any faith and which they regarded as superfluous at this critical stage in the war. They were beginning to realize, after the retreat in North Africa in 1942, the fall of Stalingrad the following January, the collapse of Mussolini and the Allied invasion of Italy that had just begun, that this had developed into a war which would be increasingly difficult to win. But Himmler's voice went on relentlessly: 'If the peace is a final one, we shall be able to tackle our great work of the future. We shall colonize. We shall indoctrinate our young men with the laws of the S.S. organization . . . It must be a matter of course that the most copious breeding should be from this racial superstratum of the Germanic people. In twenty or thirty years we must really be able to present the whole of Europe with its ruling class.' He had, he said, asked the Führer on behalf of the S.S. for the privilege of holding Germany's frontier furthest to the East: 'We shall impose our laws on the East. We will charge ahead and push our way forward little by little to the Urals.' This would keep the S.S. hard; death would always remain a possibility facing an S.S. man.

> 'In this way we will create the necessary conditions for the whole Germanic people and the whole of Europe, controlled, ordered and led by us, the Germanic people. We must be able, in future generations, to stand the test in our battle of destiny against Asia, which will certainly break out again . . . It would be an evil day if the Germanic people did not survive. It would be the end of beauty and *Kultur*, of the creative power of this earth . . . Now let us remember the Führer, Adolf Hitler, who will create the Germanic Reich and will lead us into the Germanic future.'

Himmler's determination to win his own peculiar version of the war was never stronger than during this period. He was hardened by many events, the reversals of the war, the death of Heydrich, the great challenge to his authority made by the Jews of the Warsaw Ghetto, the revolt of the students at Munich, and the Communist conspiracy in Germany of the Red Orchestra, the *Rote Kapelle*.

The *Rote Kapelle* was the name given to a network of German spies serving the Russians; many of its agents were discovered to be Germans from well-connected families, and many were working in the various Ministries. Their leader, Harold Schulze-Boysen, an unstable man who had been a poet and left-wing revolutionary in the nineteen-twenties, was working during the war in a department of Göring's Air Ministry which specialized in 'research' through telephone-tapping. This was a department which naturally enough had excited Himmler's suspicion.

Schellenberg was sent in March 1942 to Carinhall, Göring's luxurious country mansion to which the leader of the Luftwaffe retired increasingly to avoid the consequence of his lost authority.

He came to ask Göring to permit this work to be taken over by the S.D. Göring, according to Schellenberg, received him dressed in a toga but carrying his marshal's baton; fingering jewels in a cut-glass bowl, he went into a trance and managed to avoid reaching any decision likely to satisfy Himmler. The Reichsführer immediately made Göring's department the subject of an enquiry, which according to one observer was stopped by Hitler in July to avoid a public scandal. Göring hoped to close the matter amicably by giving Himmler honorary flier's wings in August, but this was the month in which the whole network of the *Rote Kapelle* came to light through the independent investigations conducted by Admiral Canaris's Military Intelligence department, the *Abwehr*, though the actual arrests of over a hundred agents were eventually undertaken by combined units made up of Canaris's Field Police and the Gestapo. In spite of the fact that the Gestapo was permitted by Hitler to prepare criminal proceedings, Himmler realized that his vast organization had failed to be the first to uncover the *Rote Kapelle*, the existence of which caused a scandal far exceeding the actual importance of this spying organization. Schellenberg in his *Memoirs* is careful to take the main credit for uncovering the conspiracy for himself and, as always, presents the story in its most colourful form.

The students' revolt in the University of Munich followed in February 1943, very soon after the series of trials of the *Rote Kapelle* agents. The students were led by Hans Scholl, a medical student, and his sister Sophie, and they distributed anti-Nazi propaganda not only in Munich but in universities elsewhere in Germany. A vicious speech made by the Gauleiter of Bavaria, Paul Giesler, in which he insulted the women students by ordering them to produce illegitimate children with the help, if necessary, of his adjutants, led to open demonstrations in the University and in the streets of Munich. But Hans and Sophie Scholl were betrayed and, after being tortured by the Gestapo, they were tried by Roland Freisler, Hitler's counterpart to the notorious seventeenth-century British Judge Jeffreys, and condemned to death along with others who had supported them. According to Hassell, the former ambassador who became a member of the German resistance movement, Himmler was driven to order a stay of execution in March in order to avoid turning his victims into martyrs, but in fact he hesitated so long in making up his mind that his order arrived too late to save them.

The challenge from the Jews themselves to Himmler's authority came from the Warsaw Ghetto, an area of some two and a half square miles in the city, containing the medieval Ghetto.[9] Round this the Nazis had built a high wall, and herded into this besieged and starving community a vast population of some 400,000 Polish Jews. In March 1942 Himmler outlined his initial scheme for the partial resettlement of the Polish Jews in a speech the full text of which does not survive;[10] there had been over three million Jews in Poland when Germany had begun the invasion, and though large numbers had fled east or been killed by the Action Groups, some two million still awaited death, including those in the Warsaw Ghetto.

When the policy of extermination came into full force during the summer of 1942, Himmler ordered the total 'resettlement' in concentration camps of the Polish Jews; the result was that between July and October over three-quarters of the Warsaw Ghetto's inhabitants were transported to camps and asphyxiated, most of them at Treblinka, the death-camp some sixty miles away. This number was as much as the limited transport or inadequate gas-chambers would allow. In October Himmler decided to turn the Ghetto itself, now reduced to some 300,000 square yards with some 60,000 survivors, into a concentration camp, but in January 1943, by which time a million Jews had been killed in six months, he spared the time to make a surprise visit to Warsaw to investigate the black market in Jewish labour which he had learned was now common practice, involving the S.S. and businessmen alike. It was, of course, inevitable that Globocnik himself was involved, the builder's foreman whom Himmler in 1939 had misguidedly reinstated as Higher S.S. Leader and Chief of Police for the Province of Lublin after his period of disgrace for illegal speculation. Himmler discovered that 24,000 Jews registered as armaments workers were in fact working illegally as tailors and furriers. He was filled with righteous indignation: 'Once more I set a final term for the resettlement: 15 February', he ordered.

The first revolt in the Ghetto began on 18 January, four days after Himmler's visit. The Jews involved in planned resistance had for long been engaged in smuggling arms from the outside world, and combat groups fired on and killed S.S. men and militia in charge of a column of deportees. This moment of resistance was suppressed with heavy casualties, and Himmler determined that the Ghetto must as soon as ever possible be totally destroyed.

In April S.S. Lieutenant-General Stroop, the police chief in

Greece, was sent by Himmler to Warsaw to evacuate the 56,000
Jews still congregated in the restricted area of the Ghetto. He entered
with armoured cars on 19 April, and to his utter surprise he found
that the Jews were able to put up a resistance that lasted for thirty-
three days. To oppose the Jewish combat units Stroop had a very
mixed force of some 2,000 men, many untrained as soldiers, and
made up of Poles and Lithuanians as well as two training battalions
of the *Waffen* S.S. Himmler, angered once more by these open signs
of resistance, ordered that the Ghetto be treated as partisan territory
and combed out 'with ruthless tenacity'.

Gradually the Jews, both armed and unarmed, were rounded up;
section by section the area was taken and the buildings destroyed.
Refugees and partisans were either flooded or smoked out of the
sewers, and the Jews not already killed or needed for immediate
work were sent to Treblinka to be gassed. The Ghetto area became
a stretch of charred and burning debris in which the last victims
strove to hide. By 16 May Stroop regarded the action as completed,
and the ostentatious report he prepared for Himmler entitled *The
Warsaw Ghetto is no More*, still survives; it is typed on paper of the
finest quality and, accompanied by many photographs, bound in
leather for preservation. Himmler's response was to order the
destruction of all ghettoes; the debris of the Warsaw Ghetto was to
be levelled to the earth and the area turned into a park. It was not
until September 1944 that the action against the other Polish
ghettoes was finally completed.

Himmler described the action in the Warsaw Ghetto in a speech
made shortly afterwards.[11]

'I decided to destroy the entire Jewish residential area by
setting every block on fire, including the blocks of residential
buildings near the armament works. One block after the other
was systematically evacuated and subsequently destroyed by fire.
The Jews then emerged from their hiding places and dug-outs in
almost every case. Not infrequently, the Jews stayed in the
burning buildings until, because of the heat and the fear of being
burned alive, they preferred to jump down from the upper stories
after having thrown mattresses and other upholstered articles
into the street. With their bones broken, they still tried to crawl
across the street into blocks of buildings which had not yet been
set on fire or were only partly in flames. Some of the Jews changed
their hiding places during the night, by moving into the ruins of

burnt-out buildings, taking refuge there until they were found by
our patrols. Their stay in the sewers also ceased to be pleasant
after the first week. Frequently we could hear from the street loud
voices coming through the sewer shafts. Then the men of the
*Waffen* S.S., the Police or *Wehrmacht* Engineers courageously
climbed down the shafts to bring out the Jews and not infrequently
they stumbled over Jews already dead, or were shot at. It was
always necessary to use smoke candles to drive out the Jews. Thus
one day we opened 183 sewer entrance holes and at a fixed time
lowered candles into them, with the result that the bandits fled
from what they believed to be gas to the centre of the former
Ghetto, where they could then be pulled out of the sewer holes. A
great number of Jews, who could not be counted, were exterminated by blowing up sewers and dug-outs.'

On 23 March 1943, Dr Korherr, who acted as the statistician of
Jewish resettlement for Himmler, presented him with a report entitled
*The Final Solution of the Jewish Question*, which contained the figures
up to the end of 1942. According to Korherr, omitting Russia and
Serbia, 1,873,549 European Jews had by then either died, emigrated
or been deported, including the victims of Himmler's 'special
treatment'. Himmler expressed his satisfaction with the report,
ordered the omission of any reference to 'special treatment', and
added that he regarded the report as 'extremely good as camouflage',
though 'at present it must neither be published nor communicated
to anyone'.[12]

Himmler's need to rid himself of the Jews became an obsession.
The ghosts of those still living haunted him more than the ghosts of
those now dead; there were Jews everywhere around him, in the
north, in the west, in the south, in the areas where his power to reach
them was at its weakest. Only in the east was he strong, where his gas
chambers were strained to their limits and his ovens choked with the
dead. On a visit paid by Himmler in October 1941 to Ohlendorf's
Action Group headquarters in Nikolaeiev he was accompanied by
Quisling's Chief of Police from Norway, and he made use of this
visit to reprimand Ohlendorf for sparing the Jews of the local
agricultural areas; he was also very concerned about the number of
Jews who escaped from the region of Odessa and infiltrated themselves among the Rumanian Jews, many of whom were deported by
the Rumanians themselves to a small Jewish reserve in the Trans-
dniestra region in former Russian territory, which by agreement

with Germany had been allocated to her Rumanian allies. Many of these Jews managed to survive the war, and German relations with Rumania were in any case to be the cause of dispute between Himmler and Ribbentrop.[13]

Rumania's Jewish population was one of the largest in Europe, amounting before her territory was readjusted to 750,000, and the record of her treatment of them before and during the period of political unrest and civil war preceding the German intervention in the country is as terrible as that of the Nazis themselves, whose Action Groups took over where the Rumanians themselves left off in the areas of Bukovina and Bessarabia, which were in 1940 ceded back to Rumania by Russia. But the small population of Jews in their pocket of Transdniestrian territory became the subject of a fearful bargaining which went on throughout the rest of the war, and involved in the end the World Jewish Congress, the Swiss Red Cross, the British (as the chilly custodians of Palestine) and the obstructive American State Department. All became involved in the greed of Antonescu and the tactics of Eichmann, who disapproved of the whole tenor of such proceedings, which in his view only compromised the 'cleanliness' of the 'final solution'.

In Bulgaria Himmler was also thwarted; the Jews, though persecuted and deprived of their property, were never deported, and even in Slovakia, after a period of large-scale deportations, the puppet government managed to halt them between July 1942 and September 1944, when the Germans themselves briefly resumed the exodus. During this period, as we have seen, the negotiations for the sale of Jews by Wisliceny and Himmler were still being conducted not only for this territory but for Hungary as well, where Eichmann was to emerge in 1944 from his shell of anonymity and live a high life in Budapest with his horses and his mistress, while supervising the deportation of some 380,000 Jews under the code name Action Hoess. Reitlinger estimates Hoess gassed over 250,000 Hungarian Jews in Auschwitz during the summer of 1944, though Hoess himself boasted the number was 400,000.

Meanwhile, Himmler had not been inactive in the north and west. In July 1942, at the height of the war, he paid a personal visit to Finland to try to enforce the deportation of more Jews. At the same time he visited Reval in Estonia, and from there sent a firm directive to Berger, his liaison officer at Rosenberg's ministry controlling affairs in the eastern territories, in order to stop the publication of a decree which would give the ultimate authority to decide who was and who was not a Jew to Rosenberg's Commissar-General and not to Himmler's Security Police. Himmler wrote to Berger: 'Do not publish the decree defining Jews. Such foolish precision ties our hands. The Eastern Territories will be freed of *all* Jews. I alone am responsible to the Führer and do not want any discussion.'

In the west Himmler's powers were far weaker; the principal German authority in France remained the *Wehrmacht*, through which the deportation of Jews had to be ordered. Although Jewish refugees rounded up in France were sent east, according to Reitlinger little more than one-sixth of the Jews with French nationality were deported during the years of occupation, though their persecution by other means was as intensive as Himmler's, Heydrich's and Eichmann's agents could make it, particularly during the period of the round-up of 1942, which was undertaken nominally as reprisals for attacks on German soldiers. When the Germans occupied the Free Zone in November 1942, negotiations for handling the Jewish question had to be undertaken with the Italians, into whose area in the South of France the Jews poured from the north, and Eichmann's attempts to secure them ended in almost total failure.

In Holland, Himmler's deportation orders worked more smoothly and almost three-quarters of the Jewish population were removed. On a report sent him by the S.S. Chief, Hans Rauter, about his deportation measures in September 1943, Himmler was able to scribble an approving *Sehr gut*. In Belgium, the impact of the S.S. was considerably lessened by the opposition to their extremism shown by General von Falkenhausen, the German Military Governor until his arrest in July 1944. In Denmark, Himmler's anti-Jewish pressures were resisted with almost entire success; he attempted during 1943 to make Werner Best, formerly on Heydrich's staff, then in Paris and now Reich Plenipotentiary in Denmark, understand that the 'final solution' applied equally to Jews in the semi-neutral territory of Denmark as to those in the east. His persuasion, however, did not reach the point of action until the period in August 1943 when martial law had to be proclaimed following riots in the docks of Odense, action by the resistance movement in Copenhagen and the revolt of the small Danish fleet. Himmler, who had by this time become Minister of the Interior, used this unrest to insist through Ribbentrop that Best start at once to seize the Danish Jews and deport them to the east. There then followed the usual unseemly evasions of responsibility in which so many administrators became expert during the latter years of the war, when the possibilities of defeat and future reprisals began increasingly to influence their actions; the round-up of Jews became, in effect, a token affair that provided ample opportunities for saving Jewish life in a country which did everything it could to protect the Jews or evacuate them to Sweden. Himmler was finally persuaded that Denmark was 'Jew-free' only after Best had done everything he could to encourage the Jews to escape. In Norway, where conditions were far less favourable for diplomatic hedging than in Denmark, two-thirds of the small Jewish population managed to elude Himmler, many escaping over the border into Sweden.

The main resistance to Himmler's obsessions occurred in the south, for the Italians were never won over to anti-Semitism; in any case there were barely 50,000 Jews living in Italy. The Italians had refused to co-operate in the South of France, and Eichmann was forced to complain once more of their 'sabotage' in Greece and Yugoslavia. Although Mussolini had created his own anti-Jewish laws in 1938 under the influence of Hitler, he did not want to become implicated in genocide. Himmler, as we have seen, was regarded by Hitler as a suitable envoy to negotiate with Mussolini, and he paid several state visits to the Duce, the last being in October 1942, of which no record survives that includes discussion of Jewish deportation.[14] Only when the Germans occupied Italy in September 1943 did Himmler gain direct access to those Jews who, having taken refuge in Rome, failed to escape the successive round-ups that followed in the capital and the north. In Yugoslavia and Greece, the proportion of Jewish losses by deportation were, in sharp contrast to Italy, extremely heavy.

'In the spring of 1942 the first transports of Jews, all earmarked for extermination, arrived from Upper Silesia', wrote Hoess.[15] They were taken across the meadows to Hoess's new gas-chambers, told to undress because they were to be disinfected, then sealed in and killed:

'There was no doubt in the mind of any of us that Hitler's order had to be obeyed regardless, and that it was the duty of the S.S. to carry it out. Nevertheless we were all tormented by secret doubts . . . I had to exercise intense self-control in order to prevent my innermost doubts and feelings of oppression from becoming apparent . . . I had to watch coldly while the mothers with laughing or crying children went into the gas-chambers . . . My pity was so great that I longed to vanish from the scene: yet I might not show the slightest trace of emotion.'

Hoess sat drinking deeply with Eichmann, trying to discover whether similar anxieties were to be found in him, but:

'he showed that he was completely obsessed with the idea of destroying every single Jew on whom he could lay his hands . . . If I was deeply affected by some incident, I found it impossible to go back to my home and my family. I would mount my horse and ride until I had chased the terrible picture away. Often at night I would walk through the stables and seek relief among my beloved animals.'

What is more revealing than these expressions of self-pity is the inability of Hoess to conceive the magnitude of the crime to which he was committed. His emotionalism, so evident throughout his writing, constantly falls ludicrously short of the nature of the tragedy which he is trying to describe, if not excuse. 'I truly had no reason to complain that I was bored', he says. 'My wife's garden was a paradise of flowers . . . The prisoners never missed an opportunity to do some little act of kindness for my wife or children, thus attracting their attention. No former prisoner can ever say that he was in any way or at any time badly treated in our house.' When offered the chance of moving to Sachsenhausen he says, 'At first I felt unhappy at the prospect of uprooting myself, . . . but then I was glad to be free from it all.' As his excuse for what he did he quotes the British saying, 'My country, right or wrong', but he lays the blame squarely on the desk of Heinrich Himmler, whom he calls 'the crudest representative of the leadership principle'. 'I was never cruel', he declares, though he admits that his subordinates frequently were so; but he was, he claims, unable to stop them. The nature of these cruelties, practised by the sadists of the S.S. and the *Kapos* who enjoyed their absolute authority over the prisoners, has been described in detail by Kogon and many others who survived imprisonment in the camps.

It is perhaps not surprising that after his initial visit in March 1941, Himmler saw the camp at Auschwitz only once more. This was in the summer of 1942, when he came to inspect constructional developments. According to Hoess, his interest lay solely in the agricultural and industrial plant. Nevertheless, he was shown something of the fearful living conditions of the prisoners and their subjection to disease and overcrowding. He was furious: 'I want to hear no more about difficulties', he said to Hoess. 'An S.S. officer does not recognize difficulties; when they arise, his task is to remove them at once by his own efforts! *How* this is to be done is *your* worry and not mine!' He contrasted the progress made by I.G. Farben in their structures; from the point of view of Hoess, Farben had the use of all the skilled labour and had priority over him for building materials.

Then Himmler turned to other matters:

'He watched the whole process of destruction of a transport of Jews which had just arrived. He also spent a short time watching the selection of the able-bodied Jews, without making any objection. He made no remark about the process of extermination, but remained quite silent. While it was going on he unobtrusively observed the officers and junior officers engaged in the proceedings, including myself. He then went in to look at the synthetic rubber factory.'

Hoess used every opportunity to voice his complaints, although he knew that 'Himmler always found it more interesting and more pleasant to hear positives than negatives.' At dinner, when Hoess told him many of his officers were utterly inadequate, Himmler merely replied that he must use more dogs. At a late-night party in the house of the local Gauleiter, with whom Himmler was staying, he became more amiable and talkative, 'especially towards the ladies'. He even drank a few glasses of red wine. The following day he watched a female prisoner whipped in the women's camp; he had in fact only the previous April personally ordered 'intensified' beatings of undisciplined prisoners. The beatings were administered on the naked buttocks of male and female alike, their bodies strapped down on wooden racks. Then, says Hoess, he 'talked with some female Jehovah's Witnesses and discussed with them their fanatical beliefs'.[16] At a final conference with Hoess he told him he could do nothing to alleviate his difficulties; he would have to manage as best he could. Auschwitz must expand, work must be increased, prisoners who could not labour must be killed. Eichmann's programme was to be intensified. He then promoted Hoess an S.S.

Lieutenant-Colonel and flew back to Berlin. He would not see Auschwitz again.

Though Auschwitz was Himmler's principal death camp, there were others in Poland and Russia at which the organized gassing and shooting of Jews, Slavs and gypsies took place during the years 1942–4.

In Auschwitz and its satellite, Auschwitz II at Birkenau, the massacres began in March 1942 and did not end until October 1944; the gas-chambers and crematoria, meticulously destroyed by Himmler in November 1944 in the face of the Russian advance, were buildings constructed in an area separated from the camp itself. The human destruction was held back by the limited capacity of these buildings and their equipment; the limit at Auschwitz, even after the construction of four new combined gas-chamber-crematoria in 1943 by Heinz Kammler, who was later to design the sites for the V-rockets, seems, according to Reitlinger, not to have exceeded some 6,000 prisoners a day. Another growing limitation was transport; the trains, their airless vans packed tight with prisoners, were shunted into sidings to avoid delay to rolling-stock with a higher war priority. Himmler and Eichmann might rage at the delays that impeded the purification of Europe, but Auschwitz before its closure consumed some two million people. Himmler's mechanized massacres far exceeded those of his hero Genghis Khan.

Himmler's off-hand treatment of Hoess is evidence that by 1942 his positive interests lay elsewhere. This was the first year of reverses for Germany, both in North Africa and on the Russian front, while at home the intensity of the Allied bombing grew even greater.

In July 1943 came the collapse of Italy and the arrest of Mussolini, and there were hasty conferences summoned by the Führer at Rastenburg, his East Prussian headquarters. Only a few days before, Hitler had met the Duce at Feltre in Northern Italy. News of Badoglio's arrest of Mussolini on 25 July reached Rastenburg in time for an all-night session, during which Hitler planned to occupy Italy and reinstate Mussolini; at the same time on the following day, when all the Nazi leaders had arrived, according to Goebbels the Führer 'ordered Himmler to see to it that most severe police measures be applied in case such a danger seemed imminent here'.

There followed a period of great confusion in Italy; the armistice with the Allies, who landed in Southern Italy early on 3 September, was not announced until 8 September, and the strategy adopted by the Allies in fact saved Kesselring's modest forces in Southern Italy from what seemed certain destruction from the combined threat of the Allied and the Italian divisions. Himmler meanwhile had been told to find Mussolini and organize his rescue, while Badoglio prevented any immediate relief of his prisoner by moving him from island to island until it was finally decided what should be done with him. In the end, early in September, when Mussolini was due by the terms of the Armistice to be handed over to the Allies, he was suddenly rescued from his final place of imprisonment on the heights of a ski resort on the Abruzzi Apennines in a brilliant operation carried out by an S.S. officer, Otto Skorzeny, after Himmler had briefed him. Skorzeny's commando party was landed by glider on the mountain top; after Mussolini had been taken from the hotel where he was held prisoner, he was flown to Vienna with Skorzeny in a small aircraft which only just managed to take off from the mountainside.

Himmler had had no illusions about Mussolini; he had been kept well informed of the situation by his agents in Rome, and Skorzeny records how much Himmler seemed to know of the position. However, once Mussolini was under arrest, the reports of his agents no longer sufficed. Himmler is said by both Schellenberg and Höttl to have consulted a group of astrologers in an effort to divine where Mussolini was hidden. They were confined, says Schellenberg, in a country house by the Wannsee and there, after the seers had consumed great quantities of food, drink and tobacco, one of their number, a Master of the Sidereal Pendulum, located Mussolini on an island west of Naples. Since Mussolini had actually been taken for a while to Ponza, this no doubt more than justified in Himmler's eyes the expenditure of S.S. time and money on the occult.

With Heydrich dead, Himmler was left to carry the full burden of his policies alone. He exercised, like Hitler himself, the leadership principle in the control of a situation of such growing complexity that, even in a dictator-state, consultation between the ministries and the co-ordination of policy with the High Command responsible for the conduct of the war would seem essential if Germany were to resolve the problems which Hitler's ambitions had brought about.

But in the place of consultation and co-ordination, Hitler chose to govern by personal decisions which were less and less affected by the advice he received. With Göring in decline and Goebbels still chafing to extend his growing influence outside the restricted field of propaganda, Hitler was surrounded by nonentities whose place in his favour still depended on their ability to support him in his fantasies of war. His strength was still great and he had not lost his cunning, but he was already in these mid-years of the war using at their limit his vast quantities of men and equipment. He weakened his fighting forces by extending them on a front that stretched two thousand miles in a curve from north to south, leaving the heart of Germany exposed to the Allied bombers from the west, which the Luftwaffe could no longer successfully oppose. For Hitler, his ultimate failure was always inconceivable, and his instinctive response to all reverses was to turn his attention from them and withdraw into the delusions of his mind. Himmler was present with both Göring and Goebbels when, at a conference held in December 1941, Hitler proclaimed himself his own Commander-in-Chief in order that he might more readily override the Army High Command. From 1942, he shut himself away from the German people and from the parading soldiers, whose saluting and massive cheers had once fed his pride and purpose. Now he saw himself as the solitary genius waging war from a succession of headquarters that lay remote from the battlefronts, first of all at Vinnitza in the Ukraine, then either at Rastenburg in East Prussia, at Zossen near Berlin itself, or in the retirement of Berchtesgaden, where the mountains reflected the peace and perfection that he craved.

Below him in the Nazi hierarchy lived Himmler, a lesser spirit but one created in the image of the man he worshipped. In place of Hitler's perverted genius, he could only offer his insatiable obsessions and his pedantic attention to detail; in place of Hitler's mesmeric leadership, his absolute devotion to his duty and his rigid insistence on a similar dedication in his subordinates. His power was based on fear; yet fear was the experience he endured himself, and it grew directly out of his dependence on others and his personal inadequacy. His nervous condition had become chronic, and only Kersten could relieve him from these disabling bouts of pain. His anxiety to destroy the Jews and Slavs and place himself at the head of a Nordic Europe brash with health was a compensation for the weakly body, the sloping shoulders, the poor sight and the knock-knees to which he was tied. His mistress and her children had renewed his sexual confidence, but sexual prowess was not his strongest point. He wore the *élite* black uniform of the S.S. or the field-grey of his fighting forces, but his private army, even in

1942, was still kept in severe check by Hitler, and his schemes for independent arms production in the camps were equally frustrated.

Hitler's reserve on recruitment for the S.S. was not to be removed till March 1943; the armoured train and the remote headquarters in Zhitomir, to which Himmler travelled so often during the years 1941–3, were a centre for directing persecution behind the lines and not for the exercise of military powers.[17]

Zhitomir, in the Ukraine, some 700 miles south-east from Berlin, was situated about sixty miles north of Hitler's headquarters at Vinnitsa. An officers' training college, set in beautiful surroundings, had been requisitioned for the Reichsführer and his staff. It was equipped, according to Schellenberg who was a frequent visitor and appreciated elaborate installations, with short-wave and telephone communications linking him to every part of German-occupied Europe. There was even a tennis court on which Himmler attempted now and then to keep himself fit. During the period Hitler was in Vinnitza, from July to October 1942, Himmler made a point of seeing him on every occasion possible, driving south in his armoured car along the *Rollbahn* connecting the two centres.

Meanwhile Himmler attempted to keep the S.S. in sound moral order. Reproving letters poured out from his headquarters: 'I note your daughter is working in your office. You should have asked me first'; 'you had better look at the Germanization files giving you evidence of intercourse between German women and incriminated Poles and other aliens'; 'I do not want you to travel round as much as you do, showing off as a great commander'; 'the Reichsführer S.S. considers it inexcusable for S.S. leaders in the fourth year of the war to get drunk'; 'Dietrich told me today that the *Leibstandarte* during its stay in France had 200 cases of gonorrhea. The men really cannot be blamed. The unit came from the Eastern front and must have been completely starved sexually . . . All units of the *Waffen* S.S. are to be provided with brothels for whose flawless medical control the unit is responsible.' At the same time unit leaders must see that the seventeen and eighteen-year-olds 'do not waste their health and strength on harlots', and arrange for 'meetings between married S.S. men and their wives, since otherwise we cannot expect these marriages to produce the required and desirable number of children'. A list of suitable hotels and inns near training camps was to be drawn up, and the expenses of visiting wives met from S.S. funds. In addition lectures on the healthy procreation of children were to be given to the men.

Himmler's thought and strategy during the middle years of the war must be understood in the light of the document he showed to Kersten at his field headquarters in December 1942, the twenty-six-page report on Hitler's state of health. He took the report, contained in a black portfolio, from a safe and gave it to Kersten under terms of the utmost secrecy. The report went into Hitler's medical history, how he had suffered from the effects of poison gas in the First World War and had been for a while in danger of blindness, and how he had certain symptoms associated with the syphilis he had contracted in his youth and which had never been cured. After lying dormant, these symptoms had re-appeared in 1937 and again at the beginning of 1942; they included insomnia, dizziness and severe headaches, and revealed that Hitler was suffering from progressive paralysis which must sooner or later affect his mind. The only treatment he was receiving was that devised by his full-time physician, Professor Theodor Morell, a former ship's doctor who had run a somewhat shady clinic for venereal diseases in Berlin until he had been discovered by Hitler's photographer, Heinrich Hoffmann, and introduced to the Führer. Hitler, as unorthodox in his attitude to medical treatment as Himmler, had taken Morell into his intimate circle in 1936, and given up his body to him for endless experiments in drugs and injections, many of which Morell patented and manufactured for his personal profit.

Orthodox treatment in a mental institution, of course, was out of the question for the Führer. 'You realize now what anxieties I have', said Himmler, 'The world regards Adolf Hitler as a strong man – and that's how his name must go down in history. The greater German Reich will stretch from the Urals to the North Sea after the war. That will be the Führer's greatest achievement. He's the greatest man who ever lived and without him it would never have been possible. So what does it matter that he should be ill now, when his work is almost accomplished.'

Only sheer anxiety had forced Himmler to reveal the report to Kersten, on whom he had come to rely, but the advice Kersten gave was unacceptable – that Hitler should retire at once and place himself in medical care, while his successor brought the war to a close. Himmler at once responded with a flood of arguments prepared for the answer he had obviously expected Kersten would give. There was no provision for a successor; the Party would be at loggerheads with the High Command; his own motives would be suspected, since it would appear he himself wanted to succeed; the symptoms observed in Hitler might well prove the result of mental and physical fatigue and not of paralysis.

'What will you do, then?' asked Kersten. 'Will you simply let the matter alone and wait for Hitler's condition to get worse and worse? Can you endure the idea that the German people have at their head a man who is very probably suffering from progressive paralysis?'

Himmler's answer was in character. 'It has still not gone far enough; I'll watch carefully and it will be time enough to act once it's established that the report is correct.'

According to Schellenberg, Heydrich had gathered together every detail about Hitler's health and habits, including the diagnoses made by his doctors; these reports had been transferred to Himmler's office after the death of Heydrich. What had no doubt led to scintillating speculation on the part of the head of the S.D. and Reich Protector in Prague, only filled Himmler with acute anxiety. Later Kersten gathered that the report about him had been specially compiled for Himmler from the files by an unnamed medical adviser of absolute integrity. Although there had always been rumours circulating about Hitler's ill-health and psychological peculiarities, the detailed facts of his case were known only to a very few persons, among whom, Kersten gathered, were Bormann and, possibly, Göring.[18]

A week later, on 16 December, Himmler discussed the situation once more with Kersten. This conversation was most significant. Kersten argued that Hitler must, for Germany's sake, retire for proper treatment; as long as he was in supreme power, it was possible at any time that his judgment would fail, and his mind become clouded by delusions and megalomania. He would suffer from loss of muscular control, and paralysis of the speech and limbs would follow. He might issue the most damaging orders while under the influence of his disease. He was a very sick man, and should be treated accordingly.

Himmler remained silent. Kersten continued his argument that Hitler should be induced to hand over his authority to a successor, and that peace negotiations should follow. To this Himmler replied that Hitler's will only decreed a successor in the event of his death, and that 'fierce quarrels over the succession' would break out between the Army and the Party if Hitler during his lifetime did not remain in absolute power. As for himself, he could never be the first to make any move against the Führer; as he put it, 'everybody would think that my motives were selfish, and that I was trying to seize power for myself.' The medical evidence, in the face of Hitler's still infallible personality, would be regarded as a fake. He must, said Himmler, be left where he was; untold harm would follow his departure. He believed that Hitler's resources of health were such that he might well overcome the disease; the symptoms he was showing were very possibly those of sheer exhaustion. All he could do for the moment was watch the Führer's condition more carefully. Kersten realized then the inherent weakness that lay behind Himmler's apparent strength.

It was during 1943 that Hitler's health suffered grave deterioration; all those who met him constantly acknowledged this. It is not clear how much Schellenberg knew of what was on the secret file; he may well have known more than he reveals. He merely remarks: 'from the end of 1943, he showed progressive symptoms of Parkinson's disease . . .; a chronic degeneration of the nervous system had set in'. As early as March, Göring expressed his concern to Goebbels about the Führer who, he remarked, had aged fifteen years during the three and a half years of war. Goebbels agreed, and comments on how Hitler never relaxed, but 'sits in his bunker, worries and broods'. He suffered now from a trembling of the left arm and leg, and he was receiving from Morell a drug compounded of strychnine and belladonna for his chronic stomach pains which, according to a later medical report, could only have harmed him and caused the discoloration of his skin that was becoming more noticeable. When not on the Obersalzburg, where his mistress Eva Braun lived her isolated life, he spent most of his time at the various remote centres from which he conducted his war, and especially at the Wolf's Lair at Rastenburg, hidden in the dark forests of East Prussia, where in the summer of 1941 he had a suite of rooms constructed in concrete and buried in the ground beneath the heavily guarded enclosure of chalets. The Wolf's Lair became a strange mixture, as General Jodl said, 'of cloister and concentration camp'.

In these concrete rooms Hitler held his incessant conferences. He ate and slept as his mood dictated, taking no exercise and seeking no entertainment except the endless repetition of his reminiscences. This helped to keep his ego in a state of ferment.

These were the conditions in which he normally received his

Ministers, Göring, Goebbels, Himmler, Ribbentrop, Speer and Bormann, when they travelled east to meet him and weave their jealous webs round what was left of his attention. It was here, for instance, that on one occasion he gave an emotional discourse on Wagner to Himmler and the members of his staff. Himmler, like the others, was drawn to him as the ultimate source of the power he had gathered over the years; each of these men was torn with doubts and anxieties. How, they all wondered, were they to retain and enlarge these powers at each other's expense? On the surface they were colleagues, bound together by their devotion to the Führer; underneath they were imperialists interested only in expanding their rival spheres of influence against the time when one or other would succeed to Hitler's place. At no time did they form an integral cabinet of executive ministers; the dangers of such organized, co-ordinated power was always instinctively realized by Hitler, the preservation of whose authority lay to a large extent in the disorganization that existed immediately beneath him, the wasteful consequences of the policy of divide and rule. When some essential matter was broached, he preferred to see his Ministers singly; when they met collectively the time was passed in trivialities or in the undiscussed reception of Hitler's long-winded commands.

Reitlinger has pointed out that Himmler's senior officers were never encouraged by him to meet and discuss their collective responsibilities. They, too, were the rivals for his favour whom he dealt with singly and separately to prevent their making common cause against him. Like Hitler, he surrounded himself with junior officers, aides whom he could replace at will, but who, by virtue of their closeness to him, achieved a power far greater than their standing. Kersten was quick to recognize the influence of men like S.S. Colonel (later General) Rudolf Brandt, Himmler's principal aide, a former male typist through whom it was necessary to pass to reach the ear of the Reichsführer S.S. Schellenberg describes Brandt as a small man of plain appearance, who tried as far as possible to look and behave like Himmler. He had a phenomenal memory for facts and began work at seven in the morning, hurrying to his master with his files and papers so that work could start while Himmler shaved. If there was bad news, Brandt would begin with the word, 'Pardon', and Himmler would stop shaving. 'He was Himmler's living notebook . . . I believe he was the only person in whom Himmler had complete confidence . . . He was the eyes and ears of his master, and the manner in which he presented a matter to Himmler was often of decisive importance.' Both Schellenberg and Kersten kept on good terms with him.[19]

Himmler's senior officers remained in their separate orbits, planets to Himmler's sun – S.S. General Ernst Kaltenbrunner, appointed head of the Reich Security Office in 1943, S.S. General Mueller, head of the Gestapo, S.S. General Pohl, head of the economic administration of the S.S. and inspector of the concentration camps, and S.S. Lieutenant-General Schellenberg, Chief of Foreign Intelligence, who was now to become Himmler's closest political adviser. He also had his retinue of specialized advisers, such as Korherr, who combined the handling of statistics with the provision of secret reports on the other S.S. leaders. This led to his being beaten-up in August 1943.

In appointing Kaltenbrunner head of the Reich Security Office on 30 January 1943, Himmler made a grave error. Apparently he brought him from Vienna, where he had been Higher S.S. Police Leader for several years, because he thought a stranger would be more tractable than one of his nearer subordinates. Kaltenbrunner, though a stupid man, was sensible enough to share the S.S. view that the war was lost and seek the quickest possible means to power, one of which was to form a working alliance with Bormann when he became Hitler's personal secretary the following April. Himmler could scarcely have foreseen this danger any more than that offered by his other principal opponent on the staff; this was Mueller, head of the Gestapo who, according to Schellenberg, was also quick to establish good relations with Bormann. Both Mueller and Bormann looked rather to Russia than to the West as the place where peace negotiations should be developed. Schellenberg regarded both Kaltenbrunner and Mueller as his enemies, only too anxious to outwit and discredit both him and probably Himmler as well. He describes Kaltenbrunner as 'a giant in stature, heavy in his movements, a real lumberjack . . . his small, penetrating brown eyes were unpleasant; they looked at one fixedly, like the eyes of a viper seeking to petrify its prey'. His hands were small, like 'the hands of an old gorilla'; his fingers were stained with chain-smoking and he drank heavily. He spoke with a pronounced Austrian accent, just as Mueller spoke broad Bavarian.

Heinrich Mueller, who had been on Himmler's staff since 1933, was a reserved, obscure man, a professional police official with piercing eyes but no marked personality. He had been described by Captain Payne Best as good-looking, though he attempted to overawe him by shouting in his face and staring at him with 'funny eyes which he could flicker from side to side with the greatest rapidity' in an attempt to mesmerize his victims. In spite of his position he would, like Hitler and Himmler, spend endless time on details, conducting individual interrogations himself because he enjoyed doing so. Schellenberg describes with disdain his squarish skull, jutting forehead, narrow lips, twitching eyelids and massive hands. At the end of the war he completely disappeared, taking refuge perhaps with the Russians, whose police methods he had always professed to admire.[20]

The first stirrings of a rumour that Himmler might be in favour at least of a separate peace with Britain is mentioned in von Hassell's diaries as early as May 1941, in the period immediately preceding the attack on Russia. Hassell had been German Ambassador to Italy from 1932–7; he was a career diplomat of right-wing views whose firm belief in friendship with Britain and the United States had brought him into conflict with Ribbentrop. He was retired from the foreign service in 1937 while he was still an active man well under sixty, and he became what Allen Dulles, America's wartime agent in Switzerland, describes as 'the diplomatic adviser of the secret opposition to Hitler'. He carried out his resistance activities under the cover of a post in economic research that he held for the German Government and which enabled him to travel in Europe with relative freedom. His acquaintance with members of the resistance, more particularly on the civilian side, was wide and the diary that he kept from September 1938 until July 1944, when he was arrested after the failure of the attempt on Hitler's life, is one of the most valuable documents that has survived from Nazi Germany.

The rumours Hassell records about the possibilities of Himmler's defection from Hitler afford the first tenuous links in a submerged chain that brought Himmler into direct contact with a section of the German resistance movement.

Carl Langbehn, a Berlin lawyer whose work took him to many countries and who at the time of the Reichstag Fire Trial in 1933 had offered to defend the Communist deputy Ernst Torgler, was a neighbour of Himmler's both in Gmund and Dahlem; they had met socially before the war through their daughters, who went to school together. Langbehn was a friendly, genial man and an excellent linguist; he became a member of Canaris's *Abwehr*; he also began at Himmler's invitation to act as an independent observer for him when he was abroad on business. At the same time, he became a channel through which a certain amount of information about Himmler reached those connected in one way or another with certain sections of the growing resistance movement. Langbehn was a friend of that extraordinary man, Professor Albrecht Haushofer, son of the notorious geo-politician who had inspired Hitler's dreams of expansion, and the man who planned Hess's flight to Britain in May 1941.

Haushofer acted as a contact-man for Hess with Karl Burckhardt, President of the International Red Cross in Switzerland, who was a friend of the Hassells. In May, just before the flight, Burckhardt told Frau von Hassell that in April he had had a visit from 'an agent of Himmler' who, during a visit to Zurich, had asked Burckhardt's opinion as to whether the British would be willing to discuss possible terms for peace with Himmler instead of Hitler. This agent was undoubtedly Langbehn, who was to make the acquaintance of the Hassells later that year, in August, and become one of their valued friends.

This circuitous series of relationships may well seem to imply that Himmler, and possibly even Hitler, knew in advance of Hess's mission to Britain. In any event Haushofer, whose part in Hess's flight was known to the Gestapo, was released on Hitler's order after only a brief detention, and he was to enjoy Himmler's protection until the end of the war. However that may be, Langbehn became a source of rumour surrounding Himmler during the darker days of the Russian campaign; from 1941 to his arrest by the Gestapo in September 1943, he had at least the temporary protection of Himmler and a calculated measure of his confidence, while at the same time, through Popitz and von Hassell, he also enjoyed direct contact with one of the principal arteries of the resistance movement. Even as early as 1938, Langbehn's influence on Himmler was sufficient to secure the release from a concentration camp of Fritz Pringsheim, the Jewish professor who had taught him law. Pringsheim was released and even allowed to leave the country.

After the initial reference to Langbehn's activities on behalf of Himmler given by Hassell in May 1941, any occasional signs of disaffection in the S.S. are noted down with wishful determination during the long period of frustration that followed the invasion of

Russia. After receiving certain evidence from a discontented junior officer in the S.S., Hassell wrote in September 1941: 'it was apparent that in Himmler's outfit they were seriously worried and looking for a way out'. In December, Langbehn told Hassell he 'had been busy trying to get people out of Himmler's concentration camps', and that this often meant arranging the payment of large sums of money. He spoke also of 'the fluid state of mind existing within the S.S.', which he felt was a strange combination of the 'barbaric Party soul' and a 'misunderstood, aristocratic soul'. S.S. leaders often made wild remarks critical of the Party, the outcome of the war, and of Hitler himself. In March 1942, Langbehn according to Hassell 'still suspects all sorts of things are being planned around Himmler', and these were no doubt the rumours that reached Ciano's lengthy ears in Rome the following month, when he noted in his diary that Himmler 'who was an extremist in the past but who now feels the real pulse of the country, wants a compromise peace'. In May Ciano added that the rumour was being spread from Prince Otto von Bismarck at the German Embassy in Rome that 'Himmler is playing his own game by inciting people to grumble.'

Various glimpses we get of Langbehn's contacts and relationships with Himmler reveal little more of Himmler's intentions. The woman Gestapo agent responsible for investigating Haushofer's connections with Britain became his friend and retailed some gossip to him just prior to Heydrich's assassination in May 1942, to the effect that Heydrich hoped to supplant Himmler. Haushofer thought this information might be useful in gaining Himmler's confidence, and Langbehn passed it on to the Reichsführer, who thanked him formally and then had the woman agent arrested for spreading false rumours. Also early in 1943, Himmler warned Langbehn to keep clear of taking any legal part in a spy trial in which he might find himself supporting the interests of Ribbentrop against those of the Reichsführer S.S.

By the middle of 1942, Schellenberg felt he had risen sufficiently in Himmler's confidence to risk discussion of the possibilities of achieving some form of negotiated peace. With Göring 'more or less in disgrace', Himmler in Schellenberg's estimation 'was, and remained to the very end, the most powerful man in the régime'. He considered a total victory was now no longer possible, and in August 1942 he had a preliminary conversation at Zhitomir with Kersten (who, on Himmler's recommendation, was treating him for nervous strain), about the best way to broach the matter with Himmler. He discovered that he had an ally in Kersten, and the following day he asked Himmler for a special appointment to discuss 'a matter that involves a most important and difficult decision'. Sometime after lunch, at which Himmler 'changed from being the cool executive to being an amusing and pleasant host', Schellenberg secured his interview. He made an elliptical approach to the difficult subject in order to prepare the ground; he began by quoting precedents for the wisdom of considering alternative solutions to every kind of problem, and then asked Himmler directly if he had in mind any alternative solutions for bringing the war to an end. After a full minute's silence, Himmler gave way to surprise and indignation, but after a while he began to listen to Schellenberg's argument that the rulers of Germany would be better advised to strike a good bargain from the vantage-ground of their present strength than wait until Germany had become so weakened by war on all fronts that her present advantages were lost. Then he joined in the argument himself:

'In my present position I might have some chance of influencing Hitler. I might even get him to drop Ribbentrop if I could be sure of Bormann's support. But we could never let Bormann know about our plans. He'd wreck the whole scheme, or else he'd twist it round into a compromise with Stalin. And we must never let that happen.

'He spoke almost as if to himself, at one moment nibbling his thumbnail, then twisting his snake ring round and round – sure signs that he was really concentrating. He looked at me questioningly, and said, "Would you be able to start the whole thing moving right away – without our enemies interpreting it as a sign of weakness on our part?"

'I assured him that I could.

' "Very well. But how do you know that the whole business won't act as a boomerang? What if it should strengthen the Western Powers' determination to achieve unity with the East?"

' "On the contrary, Reichsführer", I said. "If the negotiations are started in the right way, it will prevent just that contingency."

' "All right," said Himmler, "then exactly how would you proceed?" '

Schellenberg explained that very tentative negotiations should be conducted 'through the political sector of the Secret Service'.

Himmler, he said, must appoint an agent who had real authority behind him, and meanwhile himself work on Hitler to remove Ribbentrop and appoint a more tractable Foreign Minister. Then they looked at a map of Europe and agreed that, with certain exceptions, Germany might well have to relinquish the greater part of the territory she had occupied since September 1939 in order to retain full rights within all those areas that could be rightfully regarded as German. According to Schellenberg, when they parted in the small hours of the morning, 'Himmler had given me full authority to act . . . and had given me his word of honour that by Christmas Ribbentrop would no longer be at his post.'

Schellenberg's calculations, however, were made without sufficient regard for Himmler's extraordinary caution. He played as little part as possible in the machinations of the other leaders, and quietly resisted the open intrigues of such men as Goebbels. He preferred, as always, the secret road to power, the back way up. He was, however, according to Schellenberg, 'very discreetly striving to create a new leadership for the Reich, naturally with Hitler's approval. This policy was to ensure that all those who held leading posts in the Reich ministries, in industry, commerce and trade, in science and culture . . . should be members of the S.S.' Meanwhile he sank himself in work, absorbed himself in details, the clerk in high office hidden behind a pyramid of files. The result was that at the end of the year he refused to take advantage of the notorious memorandum on the mental instability of Ribbentrop compiled by Martin Luther, an under-secretary at the Foreign Office, who had formerly been Ribbentrop's confidant, but partly through the intrigues of Schellenberg had turned violently against him.

The time chosen by Luther to produce his report was indeed an unfortunate one; Himmler fell back into one of his moods of indecision because at that particular moment he believed Hitler's confidence in him had been shaken. In the struggle for power in Rumania, Hitler on Ribbentrop's advice had chosen to support Antonescu, whereas Himmler and Heydrich had favoured Horia Sima, Leader of the Iron Guard who, encouraged by Heydrich, had been responsible for an unsuccessful *putsch* against Antonescu in January 1941 at a time when Hitler wanted to strengthen his relations with Rumania before the coming invasion of Russia. By agreement with Antonescu, Sima had been kept a prisoner by the S.D., who managed to let him escape. Mueller did not dare to inform Himmler of the escape for a fortnight, and it was some while before the fugitive was captured. Hitler was led by Ribbentrop to believe that Himmler had known of the escape all along and was attempting through him to stir up further trouble in Rumania. If there was one thing Himmler could not bear it was the criticism or ill-will of the Führer; in any case Himmler disliked Luther, who tended to be loud-mouthed and over-familiar. While Wolff stood on one side of him warning him against Luther, Schellenberg, with his plan to depose Ribbentrop firmly in mind, stood on the other urging him not to reach a hasty decision. Himmler as usual postponed making up his mind but, as he always did when he was in any doubt, he finally took the line that offered the least risk to himself. Luther was arrested and interrogated, and Ribbentrop's face was saved.

Himmler had lacked the courage to act against Ribbentrop. He feared Hitler's admiration for the man he regarded as second only to Bismarck, exceeded the Führer's confidence in himself. Schellenberg's carefully contrived advantage was therefore discarded, and Himmler fell temporarily out of favour. In a private letter to his wife dated 16 January 1943, Bormann comments at some length on Himmler, who, he says, is 'deeply offended . . . He feels unjustly treated by the Chief'. Bormann claims that he tried to calm Himmler, whose criticism of the treatment he had received was 'very bitter, and at times acid'. Himmler, he thought, was suffering from 'nervous strain.' Later Schellenberg, to his disgust, found that Himmler wanted to discuss the whole matter openly with Ribbentrop showing, as Schellenberg put it, 'a cowardly lack of decision'. He agreed, however, that any future attempts to negotiate peace must be conducted through a neutral country. 'I don't wish to know all these details', he added. 'That's your responsibility.' Throughout this period Himmler impressed on Schellenberg that he should keep in contact with Langbehn, and it seems clear that at some stage Langbehn was being used as an agent by Schellenberg to make contact with Allied representatives in Switzerland. For instance, in December Hassell noted in his diary, 'Langbehn has had some talks with an English official in Zürich (12 December) and an American official (Hopper) in Stockholm, with the approval of the S.D.' The talks, as always, were inconclusive because the Allies required the unconditional surrender of Germany and the complete overthrow of the Nazi régime.

Meanwhile Kersten, who still had Finnish nationality, had moved with his family to Stockholm at the end of September 1943, where he was introduced to an American, Abram Stevens Hewitt, who was visiting Sweden as a special envoy from Roosevelt. Kersten soon found that Hewitt, who had become his patient, shared his view that the war should be brought to an end as soon as possible through peace negotiations, more especially as the threat from Russia was becoming so strong. Kersten offered to discuss the matter with Himmler, and on 24 October sent him a letter through the Finnish diplomatic bag.

Kersten began his letter by saying it concerned 'proposals which might have the greatest significance for Germany, for Europe, even for the entire world. What I offer is the possibility of an honourable peace.' He then went on to describe Hewitt's influential position with the American Government and the proposals for peace talks that Hewitt considered possible, but depending on conditions which were very drastic and included the abolition of Hitler's dictatorship and the Nazi Party and the appearance of the leading Nazis before a court to answer for their war crimes. 'I beg you not to throw this letter into your wastepaper basket, Herr Reichsführer,' he wrote, 'but receive it with the humanity which resides in the heart of Heinrich Himmler.' He suggested that Schellenberg be sent to Stockholm to meet Hewitt. In every paragraph he appealed to Himmler's vanity, and concluded with the challenge: 'Fate and history itself have placed it in your hands to bring an end to this terrible war.'

Kersten was also involved in encouraging the Finnish Government to retire from the war, in which they had become the unwilling allies of Nazi Germany because of their struggle with Russia. After a short period in Helsinki, Kersten returned to Stockholm, where he anxiously waited for some reply from Himmler. Schellenberg arrived in Stockholm on 9 November and met Hewitt with whom, according to Kersten, he got on well.[21] But, as usual, nothing happened when Himmler was pressed to take action.

Kersten met Himmler on 4 December at Hochwaldt, his headquarters in East Prussia. He pressed him for a decision. 'Don't torment me', he reports Himmler as saying, 'give me time. I can't get rid of the Führer, to whom I owe everything.'

Kersten played every trick he knew to inflate Himmler's vanity as 'a great Germanic leader'.

'In Stockholm Mr Hewitt is waiting for your decision', he said, 'so that he can take it to Roosevelt.'

Himmler found the conditions for the peace talks 'hair-raising'. He could not conceive of a Germany without the Nazi régime.

'How can I take the responsibility,' he said, 'when faced with the leaders of the Party?'

'You will have no responsibility towards them', Kersten pointed out. 'They will have ceased to exist.'

Himmler seemed most perturbed about the suggestion that there must be a court to try those responsible for war crimes, since he knew that the annihilation of the Jews was necessarily regarded by the Allies as the worst of the many crimes the Nazis had committed. This was not a crime at all, Himmler argued to Kersten, since it was decreed by law.

'The Führer ordered the annihilation of the Jews in Breslau in 1941. The Führer's orders are the supreme law in Germany. I've never acted on my own initiative; I've only carried out the Führer's orders. So neither I nor the S.S. can accept any responsibility.'

The removal of Hitler he regarded as 'cutting the ground from under my own feet'; the withdrawal of the German Army was an invitation to Russia or America to dominate Europe.

In the end he avoided making any decision by saying he was too tired to think. He agreed, however, that the war should be stopped, but that the conditions suggested by Hewitt were very hard.

'Your proposals aren't unacceptable to me,' he said, according to Kersten, 'except for the one about responsibility for alleged war crimes.'

In subsequent discussions on 9 and 13 December, Kersten claims that he went on pressing Himmler to make up his mind. He argued that Hitler was a sick man whose orders were bringing Europe nearer and nearer disaster. Eventually Himmler agreed to send Schellenberg to Stockholm to bring Hewitt secretly into Germany to discuss the negotiations with him.

But by the time Schellenberg eventually reached Stockholm, the time-limit for discussions set by Hewitt had elapsed; he had gone back to America. A remote chance to bring about peace had been thrown away; how far deliberately, how far through Himmler's chronic procrastination it is now impossible to determine.

During 1943 Himmler began to extend his military ambitions. The fall of Stalingrad followed by reverses in North Africa led Hitler to revoke his ban on the expansion of the *Waffen* S.S. His total losses in Russia and Africa amounted to over half a million men. After

Khahov was recaptured by the Germans in the spring, Himmler, as we have seen, spoke there in the University about the foreign recruits his S.S. men would soon find fighting beside them. Eight new divisions were formed during 1943, half of them recruited from East Europeans of whom by no means all were of German racial origin. All Rumanians of German origin were subject to conscription, to the resentment of the Rumanian Army; many of them were sent to replenish S.S. divisions elsewhere in Europe, where they were not popular. Even Bosnian Moslems were recruited, and in May Himmler made the Mufti Hajji Iman an honorary S.S. Lieutenant-General. Obviously all former S.S. standards had gone by the board, and in the same month recruitment began for an S.S. division made up of anti-Bolshevist Ukrainians, who formed part of the vast body of men numbering over half a million who had been former subjects of the Soviet Union and whom the Germans persuaded to serve in their own armies. Himmler still endeavoured to maintain his racial prejudice in the face of this rapid expansion of his forces, since he regarded all Slavs as inferior, but he welcomed into his ranks the Asiatic stock he associated with Genghis Khan. Other divisions were formed in Latvia and Estonia. By the end of the war, the number of S.S. divisions was to increase to thirty-five, representing some half a million fighting men. Allowing for losses, the numbers involved were some 900,000; of these less than half came from Germany itself, and some 150,000 were men whose racial origins were not Germanic.[22]

Although the eight months from January to 25 August 1943, when Himmler became Reich Minister of the Interior following the downfall of Mussolini and the defection of Italy, represent a period during which he had to regain the confidence of Hitler after the misunderstanding over the escape of Horia Sima – 'a considerable time', says Schellenberg – they were months in which Himmler's powers outside Hitler's court considerably increased. Although, according to Reitlinger, Himmler had no direct access to Hitler, who was spending the greater part of his time at his Wolf's Lair headquarters at Rastenburg, this does not mean he was out of touch with him. There was, however, a continuous struggle between him and Bormann for influence over Hitler, though each of them knew better than to bring the fight into the open. According to Schellenberg, who hated Bormann – 'the contrast between him and Himmler is really grotesque; if I thought of Himmler as a stork in a lily-pond, Bormann seemed to me like a pig in a potato-field' – Himmler made many tactical errors in his dealings with Bormann, which the latter merely exploited at Himmler's expense; one of these errors was the secret loan through Bormann of 80,000 marks from Party funds to help provide for the needs of his mistress Hedwig and their children.

After April 1943, when he was appointed Hitler's personal secretary, Bormann increasingly governed Hitler's daily life; he became an indispensable companion, sharing his worries, soothing his nerves, using his 'cast-iron memory' to clarify the growing complexity of Hitler's war situation and guide his decisions. As Himmler said to Schellenberg:

> 'The Führer has become so accustomed to Bormann that it's very difficult indeed to lessen his influence. Again and again I have had to come to terms with him, though it's really my duty to get him out. I hope I can succeed in out-manoeuvring him without having to get rid of him. He's been responsible for many of the Führer's misguided decisions; in fact, he's not only con-firmed his uncompromising attitude, he's stiffened it.'[23]

Schellenberg positively enjoyed embarrassing his master, and continued throughout 1943 to remind him of his promise to remove Ribbentrop:

> 'Because of the reflection of Himmler's glasses, I could scarcely ever see his eyes . . . I had therefore made a habit of always staring at his forehead, just above the bridge of his nose, and this seemed to make him strangely uneasy after a few minutes. He would start to make notes or look into the drawer of his desk in order to escape my glance. On this occasion . . . he said, "I can only remove Ribbentrop with Bormann's help, and the result would be an even more radical policy." '

Goebbels, who had personal discussions with Göring in March 1943 in the hope that some sort of group representation of the old leaders could be formed to counteract the bad influence of Bormann, Ribbentrop, Lammers and Keitel, regarded Himmler as at least a potential ally; the theory was that Göring, roused from his lassitude, should reconvene the pre-war Council of Ministers, of which he was President, and through this set up an opposing factor with Goebbels, Himmler, Speer and Ley. In May Goebbels preens himself in his diary about the praise Himmler had given to his department and agrees with his stringent criticisms of Frick, the Minister of the Interior, whose lack of leadership he deplored. On the other hand, Semmler, Goebbels's aide who kept his own diary at this time, recorded in March that Goebbels was equally suspicious of Himmler and Bormann – 'not one of those three trusts the others out of his sight'.

Not that Bormann was unfriendly to Himmler's face; he merely placed himself firmly between the Führer and Himmler, whose field headquarters in Birkenwald, East Prussia, were some thirty miles distant from the Wolf's Lair. To Bormann (whose father had once been a bandsman who, according to Ribbentrop, had often performed on the bandstands on English sea-fronts in the years before 1914), Himmler was always 'Uncle Heinrich'. As Party Chancellor, controlling the whole national Party machine, Bormann could do much in a quiet way to frustrate the influence of men as uniquely powerful as Goebbels and Himmler were to become between 1943 and the end of the war.

Himmler meanwhile built up a vast bureaucracy of his own; in addition to the *Waffen* S.S. in the field, some 40,000 men were employed by the S.S. leadership office, while the Reich Main Security Office had a strength of over 60,000. When S.S. General Heinz Guderian, the expert on armoured warfare who had been reinstated by Hitler after temporary dismissal and made Chief Inspector for Panzer Troops, met Himmler on 11 April at Berchtesgaden, he found him completely opposed to any integration of the new S.S. armoured divisions with the Army. Neither Hitler nor Himmler wanted to see the S.S., the personal army of the leadership, merged with the armed forces of the Reich. Nor could he persuade Himmler to influence Hitler in the direction of delegating more power to the Army; he 'received an impression of such impenetrable obliquity' that he gave up any thought of 'discussing a limitation of Hitler's power with him'.

Parallel with his extension of the *Waffen* S.S., Himmler turned his eyes in another direction that might assist his future powers. In April 1943 he visited the rocket establishment at Peenemünde for the first time, and met the scientist and soldier in charge of the research and development of liquid-propellant rockets, Major-General Walter Dornberger. The first experimental rocket of the pattern later known as the V2 had been successfully launched as early as October 1942, and Himmler was anxious to know more of this carefully-guarded secret weapon, for the development of which Hitler had not yet given full priority.[24] Dornberger describes Himmler's manner and appearance:

'He looked to me like an intelligent elementary school teacher, certainly not a man of violence . . . Under a brow of average height two grey-blue eyes looked at me, behind glittering pince-nez, with an air of peaceful interrogation. The trimmed moustache below the straight, well-shaped nose traced a dark line on his unhealthy pale features. The lips were colourless and very thin. Only the inconspicuous receding chin surprised me. The skin of his neck was flaccid and wrinkled. With a broadening of his constant set smile, faintly mocking and sometimes contemptuous about the corners of the mouth, two rows of excellent white teeth appeared between the thin lips. His slender, pale and almost girlishly soft hands, covered with veins, lay motionless on the table throughout our conversation.'

Dornberger soon discovered the nature of Himmler's interest.

'I am here to protect you against sabotage and treason', he said. Peenemünde was too much in the limelight; its security had become of national importance, and not merely the concern of the Army, under which its activities were formally placed. As he left, Himmler promised Dornberger that he would come back for further private discussions.

'I am extremely interested in your work', he said. 'I may be able to help you.'

The infiltration of the S.S. into the work at Peenemünde followed immediately on this meeting. Dornberger's Station Commander, Colonel Zanssen, an experienced man who had been at Peenemünde for some years, was suddenly dismissed without any reference to the Army departments concerned. This was done by order of Himmler on the most trivial charges, which the S.S. refused to authenticate. Dornberger managed to have Zanssen reinstated with the support of General Fromm, the Commander-in-Chief of the Reserve Army under whose command Peenemünde was placed. After the war, Dornberger learned that Professor von Braun, who was then one of the senior research officers at the establishment, had under an oath of secrecy been offered by Himmler full scope to develop Peenemünde if the S.S. ever took over. Von Braun had rejected the offer.

Himmler's second visit came on 29 June; he arrived driving his own small armoured car. As usual, he made a better impression in private than he did in public. Dornberger describes him at a meeting with the senior research workers:

'Himmler possessed the rare gift of attentive listening. Sitting back with legs crossed, he wore throughout the same amiable and interested expression. His questions showed that he unerringly grasped what the technicians told him out of the wealth of their knowledge. The talk turned to the war and the important questions in all our minds. He answered without hesitation, calmly and candidly. It was only at rare moments that, sitting with his elbows resting on the arms of the chair, he emphasized his words by tapping the tips of his fingers together. He was a man of quiet, unemotional gestures. A man without nerves.'

He seemed happy to talk politics in this group of men whose interests were absorbed in science and engineering. He spoke of Europe as a social and economic unit controlled by a racially-sound Germany which had come to an understanding with Britain, whose main interests lay overseas and with America. The Slav block was the great danger to Europe, and that was why Hitler had gone to war with Russia before the Slav nations had been welded into one invincible group under Russian domination. He compared the Western European worker, with his demand for leisure and a high standard of living, with the Russian worker, dedicated entirely to his factory's output and ready in time to flood world markets with cheap goods. The war was therefore just as much an economic struggle as it was military and political. They argued about the German occupation of Poland – 'Himmler's glasses glittered. Was I mistaken,' wrote Dornberger, 'or had his imperturbable, impenetrable mask of amiability fallen a little?' Poland was needed for German colonization, he said. The birth-rate of the Poles would have to be reduced until the German settlers grew sufficient in numbers to take over the territory. 'We shall arrange for the young German peasants to marry Ukrainian girls of good farming stock and found a healthy new generation adapted to conditions out there ... We must practice a rigid state-planned economy both with men and material throughout conquered territory', he added.

Dornberger and his colleagues sat both fascinated and revolted by Himmler's manner of presenting his policy, which he expressed so 'concisely, simply and naturally'. 'I shuddered at the everyday manner in which the stuff was related. But even as I did so I admired Himmler's gift for expounding difficult problems in a few words which could be understood by anyone and went straight to the heart of the matter.'

Himmler then went on to praise Stalin who, he said, Hitler considered to be his only really great adversary, and Genghis Khan, who had tried in his period to consolidate Mongol supremacy in Asia and whose blood survived in the modern ruler of Russia. They could only be conquered by the methods they understood – those practised by Genghis Khan.

They talked until four o'clock in the morning. Himmler knew the calibre of the men he was with, and that he could best appeal to them by intellectual discussion. This was conquest by the spoken word.

The following afternoon Himmler saw a successful launching of a 'V2' rocket, and he went away determined to win control of Peenemünde from the Army.

Meanwhile, in August 1943 Langbehn consented to bring a key member of one section of the German resistance movement to see Himmler. This was Dr Johannes Popitz, a scholar and an intellectual belonging to Hassell's circle, and a man of whom Goebbels was to record his grave suspicion less than a month later. 'Hitler', wrote Goebbels in his diary, 'is absolutely convinced that Popitz is our enemy. He is already having him watched so as to have incriminating material about him ready; the moment Popitz gives himself away, he will close in on him.'

In tracing the devious relations between Himmler, Langbehn and Popitz, it is impossible to know every aspect of Himmler's motives, though it is, of course, easy to speculate about them. Schellenberg, whom, as we have seen, Himmler had instructed to put out peace feelers to the Allies through Langbehn, makes no mention of Popitz in his published memoirs. Although Hassell was always doubtful about the usefulness of Himmler in any conspiracy directed solely against Hitler, there was a period when Popitz, as a member of Hassell's aristocratic circle of conspirators, managed to convince them that a risk should be taken to sound out Himmler's loyalty. In this he was encouraged by his friend Langbehn.

It must be remembered that the conspirators were by 1943 in a state of considerable frustration; no progress seemed to have been made to bring in the Army and the generals. There had since 1941 been desultory discussion of the idea of stimulating a 'palace revolution', at first through Göring and then later through Himmler, either of whom could at a later stage be removed from power once he had fulfilled his initial task in assisting with the removal of Hitler.

Langbehn was the obvious man through whom Popitz could be introduced to Himmler. According to the evidence in the indictment used at their trial in 1944, they had first met during the winter of 1941–2, shortly after Langbehn had joined the circle round Hassell. Popitz is another curious figure whose actual position it is difficult to determine; he was not a member of the Nazi Party but remained from 1933 until his arrest in 1944 Prussian Minister of State and Finance under Göring. He had been a friend of Schleicher, and it was probably at the time of Schleicher's murder by the Nazis in 1934 that he began to entertain the doubts that eventually made him one of the more ardent members of the resistance. The fact that he had once been a supporter of the Nazis and as late as 1937 accepted the golden badge of the Party from Hitler made him suspect in the eyes of many members of the resistance. Also he was politically very right-wing and favoured a return of the monarchy. But Hassell trusted him as a friend and fellow-conspirator, and it was decided by May 1943 that Langbehn should seek an appointment for Popitz with Himmler through the agency of Wolff. The arrangements were delayed owing to Wolff's illness during the summer, but eventually the meeting took place in Himmler's new office at the Ministry of the Interior on 26 August 1943.

Neither Wolff nor Langbehn was actually present at the interview, of which two accounts survive. The first is that given in the subsequent indictment of Langbehn and Popitz, and is therefore strictly slanted to conceal Himmler's part in the matter; only Popitz's very vague statements are given and no word is included of what Himmler may have said. Popitz, according to the terms of the indictment, expressed his anxiety at the corruption in high places, the inefficiency of the administration, and the impossibility of winning the war so long as Hitler, though admittedly a genius, remained in absolute power. The chances of promoting a negotiated peace should be explored, but this was not possible unless the Führer was 'surrounded by men with whom negotiations could be undertaken'. Such conditions would definitely exclude Ribbentrop. Popitz then mentioned the kind of persons he had in mind for the leadership of the Army and the Foreign Office. It was left that another conversation should be arranged at a later date. Meanwhile, in the ante-room, Langbehn expressed his fears to Wolff that Popitz would not be sufficiently outspoken to Himmler, and said that on the next occasion he wanted to be present himself. The other account of this meeting was that given by Popitz himself to a friend called Zahler a few days later. Himmler had said little, he told Zahler, but had not opposed the suggestion of negotiations being conducted without Hitler's knowledge.[25]

Langbehn then left for Switzerland to pass on the good news to his contacts in neutral territory. It was then, at this moment of cautious optimism, that the sword of Damocles overhanging every conspirator against Hitler, fell on the neck of Langbehn. As Schellenberg put it: 'A radio message about Dr Langbehn's negotiations with Allied representatives in Switzerland was intercepted, and the fact that Dr Langbehn had my blessing in this completely unofficial undertaking was mentioned, as well as Kersten's part in furthering these negotiations. Kaltenbrunner and Mueller immediately arranged for a secret investigation, but Kersten's influence with Himmler saved me from disaster.'

The interception of this radio message (which, according to Dulles, was neither British nor American in origin) meant that Himmler and Schellenberg were forced to sacrifice Langbehn, though Popitz, strangely enough, remained free until after the attempt on Hitler's life the following year. However, it seems that Langbehn was able to secure a meeting with Himmler before his arrest by the Gestapo following his return from Switzerland. Evidence for this meeting, which must have taken place before Schellenberg and Himmler had learned about the interception of the message, rests solely on Langbehn himself, who told his friend the sculptress Puppi Sarre 'that he had touched on the elimination of Hitler only in passing, that Himmler had been quite serious, had asked factual questions, but had not tried to find out any names'. But Himmler could do nothing now but protect himself and Schellenberg, whom Kaltenbrunner and Mueller were now only too ready to denounce as a British agent. Langbehn was arrested, along with his wife and Puppi Sarre.

Himmler, however, won a victory elsewhere. This was the final collapse early in 1944 of Canaris's department for military Intelligence in foreign countries, the *Abwehr*. It came as a direct result of the arrest of another anti-Nazi group centred round the widow of Dr Wilhelm Solf, a former German ambassador in Japan and a man of liberal, as distinct from right-wing, outlook. Solf, who hated the Nazis and did not fear to say so, had died in 1936 and his wife, Frau Hanna Solf, and her daughter, the Countess Ballestrem, maintained this independent outlook and were active helpers of those persecuted by the régime. They formed an intellectual circle of distinguished people, but on 10 September a Gestapo spy called Dr Reckse, who they believed to be a Swiss medical student prepared to take messages to Switzerland, was introduced at a tea-party given by Frau Solf for members of this group. Three months were allowed to elapse before the mass arrest of over seventy anti-Nazis belonging to the liberal wing of the resistance, including Otto Kiep, formerly of the German Foreign Office, and Helmuth von Moltke, who belonged to the legal section of the *Abwehr*. Attempts were also made to inveigle two other *Abwehr* agents, Erich and Elizabeth Vermehren, who were close friends of Kiep in Berlin, to return from their base in Istanbul for interrogation. Knowing of Otto Kiep's arrest, they sought asylum with the British, and were flown to Cairo.[26]

Hitler was now strongly advised by Himmler to dispense with the *Abwehr*, since it seemed so persistently to be staffed by intellectuals who were opposed to the régime. On 18 February 1944 Hitler broke up the organization and announced that the German Intelligence Service was to be unified. Later in the year the various sections of the *Abwehr* came finally under the authority of the Gestapo and the S.D., and in May Himmler gave one of his standardized speeches at Salzburg to the principals of Canaris's former department. He derided the very term *Abwehr* as defensive, whereas a truly German Intelligence service, he said, should obviously be aggressive. The inspiration of the Führer made defeatism impossible; Himmler even went so far as to welcome the idea of invasion because it would enable Hitler's armies to drown the invaders 'in the seas of their own blood'. D-Day came two weeks later.

Canaris was not immediately disgraced by the collapse of the *Abwehr*. He was transferred and made chief of the Office for Commercial and Economic Warfare, a suitably remote position for a man who was too involved in well-meaning personal intrigue to be an efficient master either of spies for the Nazis or agents for the resistance. The *Abwehr* had been a failure, staffed by amateurs and used as a convenient cover by a number of members of the resistance, such as the Pastors Dietrich Bonhoeffer and Bethge, Hans Bernd Gisevius, Otto John and Josef Müller. 'His subordinates were able to twist him round their little finger', wrote Schellenberg of Canaris, whose company he always enjoyed in spite of their dubious official relationship. A vast dossier against Canaris had been built up over the years against the time when Himmler should decide on the destruction of this man he professed to admire. The long delay in taking action led Schellenberg, the expert in suspicion, to sense that Canaris had some secret hold over Himmler. He was allowed to continue unassailed until after the attempt on Hitler's life in July, when Schellenberg was sent to arrest him.

Langbehn remained imprisoned without trial until after the attempt on Hitler's life the following year; he was the subject of speculation alike by the Nazis and the members of the resistance. Popitz's attempt to enquire after his fate from Himmler met with no success, and Popitz himself was regarded with suspicion by many members of the resistance who knew in any case that he was dangerous because he was being closely watched. Interrogation recurred month after month, duly noted by Hassell, but it was in Himmler's interest to keep the enquiries as obscure as possible. At least at this stage Langbehn was not tortured, and this could only have been the result of orders from Himmler.

Early in November 1943, Himmler had a long conversation with Goebbels in which they agreed that Ribbentrop's inflexible foreign policy was deplorable, and they joined in the usual diatribe against the High Command. Then Himmler began to whitewash his own position with regard to the resistance; he told Goebbels all about the existence of a group of enemies of the State, among whom were Halder and possibly also Popitz. This circle, he said, would like to contact England, by-passing the Führer. Himmler must have aquitted himself well: 'Himmler will see to it that these gentlemen do no major damage with their cowardly defeatism', wrote Goebbels. 'I certainly have the impression that the domestic security of the country is in good hands with Himmler.'

# VI

# *The Miraculous Hands*

The curious relationship between Kersten and Himmler lasted for six years and became the single most powerful influence in Himmler's life after the death of Heydrich. Even the strongest man placed in a position of unique responsibility normally needs the support of advisers, though he may turn these men into shadows of his own personality, expecting from them confirmation of every opinion he happens to hold. Some men in positions of supreme authority need someone whom they respect to stay close to them and fulfil their need for a confessor who can help them purge their consciences when their ruthlessness has led them to take actions of which they are uncertain, if not ashamed.

Kersten, as we have seen, was forced against his will to become Himmler's confessor as well as his masseur. The relationship which grew up between them was one which neither could have forecast. Kersten has been described by his biographer, Joseph Kessel, as 'mild-mannered with kind eyes and the sensual mouth of one who loves the good things of life'. In his gentleness lay his great strength: to patients seized by pain, much of which was neurotic in its origin, he seemed like an angel sent to bring them swift relief. Their gratitude was profound, and was increased by the speed with which his treatments had their effect. His patients all idolized Kersten, making of him a kind of saint on whom they showered their gifts and bestowed their praises.

A patient suddenly relieved of pain often turns to the man who has cured him with an urge to ease his mind. The mood of relaxation that follows treatment acts as a solvent to confession. Kersten, mild-mannered though he was, appeared to Himmler as a saviour, an indispensable, reassuring worker of miracles on whom he relied and whom eventually, in his own peculiar way, he loved. It was Kersten,

in fact, who enabled Himmler to carry the unnatural burden which
eventually proved to be far beyond his limited strength of character.
Kersten has described the situation very clearly himself:

'Anybody today who holds some very responsible position –
political, administrative, industrial or in any other sphere of
public life – is constantly obliged to impose on himself physical
and psychic stresses which are not only unaccustomed, but may
even be described as unnatural. The result is to be seen in the
frightening increase of illnesses in these classes due to the wear
and tear of civilization: today the term "occupational disease"
has been coined . . . A practice extending over many years has
convinced me that men who are obliged to make such inroads on
their physical and psychic powers can nevertheless be maintained
in health and happiness through a regular course of my physio-
neural therapy, so that they can be equal to the heavy tasks
constantly imposed upon them. It was always my sincerest wish
to be at hand, unremitting in helping and relieving pain.'[1]

Although Kersten used his growing influence over Himmler to
save thousands of lives, his attendance on the head of the S.S. and
the Gestapo during the worst years of his criminal career made him
a controversial figure both during and after the war. Kersten began
his treatments of Himmler unwillingly; he was, like everyone else,
alarmed even at the thought of meeting him. But the needs of
Himmler as a patient soon overcame Kersten's initial antipathy, and
almost immediately he sensed Himmler's need for a confidant. The
moment he was relieved of pain, Himmler began to unburden his
mind. He wanted someone to whom he could talk. Who better than
this Finn from Holland who looked at him with a calm and confident
smile and seemed like some wise man – a 'magic Buddha', as
Himmler once called him. The Reichsführer was deeply shamed of
his illness, and the fact that only a few of his intimate staff knew of
his suffering placed Kersten at once in a privileged position.

Kersten kept notes of everything that passed between Himmler
and himself, as well as of the conversations he had had with other
leaders of the S.S. His principal allies were Brandt, Hitler's secretary,
and later Walter Schellenberg. In Kersten's memoirs we come
nearest to understanding Himmler as a man and evaluating the
peculiar views he acquired as a result of his scholarship. He talked
to Kersten on every subject that occupied his thoughts. As far as

his time permitted, Himmler was an assiduous reader, though, like Hitler, he used books only to confirm and develop his particular prejudices. Reading was for him a narrowing, not a widening experience. He saw himself as a teacher and reformer born to change the world.

The study of medicine along the lines he favoured was a constant subject for discussion with Kersten. He was against the conventional remedies put on the market by industry for private profit. He believed in herbal remedies that came straight from natural sources, and he had for long been a serious student of medieval herbalism. Kersten could not help being impressed by his knowledge, but scarcely by his conclusions. Himmler fancied himself as a medical adviser and he was always prepared to prescribe such natural remedies as applying a wet, cold stocking to the forehead to cure a headache. Kersten acknowledged that Himmler knew a certain amount about the subject, but the reforms he planned to introduce after the war would have staggered the medical profession had they known them. He intended to enroll in the S.S. the doctors who believed in homoeopathic remedies so that they might form effective shock troops to coerce the rest of the profession into seeing sense, while the German public were to be encouraged to grow their own health remedies in their back gardens. Meanwhile he experimented as far as he could with dietary and health practice in the S.S. and the *Lebensborn* movement.

It was natural for Himmler to see the future of society in terms of people of chosen blood. He believed that the healthiest and most intelligent and industrious stock originated from the land, and he wanted to found a vast European system of state farming to provide the right environment for the universal aristocracy of the future. Politicians, civil servants, scholars and industrialists alike would all be expected to keep in active contact with the land in addition to their urban professions. 'Their children', he said, 'will go to the country as a horse to pasture.' Kersten raised all the obvious objections to this, saying that the nation's agriculture would be jeopardized by the ignorant activities of these amateur, weekend farmers. Himmler hoped to overcome this weakness by means of professional bailiffs, who would in the end be responsible for the maintenance of the farms. As for the industrial workers, they would have state allotments on which to dig and flourish, and all soldiers would automatically have the status of peasants. The S.S. would

arrange everything, he said. 'Villages inhabited by an armed peasantry
will form the basis for the settlement in the East, the kernel of
Europe's defensive wall.'

The focus of Himmler's political vision was centred in the past
as he understood it. The vision had a deadly simplicity about it,
taking no account of the organic growth of the many different
peoples who had evolved the present divisions of Europe during
centuries of war and political barter. Europe, he held, must be
dominated either by the Germanic races or the Slavs; this was
Himmler's set belief. It always seemed to him utterly unreasonable
for the Germanic English to side with the alien Slav against their
racial brothers. As he put it to Kersten:

> 'Our measures are not really so original. All great nations have
> used some degree of force or waged war in acquiring their status
> as a great power, in much the same way as ourselves; the French,
> the Spanish, the Italians, the Poles, to a great extent, too, the
> English and the Americans. Centuries ago Charlemagne set us
> the example of resettling an entire people by his action with the
> Saxons and the Franks, the English with the Irish, the Spaniards
> with the Moors; and the American method of dealing with their
> Indians was to evacuate whole races . . . But we are certainly
> original in one important point: our measures are the expression
> of an idea, not the search for any personal advantage or ambition:
> we desire only the realization on a Germanic basis of a social ideal
> and the unity of the West. We will clarify the situation at whatever
> cost. It may take as many as three generations before the West
> gives its approval to this new order, for which the *Waffen* S.S.
> was created.'[2]

Had Nazi Germany won the war, this would have been the
pattern of Europe which Himmler intended to impose by force had
he succeeded Hitler as Führer; his aim was for Germany to set up a
large economic confederation of European and North African states
led by Germany and representing a total population and power three
times greater than that of the United States. Kersten carefully
recorded Himmler's statements:

> 'The European empire would form a confederation of free states,
> among which would be Greater Germany, Hungary, Croatia,
> Slovakia, Holland, Flanders, Wallonia, Luxemburg, Norway,
> Denmark, Estonia, Latvia, Lithuania. These countries were to

govern themselves. They would have in common a European currency, certain areas of the administration including the police, foreign policy and the army in which the various nations would be represented by national formations. Trade relations would be governed by special treaties, a sphere in which Germany as the economically strongest country would hold back in order to favour the development of the weaker ones. Free towns were also envisaged, having special functions of their own, among them the task of representing a nation's culture . . .

'When Bolshevism had been extirpated in Russia, the Western Territories would come under German administration modelled on the Marches which Charlemagne had instituted in the east of his empire; the methods followed would be those by which England had evolved her colonies into dominions. When peace and economic health were fully restored, these territories would be handed back to the Russian people, who would live there in complete freedom, and a twenty-five year peace and commercial treaty would be concluded with the new government.'[3]

The great expanse of Russia was to be partitioned and placed under the administrative control of Germany, Britain and the United States, after these nations had come to terms with Hitler. Germany would control the area up to the River Ob, while the English were to have the areas between the rivers Ob and Lena. The Americans would be allocated the region east of the Lena and including Kamschatka and the sea of Okhotsh. As Himmler told Kersten early in the war, Germany had no intention of weakening England's position as a great power. On the contrary, England was to be one of the cornerstones in the new Germanic Europe. The British fleet would protect Europe at sea while the Germanic armies would protect the land. Himmler's theories, geared only to the past, found difficulty in defining a creative future for America. As Kersten puts it, 'The whole American way of thinking was so alien to him that he could not even begin to understand it.'

Once Europe had been stabilized as the political, economic and cultural centre of the world, governed by a landed aristocracy and policed by a soldier-peasantry, the spread of the pure Germanic stock by intensive breeding would begin. The germs for this brave Germanic world had already been established in the original S.S. marriage and breeding codes and in the conception of the *Lebensborn* movement. 'I regard the S.S. as a tree that I have planted', said

Himmler to Kersten, 'which has roots deep enough to defy all weathers.' This *élite* must be established in every nation capable of producing a pureblooded Nordic stock; where this did not exist, it must be provided by settlements of Nordic immigrants.

Alongside the men, Nordic womanhood was to be developed, the 'Chosen', as Himmler called them, 'the strong, purposeful type of women', the best of them trained in Women's Academies for Wisdom and Culture and acting as representatives of Germanic womanhood throughout the world. The true Nordic woman would be willing to be directed into a suitable marriage designed to promote the ideal growth of the human race. Himmler maintained 'that men could be bred just as successfully as animals and that a race of men could be created possessing the highest spiritual, intellectual and physical qualities.' When he saw blond children, says Kersten, 'he became pale with emotion'.

As the best of Germany's manhood was dying at the front, both Hitler and Himmler agreed that a stand must be made after the war to change the marriage laws and introduce legalized bigamy. The good stock so cruelly lost in war must at all costs be replaced.

'My personal opinion', said Himmler to Kersten in May 1943, 'is that it would be a natural development for us to break with monogamy. Marriage in its existing form is the Catholic Church's satanic achievement; marriage laws are in themselves immoral. . . . With bigamy each wife would act as a stimulus to the other so that both would try to be their husband's dream-woman – no more untidy hair, no more slovenliness. Their models, which will intensify these reflections, will be the ideals of beauty projected by art and the cinema.'

Himmler's open and happy relationship with Hedwig, who at the time he was talking to Kersten on this subject had already borne him one child and was soon to become pregnant with her second, no doubt encouraged him to regard bigamy in a favourable light, both personally and politically. He loved to enlarge on this dream of multiple family life:

'The fact that a man has to spend his entire existence with one wife drives him first of all to deceive her and then makes him a hypocrite as he tries to cover it up. The result is indifference between the partners. They avoid each other's embraces and the final consequence is that they don't produce children. This is the reason why millions of children are never born, children whom the state urgently requires. On the other hand the husband never dares to have children by the woman with whom he is carrying on an affair, much though he would like to, simply because middle-class morality forbids it. Again it's the state which loses, for it gets no children from the second woman either.'⁴

He attacked fiercely the fact that illegitimate children were denied the full rights due to them as their father's offspring, and the social disgrace the unmarried mother had to endure seemed to him intolerable:

'A man in this situation has no access to his child. He's up against the law again if he wants to adopt the child, so long as he has children of his own or even has the possibility of having them. In other words, the law is in direct contradiction to our crying need – children and still more children. We must show courage and act decisively in this matter, even if it means arousing still greater opposition from the Church – a little more or less is of no consequence.'⁵

His rooted objection to homosexuality among S.S. men invariably led to habitual offenders being confined in concentration camps. The homosexual was only useful in a degenerate society where breeding was to be discouraged. A Nordic homosexual was 'a traitor to his own people', and he refused to listen to Kersten's advocacy of psychiatric treatment for men with homosexual tendencies who were capable of redirection to normal sexual relations. Particular trouble arose over one dedicated officer who was discovered in 1940 to be advocating the formation of a homosexual *élite* within the S.S.; Himmler was horrified and prevailed on Kersten to interview the man and report on his case.

Himmler's hostility to the Christian religion, and especially to the Catholic Church, led him to make his own particular form of study of other religions. This again drew him back into the past. He liked occasionally to entertain German scholars and challenge them with his ideas. He enjoyed discussion and friendly controversy, and he was not bigoted enough to refuse Gudrun, his daughter, her right to say Christian Grace before meals. He searched the sacred books of other faiths for ideas which would support his own acquired beliefs. He studied the *Bhagavad-gita* (which he particularly admired, observed Kersten, for its 'great Aryan qualities') and the books of the Hindu and Buddhist creeds, while his interest in astrology was well-known.

When Kersten, who was himself interested in comparative religion, asked him in the summer of 1942 whether he had any religious belief at all, Himmler was indignant that Kersten should even doubt that he had. It was only common sense, he said, to believe:

'that some higher Being – whether you call it God or Providence or anything else you like – is behind nature and the marvellous order in the world of man and animals and plants. If we refused to recognize that we should be no better than the Marxists . . . I insist that members of the S.S. must believe in God. I'm not going to have men around me who refuse to recognize any higher Being or Providence or whatever you like to call it.'

He longed, he said, to be Minister for Religious Matters and 'dedicate myself to positive achievements only . . . Of course it's pleasanter to concern yourself with flower-beds rather than political dust-heaps and refuse-dumps, but flowers themselves won't thrive unless these things are seen to'. He spoke of the Gestapo as 'the national charwoman', cleaning up the state. Meanwhile, he took the *Bhagavad-gita* to bed with him; it gave him comfort to read this: 'It is decreed that whenever men lose their respect for law and truth, and the world is given over to injustice, I will be born anew.' That, he said, 'was absolutely made for the Führer . . . It has been ordained by the *Karma* of the Germanic world that he should wage war against the East and save the Germanic peoples.' In his more colourful and sentimental moments he saw Hitler, like the notorious picture postcard of the Führer, as a saint in armour whose head was haloed with light, a throw-back to the legendary Knights of the Holy Grail and the story of Parsifal. As for Himmler, he was proud to associate himself with the reincarnation of Henry the Fowler, on whom he tried to model himself. Yet in spite of his hostility to the Catholic Church, he foresaw the elevation of the Führers of the future through a system of election similar to that used in electing the Pope.[6]

Kersten studied Himmler's character closely with the intention of controlling him in so far as he could, and began to introduce the question of the Jews into their discussions. Himmler was quite prepared to discuss this subject in the same way as he discussed any other, with an apparent rationality which soon became irrational. Just as the growth of freemasonry was obnoxious in a healthy nation because it represented a powerful, self-seeking secret society intent on spreading its own power and influence inside the State, so the development of powerful Jewish interests in Germany seemed to Himmler like a cancerous growth that had spread its parasitic network through the natural economy of the land. This conception of the alien Jew sapping the vitality of the German nation had become an obsession with Himmler, as with all the more bigoted Nazis. None of Kersten's arguments, which Himmler was quite prepared to hear, moved him in the slightest from this predetermined and irrational obsession. He could not tolerate what he regarded as Jewish infiltration into the German economy and culture entirely for racial and political ends. The two races, the two worlds, he said, could never mingle; they must be separated by force before further irreparable harm was done.

It was this obsession, combined with his academic passion for 'neatness', that converted Himmler from the idea of the expulsion of the Jews from the Germanic territories and made him favour their absolute destruction through genocide.

Himmler was a man of violence, not by nature, but by conviction. Although, like Kersten, he took part in hunting as a manly sport, he was a poor shot, and he could never understand Kersten's passion for deer-stalking. 'How can you find any pleasure, Herr Kersten,' said Himmler, 'in shooting from behind cover at poor creatures browsing on the edge of a wood . . . Properly considered, it's pure murder.'

He practised hunting, however, because it was a traditional Germanic sport, and because the game must be 'kept within bounds'. But he despised the theatrical sportsman, like Göring, who turned hunting into an egotistical cult. Children, he believed, should be brought up to love animals, not to kill them merely for sport.

The destruction of human beings, who were themselves so much more destructive than the animals, was in fact forced on Himmler, and he accepted this fearful task because he believed it to be the only, as well as the 'final', solution to the problem of securing the racial purification of Germany which remained his deep-rooted ideal. Belief in the maintenance of racial purity in the modern world, if it is to be carried to its logical conclusion, must lead either to complete segregation or to genocide. Himmler, in the circumstances of total war, came to accept genocide as the only solution. The primitive hatred and fear from which such absolute ideas originate forced Himmler, who was neither primitive nor passionate by nature, to take the supreme crime of mass murder upon his uneasy conscience.

Kersten discovered what was affecting his patient as early as November 1941: 'After much pressure . . . he told me that the destruction of the Jews is being planned.'

The admission put Kersten himself in a position of responsibility for which he was utterly unprepared. So far he had managed to persuade Himmler to release a few men from imprisonment as a personal favour to himself. The problem which he faced now was crime on a scale he did not know how to approach; he could only react at once against the raw fact that Himmler had unwillingly revealed to him:

'Filled with horror, I emphatically begged Himmler to give up this idea and the plan to be discerned behind it. The suffering and counter-suffering were not to be contemplated. To this Himmler answered that he knew it would mean much suffering for the Jews. But what had the Americans done earlier? They had exterminated the Indians – who only wanted to go on living in their native land – in the most abominable way. "It is the curse of greatness that it must step over dead bodies to create new life. Yet we must create new life, we must cleanse the soil or it will never bear fruit. It will be a great burden for me to bear." '[7]

Himmler spoke of the Jewish concept of 'atonement' and the Jewish saying of 'an eye for an eye and a tooth for a tooth'. Had not the Jews been responsible, he argued, for millions of dead in building up their empire?

Himmler took his own time to adjust the necessity for genocide to his code of morality. He did so deliberately and painfully. As he said to Kersten, 'It's the old tragic conflict between will and obligation. At this moment I am learning how terrible it can be . . . The extermination of people is unGermanic. You can demand everything from me, even pity. But you cannot demand protection for organized nihilism. That would be suicide.'

As he watched Himmler absorb the necessity to commit this crime into the niceties of his conscience, Kersten got ready to use his increasing influence over the Reichsführer S.S. to keep his mind uneasy. This, he knew, was the only weapon he possessed with which to fight this man, whose soft but obstinate nature was only too familiar to him. He used every device he could to keep his patient pliable. But for the next two years the momentum of the war overcame him; he was able to ease a few individuals out of Himmler's prison-camps, but not a whole race. Only in 1944, when the prospect of Germany's defeat became evident to Himmler's unwilling eyes, did Kersten's struggle to turn the liberation of single individuals into that of large numbers begin to succeed.

The accuracy of his understanding of Himmler was therefore of the highest importance to his ultimate success. The superficial judgment passed on by Himmler to so many people, that he was like a teacher misplaced in a position of political power, was right only if the conception of a teacher is limited to an instructor and not an educator. Himmler was a born instructor, lucid and, within the limits he imposed on himself, well-informed. But in spite of his abundant and wide-ranging interests he was an informed not an educated man. He was always, as Kersten observed, using his knowledge to produce a set doctrine about which he loved to lecture any audience he could reach. Yet Kersten found him 'not at all overbearing in these lectures of his, but quite amiable and not without a touch of humour'. In fact he encouraged his subordinates to express their opinions and argue respectfully with him, much as a headmaster whose opinions were hidebound might encourage his sixth-formers to debate with him so that he might have a good excuse to express his own opinions.

Fundamentally, however, Himmler's character was deadly serious, in the direst meaning of these words. Like many men, he learned how to strengthen the weakness of his nature by fostering obsessions on which he could constantly lean for protection against his conscience and his reason. He used prejudice to lighten his burdens; if he needed an excuse for the exercise of kindness to a prisoner he would ask for a photograph and let clemency rule if the prisoner proved to be blond and Nordic. He could not tolerate his own physical weakness and ill-health, and yet he increasingly gave way to it in the refuge of Hohenlychen, to which in the end he would retire to recuperate from a cold. Kersten learnt exactly how to insert his subtly devised wedges with the grain of Himmler's conscience, and he often gained concessions from him which might seem impossible. For Himmler lacked by nature the ruthless barbarity that his reason admired and that he extolled in the notorious speeches he made when the public image of the Reichsführer S.S. had to be maintained. His family background and training taught him only the meticulous honesty, industry and sense of public service expected of the German teacher, the subordinate soldier and the civil servant. As a man of action Himmler was quite useless; as a soldier disastrous; as an administrator industrious, pedantic and obsessed by the desire to surround himself with the protective cover of administration.

Like all Nazis, he was an authoritarian who derived his inflexibility from obedience to his chosen leader. On the belts of the S.S. he had the phrase inscribed: 'My honour is my loyalty.' Hitler's influence over him was paramount, and he anxiously fulfilled every task the Führer gave him until the utter impossibility of doing so shattered the narrow energies of his spirit. In this, as Kersten observed, he confused statesmanship with the obedience of a bodyguard. In no essential matter did he ever dare to contradict Hitler to his face, and the difficulties both Kersten and Schellenberg encountered in their pursuit of Himmler's weakness were due to the deep doubts he entertained of how best to reconcile loyalty to Hitler with loyalty to the fulfilment of the future of the German race. This conflict built up in him to fearful proportions when he realized that the Führer was a sick man who might have to be dispossessed for his own ultimate good and that of Germany. The increasing rage of the Führer as his sickness took possession of him only induced in Himmler the nervous condition which brought on the agonies of cramp. His subservience was complete, and as his tasks became more impossible to fulfil he dreaded the very thought of entering Hitler's presence, where as like as not he would be reduced to a tongue-tied inability to speak at all.

In his private life he was simple and as kind as he knew how. He was considerate to his wife, in love with his mistress, and devoted to his children. He despised money and did his best, as far as wholly private expenditure was concerned, to eke out his living on his small official salary of some £3,000 a year in the values of the time. It is significant that when, during 1943, Kersten obtained an inexpensive watch for Himmler in Sweden, the Reichsführer S.S. thanked him, gave him M. 50 on account and promised to settle the rest of his debt when he received his next salary cheque. Although Himmler liked food, he ate and drank and smoked with extreme moderation, and expected all those in his service to do the same. He loved a life of hard labour and devotion to a narrow ideal which seemed to him moral and which was partly inherited from others and partly of his own creation.

He no more understood the evil he was generating through the S.S. and the Gestapo than a rigid Victorian moralist understood the repressive cruelty he must be imposing on the innocent members of his family. To the last he failed to understand why his name became so hated. He believed he was a good man who, if he had made mistakes, had made them in a noble cause. He dictated his memoranda from his various headquarters without any human consideration for the moral degeneration of his agents or the suffering of his victims. His efficiency was in his mind, and the chaos he caused was the result of enforcing what was at once both utterly cruel and administratively impossible.

As a man he was at the same time mediocre and extraordinary. Had he stayed in his rightful place in society he could have been an over-efficient and priggish executive, a small-time official or minor educationalist. But Himmler was not altogether mediocre. He possessed a fanatical vision and energy and an image of himself as a figure in power politics which made him in ten years one of the masters of Europe. A nonentity could not have become one of the most feared men in the history of modern times. Yet he failed utterly to develop a personality to match the scale of his office. He remained to the end a small, middle-class man, a petty bourgeois figure whose appearance made men laugh, a minister so utterly servile to his leader that he could not bear the thought of an ill-word or a reprimand.

If he did not consciously recognize this deep division in his nature, the nervous condition of his body did. This Kersten knew, and it gave him access to a certain degree of power over his patient which he tried to explain after the war:

'His severe stomach-convulsions were not, as he supposed, simply due to a poor constitution or to overwork; they were rather the expression of this psychic division which extended over his whole life. I soon realized that while I could bring him momentary relief and even help over longer periods, I could never achieve a fundamental cure . . . When he was ill I first came into contact with the human side of Himmler's character. When he was in good health, this was so overlaid with the rules and regulations which he invented or which were imposed upon him that nobody, not even his closest relations, could have got anything out of him which ran counter to them. In the event of any conflict arising he would have behaved, even to his own relations, exactly as the law demanded. His blind obedience was rooted in a part of his character which was quite inaccessible to other emotions.

'As this obedience to law and order was, however, really based on something quite different, namely on Himmler's ordinary middle-class feelings, it was possible for anybody who knew how to penetrate to those feelings to come to an understanding with him – even to the point of negotiating agreements with him which ran counter to the Führer's orders. Because he was utterly cut off from his natural roots and needed somebody on whom to lean, he was happy to have a man beside him who had no connection with the Party hierarchy, somebody who was simply a human being. At such moments I was able to appeal to him successfully.'[8]

Himmler, therefore, behind the mask of secrecy and power, was a man dominated as much by fear as by ambition. He tried hard to live in accordance with an image for which he was utterly unfitted. Few men in human history have shown to the extent that Himmler did what terrible crimes can be committed through a blind conviction that such deeds were both moral and inevitable.

# VII

# *Slave of Power*

News of the Allied landings in Normandy in the small hours of the
morning of 6 June, two days after the liberation of Rome, came as a
surprise to the Nazi leaders. Hitler was in Berchtesgaden, and
Rommel, who was in command of the Army Group controlling
Holland, Belgium and Northern France, was spending the night at
his home in Ulm. Göring was resting at Veldenstein, one of his
castles in the south, when he received the telephone call from his
*aide* Brauchitsch that hurried him by road to a situation conference
held during the afternoon at Klessheim, a baroque palace near
Salzburg where Hitler had acted as host to Mussolini and Ciano in
1942, and bullied Horthy in 1944. The conference was attended by
Himmler, who came from his special train stationed near Berchtesgaden which he was using as his headquarters during the times
Hitler was on the Obersalzburg, while Ribbentrop travelled from
Fuschl, his summer palace near Salzburg where, according to
Schellenberg, he had been brooding on the idea of shooting Stalin
with a revolver disguised as a fountain-pen. Meanwhile, Hitler had
gone to bed after hearing the news from France, leaving an order
that he was not to be disturbed.

No record survives of what Himmler, Göring and Ribbentrop
discussed at this meeting. Only the circumstance of an invasion
could have brought these three together without the master-presence
of Hitler, who did not emerge from his retirement to face his generals
in France until 17 June, when he summoned Rundstedt and Rommel
to a conference at Margival, near Soissons, the day after the first
V-weapon had been launched against London. According to
General Speidel who was present, Hitler looked 'pale and sleepless';
his restless fingers played with coloured pencils and, when they ate,
he swallowed a sequence of pills and medicines after bolting down a

plate of rice and vegetables. He broke his promise to visit Rommel's Group headquarters two days later, returning to Berchtesgaden the same night that a stray V-bomb turned off course to London and exploded near his bunker. Instead, he received Rundstedt and Rommel on the Obersalzburg on 29 June, a week after the Russians had begun their major offensive; he rejected their appeal to end the war and lectured them on his miracle weapon. On 1 July Rundstedt was replaced by Kluge. Rommel, left alone, warned Hitler in a letter dated 15 July that defeat in France was now inevitable; two days later he was severely wounded in his staff car by a low-flying aircraft.

The situation could scarcely be worse on both fronts. By early July the Russians had reached Polish territory and were threatening East Prussia. Himmler continued in the south, where Hitler remained brooding until 14 July, when he transferred his headquarters to the Wolf's Lair at Rastenburg in East Prussia. Himmler followed him north, but was not present at his first staff conference on 15 July, the day Hitler authorized him to form fifteen new S.S. divisions to replace the losses on the Eastern front, an order that in fact antici-pated by five days his appointment as Commander-in-Chief of the Reserve Army, a post from which General Fromm was to be dis-missed on 20 July. It was here, too, on 20 July that the group of senior officers in the Reserve Army almost succeeded in killing Hitler at his mid-day conference and achieving a *coup d'état* in Germany.[1]

A briefcase holding a time-bomb was planted by Colonel the Count von Stauffenberg, Fromm's Chief of Staff, under the Führer's conference-table. At 12.42 the bomb exploded, ten minutes after Stauffenberg had broken the capsule holding the acid which ate through the wire controlling the firing-pin. But the briefcase under the table had been inadvertently pushed by another officer to a position which shielded Hitler from the worst effects of the blast. Two minutes later Stauffenberg passed successfully through the first check-point at Rastenburg on his way to the aircraft which was to fly him back to his fellow-conspirators at the Bendlerstrasse, the War Office in Berlin. He believed Hitler was dead.

Neither Himmler, Göring nor Ribbentrop were at the conference at the time of the explosion, and Goebbels was in Berlin. Göring was at his headquarters fifty miles away. Himmler's centre in East Prussia was the villa Hagewald-Hochwald, at Birkenwald, on the Maursee lake; his official train was stationed nearby. Kersten had

Felix Kersten

Kersten with Himmler

given him treatment during the morning; Himmler told him that he believed the whole course of the war would be affected by the troubles developing between the Americans and the Russians. Kersten then went for a long walk, lunched in the peaceful setting of the villa and later slept in his compartment on the train.

Himmler was at Birkenwald at the time of the explosion; he was summoned immediately by 'phone, and his bodyguard Kiermaier remembers the rough journey they made at speed over the uneven country roads, covering the twenty-five kilometres in about half an hour.

It had been arranged that General Fellgiebel, the Army Chief of Signals, who was one of the conspirators, should send a signal in code to the generals at Army headquarters at the Bendlerstrasse in Berlin immediately after Hitler's death, so that the complex operation of the *coup d'état* could be put in motion; after this he was to sever Rastenburg's communications with the outside world for as long as he could. After seeing the bomb explode, Stauffenberg had jumped into his car and left for the airport in the full belief that Hitler was dead. But a few moments later Hitler, Keitel and the other survivors emerged dazed, shocked and wounded from the shattered building, and Fellgiebel, not knowing what to do for the best, joined the running men who rushed to help the Führer and tend the injured officers. By Hitler's express orders no news of the explosion was to be given to the outside world, and the S.S. took charge of the area. Fellgiebel found it impossible to report what had happened to the Bendlerstrasse.

The conspirators were left without news of any kind until 3.30 in the afternoon, when Thiele, Chief of Signals at the Bendlerstrasse, managed to get a vague message from Rastenburg that the attempt had taken place. The measures for the *coup d'état* under the code name Valkyrie were put into operation. Meanwhile Stauffenberg had been flying back to Berlin confident that his great mission had at last been accomplished.

Himmler arrived at Rastenburg shortly after 1.15 and took immediate action. He telephoned Gestapo headquarters in Berlin and ordered a posse of police investigators to fly at once to Rastenburg. After this it appears that communications with Berlin were shut down by order of Hitler until round 3.30, the time when Thiele managed to telephone from the Bendlerstrasse. Shortly after this, Keitel was able to inform Fromm that Hitler was not dead.

Fromm immediately attempted to cancel the Valkyrie operations that the conspirators had launched in his name as Commander-in-Chief. This was too much for the conspirators, and they placed him under arrest. At Rastenburg, Himmler had by now traced the origin of the bomb to Stauffenburg. He telephoned Berlin, where Stauffenburg had landed about 3.45, to order the Count's arrest either at the airport or the Bendlerstrasse, but the S.S. Colonel who drove to the Bendler-strasse at 5.30 with two subordinates to carry out the order only found that it was he himself who was put under arrest.

Himmler still believed that he was dealing with an attempt on Hitler's life by an isolated man or at most by a small group in the resistance; he did not yet realize that a military *coup d'état* was actually in operation in Berlin. Had he done so, he would not have accompanied Hitler to meet the train bringing Mussolini on a visit to Rastenburg, which it seemed to Hitler unnecessary to postpone. Indeed, he needed an audience to whom he might boast of the special 'Providence' that had in its wisdom seen fit to preserve him, even though the audience was only an aged and fallen führer on whom the same Providence had evidently ceased to smile. With Himmler still in anxious attendance, Hitler and Mussolini stared wonderingly at the wrecked conference room which the bomb had destroyed, and it seemed that a miracle had manifestly occurred. Himmler asserted later that his re-conversion to belief in God happened at this moment.[2]

Now that communications with Berlin had been restored, it was soon realized that a major upheaval was taking place in the capital. Before taking tea with Mussolini and the remaining Nazi leaders at five o'clock, Hitler ordered Himmler to fly at once to Berlin. With a sudden burst of decision he gave the faithful Reichsführer S.S. formal control of the security of the Reich and made him Commander-in-Chief of the Reserve Army in the place of Fromm. This gave Himmler what he most desired, direct access to the Bendlerstrasse and a command at last in the Army itself. His last words to Hitler were overheard: 'My Führer,' he said, 'you can leave it all to me.'

Nevertheless, he moved with pronounced caution for a keen soldier sent on an urgent and dangerous mission. While Hitler entertained his guests at what proved to be a socially disastrous tea-party, Himmler returned to Birkenwald before leaving for Berlin. Kersten was wakened from his long afternoon nap by Himmler's

driver bursting in on him with the news from Rastenburg; he got up
at once and hurried to Himmler's study in the villa, where he found
him sorting and destroying certain papers. 'Now my hour has come',
said Himmler. 'I'll round up all that reactionary gang; I've already
given orders for the arrest of the traitors. By preserving the Führer,
Providence has given us a sign. I am flying immediately to Berlin.'

When he eventually reached Berlin late that evening after landing
at a remote airport, he was far too wary to go to the Bendlerstrasse,
the headquarters of his new command. He went straight to Goebbels
who, as the senior Nazi Minister in Berlin, had been taking vigorous
action against the conspirators ever since he had learned the truth
of the situation in Rastenburg. In his dealings with the unit of the
Berlin Guards Regiment initially detailed under the command of
Major Remer, an ardent Nazi, to arrest him, he reversed the whole
situation and put Remer on the telephone to Hitler. Hitler promoted
Remer a Colonel for his loyalty and placed the safety of Berlin in
his charge. He told him to obey only Goebbels and Himmler, his
new Commander-in-Chief who was at that moment on his way to
Berlin. Meanwhile, following Hitler's instructions, Goebbels had
arranged for a preliminary announcement of the Führer's survival
to be broadcast at 6.30, and two hours later Keitel sent a teleprinter
to all Army Commands announcing Himmler's appointment and
insisting that only commands issued with the authority of the
Führer or Himmler were to be obeyed. Stauffenberg, who was valiant-
ly trying to maintain the *coup d'état* at the Bendlerstrasse by tele-
printer and telephone, gradually found the wind stolen from his sails.
Only in France and Austria were active steps taken to join in the
*coup d'état*. The conspiracy had been a valiant effort on his part and
that of General Olbricht, Fromm's Head of Army Supplies. At nine
o'clock it was announced on the radio that Hitler would speak to his
people later that night.

So by the time Himmler reached the centre of Berlin from the
airport, the essential danger was over. He was forced, however, to
arrange for Hitler to countermand a number of hysterical instructions
sent by Bormann to the Gauleiters, ordering them to arrest the
Army commanders in their areas. When a commando unit under
Skorzeny finally reached the Bendlerstrasse around midnight, they
found that Fromm, having been freed to resume his command, had
held a summary court-martial of the men who earlier in the day had
arrested him, and that Beck, Olbricht and Stauffenberg, together

with certain others of the inner corps of conspirators had already
been shot or forced to commit suicide. Skorzeny forbade any further
executions, in the name of Himmler, the new Commander-in-Chief.

Himmler meanwhile had set up his own court of enquiry at
Goebbels's official residence in the Hermann Göring Strasse. Together the two Ministers examined the men brought before them by
the S.S., including Fromm himself. The interrogation went on
throughout the night, broken only by the need to listen to Hitler's
speech on the radio, which was broadcast at one o'clock in the
morning. Goebbels was furious at the wording of this statement,
which Hitler delivered in a harsh and weary voice, vowing brutal
vengeance on the men who had betrayed him.

The following day Bormann was forced to rectify his error of the
night before and transmit less ambiguous instructions which supported Himmler's new authority. Kaltenbrunner was empowered by
Himmler to take charge of the interrogations that followed in
preparation for the first phase of the trials which began on 7 August
in the Peoples' Court. Roland Freisler, President of the Court,
controlled the proceedings, and the first group of conspirators,
tortured, unshaven and dressed in old and ill-fitting civilian clothes,
were pressed into the courtroom for an examination which was
designed to degrade them before the film cameras set up to record
their trial by order of a Führer obsessed by the need for vengeance.
Beck, Olbricht and Stauffenberg, the leaders of the conspiracy, were
mercifully dead; but their seconds in the courtroom, including
Field-Marshal von Witzleben, who was pushed forward to face
Freisler's vicious ridicule in unbraced trousers, the Generals
Hoepner and Stieff, and Stauffenberg's cousin, Peter Yorck von
Wartenburg, were examined in turn and then condemned to hang
naked before the recording lens of a film camera; each of them was
strangled by a loop of piano wire suspended from a meat hook.
They died on 8 August one by one in the confined space of a small
room in the Plötzensee Prison, and it is said some of the men executed
hung struggling for five minutes on end before their agony ceased.
Hitler watched the record of the executions that night in the pro-
jection room at the Reich Chancellery; even Goebbels, hardened
as he was, could not look at such fearful suffering. All the prints of
this film were subsequently destroyed.

From the point of view of Himmler and his agent Kaltenbrunner,
preparation for the trials represented a prolonged series of interro-

gations that lasted throughout the final months of the war. These interrogations led to more and more arrests and executions; the final death-roll will never now be known, though the number rose into the hundreds.[3] The victims included many of the most distinguished members of the resistance, some of them kept alive until the last few days of the war and then killed in the very face of liberation because their tragic testimony would have added weight to the overburdened guilt of the Nazis.

Von Hassell was hanged on 8 September 1944, Langbehn executed on 12 October, Popitz hanged on 2 February 1945, Nebe of the S.S. executed on 3 March. Rommel, Hitler's and Germany's ideal general, was compelled to commit suicide on 14 October. Pastor Dietrich Bonhoeffer was executed on 9 April, the same day as Admiral Canaris.

Himmler made his first public comment on the events of 20 July in an address to a group of Gauleiters and other officials assembled at Posen on 3 August; both Bormann and Goebbels were present. He spoke with a scathing, self-protecting irony of what had happened between himself, Langbehn, whom he called the middleman, and Popitz:

> 'We let this middleman chatter, we let him talk, and this is more or less what he said: Yes, it was of course necessary that the war should end, we must come to peace terms with England – following the opinion of the day – and the first requisite is that the Führer must be removed at once and relegated by the opposition to an honorary president's place. His group was quite certain that no action of this kind be carried out against the S.S.'

He had told Hitler of the matter, and they had laughed together; the appointment with Popitz, however, had not been very revealing. So Langbehn was arrested:

> 'At last I pulled in the middleman. Since that time, nine months ago, Herr Popitz looks like a cheese. When you watch him, he is as white as a wall; I should call him the living image of a guilty conscience. He sends me telegrams, he telephones me, he asks what is the matter with Dr X, what has happened to him; and I give him sphinx-like replies so that he does not know whether I had anything to do with what happened or not.'[4]

Himmler, as might be expected, poured ridicule on the whole civilian part in the conspiracy, from Langbehn and Popitz to Kiep and the Solfs. 'We knew about the present conspiracy for a very long time', he said. As for the generals, he was equally scathing, 'Fromm', he declared, 'acted like a vulgar film scenario', and he made the whole Army seem responsible for the conspiracy. He claimed that Stauffenberg was preparing to loose the inmates of the concentration camps upon the people of Germany. 'It meant that in the next two or three weeks crime would blossom and the communists would reign over our streets.'[5]

These words were meant for public hearing. In private, Himmler was most careful to ensure that the trial of Langbehn and Popitz was kept as secret as possible. When the hearing occurred in the autumn, Kaltenbrunner sent a letter to the Minister of Justice:

> 'I understand that the trial of the former minister Popitz and the lawyer Langbehn is to take place shortly before the Peoples' Court. In view of the facts known to you, namely the conference of the Reichsführer S.S. with Popitz, I ask you to see to it that the public be excluded from the trial. I assume your agreement and I shall dispatch about ten of my collaborators to make up an audience.'[6]

Though both Langbehn and Popitz were condemned to death, Popitz was kept alive until the following February in case more information could be got from him. Langbehn, as we have seen, died in October; he was tortured before the death sentence was carried out.

In his talk to the Gauleiters and other high officials at Posen, on 29 May 1944, Himmler was unusually direct in his reference to the *Judenfrage*, the Jewish problem. He adopted the frank manner of speech he favoured with his more intimate audiences, the audiences in fact that he most enjoyed addressing. Extermination, he explained, was a hard and difficult operation:

> 'Now I want you to listen carefully to what I have to say here in this select gathering, but never to mention it to anybody. We had to deal with the question: what about the women and children? – I am determined in this matter to come to an ab-

solutely clear-cut solution. I would not feel entitled merely to root out the men – well, let's call a spade a spade, for "root out" say kill or cause to be killed – well I just couldn't risk merely killing the man and allowing the children to grow up as avengers facing our sons and grandsons. We were forced to come to the grim decision that this people must be made to disappear from the face of the earth. To organize this assignment was our most difficult task yet. But we have tackled it and carried it through, without – I hope, gentlemen, I may say this – without our leaders and their men suffering any damage in their minds and souls. That danger was considerable, for there was only a narrow path between the Scylla and Charybdis of their becoming either heartless ruffians unable any longer to treasure human life, or becoming soft and suffering nervous breakdowns.'

He promised the Gauleiters, whom he called 'the supreme dignitaries of the Party, of this political Order of ours', that 'before the end of the year the Jew problem will be settled once and for all.' He concluded:

'That's about all I want to say at the moment about the Jew problem. You know all about it now, and you had better keep it to yourselves. Perhaps at some later, some very much later, period we might consider whether to tell the German people a little more about all this. But I think we had better not! It's us here who have shouldered the responsibility, the responsibility for action as well as for an idea, and I think we had better take this secret with us into our graves.'

Nineteen forty-four was the year in which Himmler established his highest prestige with Hitler and finally won from him a command on the battlefield in addition to control of the Reserve Army and the *Waffen* S.S. Yet he was realistic enough at the same time to modify his position over the Jews. There were many practical reasons for this. The machinery of slaughter was becoming increasingly difficult to operate now that the adversities of war were gathering momentum. By the spring of 1944 it was conceivable that areas such as Auschwitz might eventually be overrun by the enemy; with the heavy losses of men and equipment the attempts to mobilize the labour of the prisoners became more urgent. At the same time, an increasing pressure was being brought to bear on Himmler to relent, and this matched a growing fear in his own mind that the revulsion of the world outside Germany to the genocide associated most directly with his name would tell against him if he were ever able to put himself forward as Germany's negotiator with the Allies in the West.

Himmler never understood the nature of the abhorrence in which his name was held, nor realized the extent of it. He believed that a few apparent gestures of goodwill would be sufficient to re-establish his unfortunate reputation in the West, though the announcements made in America during the summer that there would be trials for war crimes once hostilities were over must have reached his ears.

Himmler began to think again. The constant humanizing influence of Kersten and the intrigues of Schellenberg designed to edge his master into becoming a peace negotiator, combined to make Himmler retreat to some extent from the absolute position he had held in 1943. The first change of policy was, as we have seen, second only to genocide itself in its inhumanity – extermination of unwanted peoples through work. Then came the attempted sale of certain Jews, negotiated on the one side in order to save lives and on the other to gain either money or commodities useful for the war.[7] The first important negotiations of this kind were those undertaken by Yoel Brand on behalf of the Hungarian Jews, whom the Nazis had finally succeeded in adding to their victims in 1943. In May 1944 Eichmann offered Brand the lives of 700,000 Hungarian Jews in exchange for 10,000 lorries which the Allies were to deliver to Salonika; this was the first form of barter to be suggested and came to nothing. It was to be followed by other proposals equally appalling, such as Eichmann's subsequent offer on behalf of Himmler to receive 20 million Swiss francs for the lives and liberties of 30,000 Jews. This last proposal led to the actual transfer of 1,684 Rumanian Jews, who reached Switzerland in August and December 1944, and a further 1,000 Hungarian Jews the following February, for all of whom Himmler received through the Swiss President, Jean-Marie Musi, 5 million Swiss francs subscribed through international Jewish charity. These developments were assisted by the proposals Himmler received from a Madame Immfeld to settle liberated Jews in the South of France. The negotiations for the transfer of the money were most complicated and were in fact hindered by the action of the U.S. State Department. Information about this pitiful sale was eventually to reach the ears of Hitler. But by this time, as we shall see, Himmler was deeply involved in negotiations with the Red Cross.

Schellenberg, having reached that stage in his post-war memoirs when he was most determined to promote himself as the humane peace negotiator, describes in some detail how he brought Musi and Himmler together on a number of occasions during the winter of 1944–5. At the first of these meetings, Musi persuaded Himmler to accept money instead of equipment and medicines, while at a second conference, which Schellenberg says took place on 12 January in the Black Forest, the following terms were agreed:

'Every fourteen days a first-class train would bring about 1,200 Jews to Switzerland. The Jewish organization with which Herr Musi was working would give active support in solving the Jewish problem according to Himmler's suggestions. At the same time, the beginning of a basic change in the world-wide propaganda against Germany was to be brought about. According to my suggestion, it was agreed that the money should not be paid over directly to the International Red Cross, as had originally been decided, but should be handed to Musi as a trustee.'[8]

This was the plan that led to the dispute with Hitler, which Schellenberg claims was deliberately fostered by Kaltenbrunner: 'Hitler immediately issued two orders: that any German who helped a Jew, or a British or an American prisoner to escape would be executed instantly.'

Hitler summoned Himmler, told him what he thought of his action in terms that Himmler was never to forget and, according to Kurt Becher, Himmler's agent in the commercial negotiations over the Jews, gave his notorious order that 'no camp inmate in the southern half of Germany must fall into enemy hands alive'.[9]

Meanwhile, with Hungary in the autumn on the eve of capitulation to Russia, the deportations began once more. Himmler employed Hoess, now Deputy-Inspector of Concentration Camps, to act as one of the supervisors who were supposed to ensure reasonable humanity. Budapest fell in December with a considerable Jewish population still left there alive.[10] Himmler had permitted an International Red Cross Mission to make a highly restricted inspection of Auschwitz in September, and in October and November there is evidence that he was trying to halt the massacres, or at any rate shift the responsibility for them onto the shoulders of his subordinates. He began, according to Becher, by issuing an order to Pohl and Kaltenbrunner 'between the middle of September and the middle of October': 'By this order, which becomes immediately operative, I forbid any liquidation of Jews and order that on the contrary, care should be given to weak and sick persons. I hold you personally responsible even if this order should be not strictly adhered to by the subordinate officers.'[11] This was followed on 26 November by an order which Becher is also responsible for recording: 'The crematoria at Auschwitz are to be dismantled, the Jews working in the Reich are to get normal Eastern workers' rations. In the absence of Jewish hospitals they may be treated with Aryan patients.'

The Red Army were not to reach Auschwitz and its associate camps until the end of January 1945; when they arrived they found that the evacuation of the vast body of prisoners to the west, which had begun as early as the previous September, had been all but completed, and there were less than 3,000 invalids left for them to tend. According to Reitlinger, the central camps and their satellites inside Germany numbered over a hundred at the beginning of 1945, and still held, in conditions which were now deteriorating beyond all control, 500,000 'Aryans' and 200,000 Jews. Their fate remained now in the balance; Himmler wanted to use them as his bargaining point with the Allies, while Hitler and Kaltenbrunner seemed equally determined they should die before there was any chance of their final liberation.

Himmler had always covered his weakness of character and indecision by assuming a mask of strength. The rank and uniform of an Army Commander fulfilled his need to prove to himself that he was a resolute man of action. Just as he had forced his inadequate body to reach the required standard in athletics, he braced himself now to become a general in the field of battle.

He was completely unsuited either in mind or body for such a task. But he had a purblind faith in himself, and the doubts that always welled up from hidden sources in his mind and conscience were quelled by his able advisers. If Kersten was at his side to convince him of his humanity and Schellenberg always ready to persuade him he was a diplomat, Skorzeny, the genius in commando tactics, was there in his service to make him feel a general. His instinctive need was to compensate for anything that might go wrong – the death or derangement of Hitler, the machination of the generals, the collapse of the German Army, the chicanery of Goebbels or of Göring, the uncertain powers of Bormann as the controller of Hitler's court; he tried to allow for everything in the process of keeping himself at the centre of the spiders' web of Nazi intrigue. No wonder his head ached and the nerves of his stomach were knotted with cramp. But Kersten was there to relieve him. In the Nazi hierarchy, the man whom Germany feared most after Hitler was himself the greatest victim of chronic doubts and fears.

At this moment he needed the reassurance of some new and active occupation which would release him from the constraint of his own nature. He would become a field commander. In July, as we have seen, Hitler in a moment of great national insecurity had impulsively given him the doubtful command of the Reserve Army, a melting-pot of units mainly composed of the older age-groups still in uniform, of men who had been wounded but not released from service and army trainees who had never seen action at all. For Himmler command of such forces spread over Germany was a beginning but not an end. He needed far more than this to consolidate his power and secure his ego. Nevertheless, he set out to make the men of his new command observers of National Socialism by increasing the number of National Socialist Control Officers, and he initiated new Army divisions to be called by such names as the Peoples' Grenadiers (*Volksgrenadier*) and the Peoples' Artillery (*Volksartillerie*).

The Party Control Officers, of whom Lieutenant Hagen had proved so notable an example when he had brought the Bendlerstrasse conspiracy to Goebbels' notice on 20 July, were in effect commissars attached to the Army to ensure the political education of the men. Himmler addressed a group of these political commissars a few days after the attempt, spurring them on to take violent action against all defeatists and deserters: 'I give you the authority to seize every man who turns back, if necessary to tie him up and throw him on a supply wagon . . . Put the best, the most energetic and the most brutal officer of the division in charge. They will soon round up such rabble. They will put up against a wall anyone who answers back.'[12] Such talk as this prepared Himmler to issue his notorious decree of 10 September that the families of those who deserted to the enemy would be shot:

'Certain unreliable elements seem to believe that the war will be over for them as soon as they surrender to the enemy. Against this belief it must be pointed out that every deserter will be prosecuted and will find his just punishment. Furthermore, his ignominious behaviour will entail the most severe consequences for his family. Upon examination of the circumstances they will be summarily shot.'[13]

During August Himmler finally gained control of the V-weapons.[14] According to General Dornberger, the head of the project at Peenemünde, Himmler had in September 1943 appointed S.S. Brigadier Dr Kammler, who was in charge of building projects for the S.S., to supervise any buildings needed for the development of the V-weapons. Kammler was there, says Dornberger, to act as a spy, and he is described as an energetic, Machiavellian figure, handsome and utterly without conscience. Kammler's purpose was to supersede Dornberger as controller of the project, nominally taking over on behalf of Himmler. Dornberger worked under Fromm, the Commander-in-Chief of the Reserve Army, and Himmler naturally saw his opportunity to take action after his appointment to succeed Fromm following the attempt on Hitler's life. On 4 August he formally took over at Peenemünde and appointed Kammler his Special Commissioner in charge of the entire programme. The development of the secret weapons continued to be seriously retarded by the constant intrigue to which it had all along been subject.

Himmler's second bid for power on the fighting front was won in the teeth of opposition from Guderian, Hitler's new Chief of Staff, barely two weeks after the explosion at Rastenburg, when the Poles in Warsaw revolted on what seemed to be the eve of liberation by the Russians. As Guderian himself describes it: 'I requested that Warsaw be included in the military zone of operation; but the ambitions of Governor-General Frank and the S.S. national leader Himmler prevailed with Hitler . . . The Reichsführer S.S. was made responsible for crushing the uprising . . . The battle which lasted for weeks was fought with great brutality.'[15]

Himmler sent S.S. Group-Leader von dem Bach-Zelewski with S.S. and police formations to fight in the streets of Warsaw, reinforced by the White Russian officer Kaminski and his S.S. brigade of some 6,500 Russian prisoners-of-war. These men were sent on the mission because their hatred of the Poles was well known. The Russians committed atrocities of such a nature that Guderian stated after the war that he had felt forced to persuade Hitler to withdraw them from Warsaw, while Bach-Zelewski claimed later that he had had Kaminski executed.[16] Hitler, with memories of the revolt in the Ghetto during 1942, ordered Himmler to raze Warsaw to the ground, but the tragic and futile revolt continued until the beginning of October without any assistance from the Russian armies stationed on the Vistula, which flowed right through the heart of Warsaw. In his speech at Posen on 3 August, Himmler went so far as to praise the Kaminski brigade for its resource in looting German Army supplies that had been abandoned. Later, in the autumn, Himmler proposed that Budapest should be treated like Warsaw when the Russians were approaching the city. Himmler declared Budapest to be a centre of partisan warfare in order to keep the campaign within his jurisdiction and that of his favourite commander, Bach-Zelewski.

The use of these Russian forces did not in fact appeal to Himmler. He was bitterly hostile to the renegade Russian general Andrei Vlassov, who as a Ukrainian was ready to fight against Stalin. The Army was anxious to exploit this disillusioned Red general, who had been captured in the spring of 1942, and use him to recruit the Cossacks to fight against the Red Army. In April 1943 Vlassov became in effect the organizer of so-called Free Russian forces in Smolensk. Himmler was outraged. In his speech at Posen on 4 October he attacked Vlassov for his boasts that only Russians could defeat Russians and that he could muster an army of 650,000 deserters to fight alongside the Germans.[17] Later, in the more informal but also more revealing talk he gave to the group of Gauleiters and senior officials at Posen on 25 May 1944, he described how Fegelein made fun of a Russian general by treating him as an equal and calling him 'Herr General', praising him until he had managed to get all the information he needed from him. 'We were well aware of the Slav's racial characteristic that he particularly likes to hear himself talk', sneered Himmler:

> 'All of which proves you can have that sort of man quite cheaply, very cheaply indeed . . . All that fuss about Vlassov has really frightened me. You know I'm never pessimistic and not easily excitable. But this thing seemed to me downright dangerous . . . There were fools among us who would give that shifty character the arms and equipment which he is meant to turn against his own people, but quite possibly, when the occasion comes, he will turn against us.'

After the attempt on Hitler's life, Himmler commissioned Gunter d'Alquen, who was now Head of Army Propaganda, to organize the Russian deserters under Vlassov, but in the end only two divisions were formed in place of the twenty-five divisions of which Vlassov spoke, and the German Army kept its own Cossack divisions intact. Himmler was only induced to support Vlassov's claim to be a Ukrainian de Gaulle because he was ready to claim jurisdiction over these Free Russian forces if ever they were brought up to full strength, incorporating them into the *Waffen* S.S. This, however, never happened. By the time Vlassov went into action Himmler was wholly absorbed in the task of survival. Vlassov was eventually captured by the Red Army and hanged.

With his appointment as Commander-in-Chief of the Reserve Army, Himmler also founded with Bormann the *Volkssturm*, the German Home Guard, which was to act as a civilian defence force in the case of invasion. This was followed in November by plans for the Werwolf,[18] the future resistance force which Himmler hoped would operate if Germany were ever occupied. In so far as Himmler drew near to anyone, it was to Goebbels, whom Hitler had made Plenipotentiary for Total War when he had visited him to see the sacred bombed-site at the Wolf's Lair. With the Army High Command in disgrace, the two men, one a life-long civilian and the other a chief of the secret police who had never commanded a platoon on the battlefield, planned to share out the war effort between them. Goebbels's aide von Oven claims that Goebbels said in November, 'The army for Himmler, and for me the civilian direction of the war! That is a combination which could rekindle the power of our war leadership.'[19] Between them they planned the redistribution of German civilian labour and the recruitment of a million men, half of them from Göring's Luftwaffe, who would be drafted and trained in the ranks of Himmler's Reserve Army. In effect, Himmler became Minister of War, though Hitler did not grant him the title.[20] But he permitted him the particular honour of delivering the annual speech of Party commemoration in Munich on 9 November, which showed that in Hitler's eyes Himmler was fully established in the forefront of the Nazi leadership.

Goebbels's vicious ruthlessness in the exercise of power appealed to Himmler, whose nature craved for a similar measure of courage and decision. Once Goebbels had decided what he wanted, neither fear nor scruples deterred him. If von Oven is to be believed, Goebbels too was considering who best might govern Germany along with himself if Hitler were no longer in power – not Göring, certainly, who neglected his duties so shamefully; not Bormann,

that second-rate climber, but Himmler? Here Goebbels paused
before reaching the inevitable negative. Recently, he decided,
Himmler had become too arbitrary (*eigenwillig*). But while treason-
able thoughts were to nibble uneasily at Himmler's conscience until
the day Hitler died, they were firmly rejected by Goebbels, if they
were ever entertained at all, as untenable. Goebbels realized what
Himmler was incapable of grasping, that there could be no place at
all for such a man as himself in a Germany without Hitler.

Himmler also managed to keep on what appear to be easy terms
with Bormann, whom Guderian described as the 'thick-set, heavy-
jointed, disagreeable, conceited and bad-mannered' *éminence grise*
of the Third Reich. Himmler's mistress Hedwig, whose pet name was
Häschen, had become friendly with Bormann's wife, Gerda, the
mother of their eight children and the apple of her husband's sentimental eye. Himmler appears as 'Uncle Heinrich' in the letters
Bormann dutifully sent home during this period, and Gerda writes
in September to say how happy Häschen and her children Helge
and Gertrud are in their new home in the Obersalzberg.[21] Now that
Häschen is a neighbour the older children can play together. 'Helge
is a lot taller than our Hartmut', writes Gerda, 'but much slimmer
and thinner. In his movements and general build he is as much like
Heinrich as Hartmut is like you, but I can't see the facial likeness
any more. The little girl, however, is ridiculously like her father.
Häschen has some photos from Heinrich's childhood where he looks
exactly the same. The baby has grown big and sturdy, and is so
sweet . . .'

In October we get a domestic glimpse of Himmler from Bormann:
'Heinrich told me that yesterday he had been hanging pictures,
doing things about the house, and playing with the children the
whole day long. He didn't accept any telephone calls either, but
devoted himself quite comfortably to his family for once.' According
to Bormann: 'Uncle Heinrich apparently is very pleased at the way
Helge bosses everybody; he regards this as a sure sign of a leader of
the future.'

Gerda sees Himmler and her husband as an affectionate team of
disciples serving their master. 'Oh, Daddy,' she writes to Bormann
at the end of September, 'it doesn't bear imagining what would
happen if you and Heinrich didn't see to everything. The Führer
would never be able to do it all alone. So you two must keep well and
take care of yourselves, because the Führer is Germany, but you are

his selfless comrades-in-arms . . .' Her view of these two men must
remain unique in Nazi history, but Bormann's terms of endearment
for his wife (beloved mummy-girl, sweetheart mine, dearest heart,
all-beloved) only encouraged her to dream of the roses round the
door of Hitler's headquarters, especially when he describes the fun
he and Himmler have together in Berlin:

> 'Last night Himmler and I – Himmler had his evening meal
> with me together with Fegelein and Burgdorff – laughed till we
> cried at those two funny birds – they are like a pair of naughty
> boys. And Burgdorff is 49, and will soon be made a General in
> the Infantry. Fegelein told his boss what it was like to be shouted
> at by him over the telephone: just, Fegelein felt, as if white steam
> were puffing from his ears . . . You can imagine what fun we had.'[22]

Other references to Himmler in Bormann's letters home show the
new-born general in action. On 3 September: 'Heinrich H. drove
to the West Wall yesterday; we are in daily communication by
telephone. He is tackling his task of C.-in-C. of the Reserve Army
with magnificent energy.' Gerda sent Himmler an encouraging
message through her husband. On 9 September: 'I have told H.H.,
who telephones once a day, that you are glad to know he's there,
because you think this will solve the problem. It gladdened his heart,
and he sends you his warmest regards . . .' However, Hitler's
irregular hours of work did not suit Himmler. Bormann is amused:
'Himmler is always quite shocked at our unhealthy way of living.
He says he has to be in bed by midnight, at least as a rule. And we
go on working till four in the morning, though we do stay in bed a
little longer. But this is just the old, old story . . .'

Then, on 31 October, Bormann writes: 'At my request, Uncle
Heinrich is going to the Ruhr on 3 November . . . to put things in
order.'

This forecast Himmler's ineffectual intervention on the Western
Front. On 10 December Hitler appointed him Commander-in-Chief
of Army Group Rhine. The reason why he was ever appointed at all
has been the subject of many and varied speculations. Guderian's
view is typical: the command was given at Bormann's suggestion in
order to ruin Himmler by putting him in a position which would
expose his incompetence. Another view was that it was the only way
to move Himmler's Reserve Army to the battlefront. There is also

Hedwig

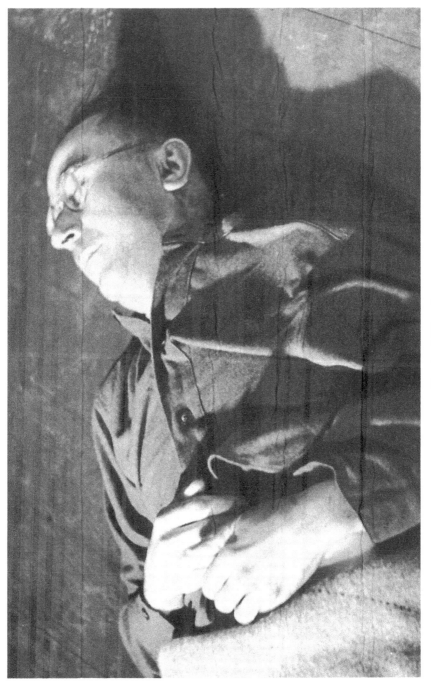

Death of Himmler

the most obvious explanation, that Hitler thought this loyal and energetic man would be successful where the generals had failed. Hitler always distrusted the experts.

Strangely enough, the appointment deprived Himmler of immediate authority over the counter-offensive in the Ardennes planned by Hitler in October to be carried out by the S.S. General Sepp Dietrich, to whom Hitler gave the command of the Sixth Army, a special Panzer formation under Rundstedt, the Commander-in-Chief in the West. It has been suggested that Himmler's command was given him in order to divert any attempts he might make to interfere with Dietrich's strategy. Rundstedt was particularly sensitive to interference from Himmler, who had been tactless enough during one of his tours of inspection to send Rundstedt orders which he signed as 'Supreme Commander in the West.' As General Westphal, Rundstedt's Chief of Staff, puts it, 'Although we never discovered whether Hitler had in fact appointed him as such for a time, his rival authority was speedily eliminated.'[23]

Sepp Dietrich's S.S. Panzer Army was hardly what it sounded; one-third of his armoured divisions was recruited from the Peoples' Grenadiers, another third from the *Waffen* S.S. The campaign was a failure, even though Skorzeny was brought in to form a special brigade operating directly under Himmler, who assumed his command in the west only a few days before the offensive. The Allies learned in advance that Skorzeny had been ordered to send English-speaking Germans dressed in Allied uniforms as spearheads behind the enemy lines. Skorzeny's men penetrated far, wide and deep, but the effort was soon lost when Sepp Deitrich's armour, which was bogged down in the winter countryside, failed to follow and support them. Himmler's hastily improvised forces, their commanders including Bach-Zelewski of Warsaw, undertook little fighting. He attempted to take Strasbourg with his untried army and failed. He was rescued from this inglorious situation by being posted to the command of the Vistula Army Group in the east. He left on 23 January, taking Skorzeny with him. According to the scornful General Westphal, he left behind him 'a laundry-basket full of unsorted orders and reports'.

Himmler had been based in the Black Forest. As Bormann put it in a letter to his wife: 'he has his quarters – that is to say, his train – either in the vicinity of one of the Murgtal tunnels or near Triberg'. Hitler's headquarters for the offensive were at Bad Nauheim 150 miles away, but Himmler kept in touch. On Christmas Eve he was present at a dinner party, sitting next to Guderian, a hostile critic, who noted that Himmler seemed to share Hitler's delusions about the East:

> 'He harboured no doubts about his own importance. He believed that he possessed powers of military judgment every bit as good as Hitler's, and needless to say far better than those of the generals. "You know, my dear Colonel-General, I don't really believe the Russians will attack at all. It's all an enormous bluff. The figures given by your department . . . are grossly exaggerated. They're far too worried. I'm convinced there's nothing going on in the East." There was no arguing against such *naïveté*.'

This apparent lack of concern for the situation in which Germany was placed permeated those under the influence of Hitler, who seems to have spent his evenings looking at films while his staff entertained each other at parties. Himmler gave a reception for Rundstedt and Bormann on 29 December, after which his guests returned to their own quarters – some distance from Himmler's – for 'music, dancing and gaiety'. 'I did not dance', writes Bormann to his wife, 'but you ought to have seen Jodl.'

Himmler nevertheless continued to watch over the self-discipline of those whose conduct he felt he should influence. In January he had written to Rauter, his representative in Holland: 'I herewith order you to carry out your reprisal and anti-terror measures in the sharpest possible manner. Failure to do that would be the only misdemeanour you could possibly be guilty of. If there are complaints about your severity, that's an honour to be proud of.' In May 1944 he had written to Pancke, his Chief of Police in Denmark: 'Will you please see to it that your wife adopts more modest and inconspicuous standards of living . . . I must ask you to educate your wife so that she refrains from trumpeting her personal opinions on this or that political event . . . I am not altogether convinced that, so far as your marriage is concerned, you have assumed leadership of your young wife to the extent I expect from a senior S.S. leader. Heil Hitler!' In August he had sent a scathing signal to the Military Governor of Cracow: 'I thoroughly disapprove of your orders which seem only concerned with evacuation. I demand supreme fortitude from all members of the administration. Getting your luggage away is supremely unimportant!' When he himself was in trouble on the

Western front, it did not prevent him writing a painful letter to S.S. General Höfle on 12 January, after deciding against sending a severe reprimand drafted on 30 December. His revised letter began: 'According to my custom I have been brooding over a letter to you dictated more than a fortnight ago, and I have decided to write you a more personal letter instead, giving you one more chance.' This letter ends: 'Had I imagined how much this command that I confided to you exceeds your mental strength I would have spared both you and myself this grief.'

Letters and memoranda survive from Himmler's files which show he must have been aware of the failure of the S.S. to commit the heroic self-sacrifice he wanted to impose on them. For example, an anonymous letter dated 14 January 1944 denounced the graft, fraud and theft in which many leading members of the S.S. indulged; the writer claimed he was an old man whose sons were all at the front and whose home was destroyed in the air-raids. The letter, which is plainly a serious one, lists about a dozen S.S. officers who were, the writer claims, betraying the Fatherland through their luxurious living. Ten days later, on 24 January, a senior S.S. officer writes to point out the folly of calling up men from the armament industry when the shortage at the front is not of men but munitions. On 16 February S.S. General Hofmann writes from Stuttgart to ask what is to be done with the surplus masses of foreign labour who have become a serious burden to the Reich now that the frontiers are contracting so rapidly and there is no work for them to do. Should they be abandoned to the enemy? There is no record of any reply to this letter.

On 23 February Himmler is himself writing to Bormann, whom he addresses as 'Dear Martin', about a report he has received from a young S.S. officer in Weimar, Wilhelm Vermöhlen, on the poor morale of leading Party members who have been the first to take flight.

Himmler's appointment on the battlefront coincided with Hitler's disastrous policy of giving both Göring and Himmler direct command over their respective Luftwaffe and S.S. fighting forces. The Army had no disciplinary power over these divisions, which reported to their own leaders. Only for tactical purposes did they come under the direction of the Army. Himmler, like Göring, was now free to intervene on matters of strategy and object to orders given by the Army Commanders in so far as these affected his own men.

According to Westphal, Himmler issued 'a deluge of absolutely puerile orders', but the professional soldiers were directed by Keitel to take note of Himmler's 'new methods of leadership'. Himmler was 'hag-ridden by a pathological distrust' and never hesitated to blame the Army for the failure of his own impractical orders because 'he always felt he was being put at a disadvantage'. Westphal claims he was wasteful of supplies sent to him:

'He was in any case receiving greater quantities than were allotted to other sections of the front, because otherwise it was feared he would ring up Hitler and have all the munition trains diverted to his sector. Yet he fired off every shell that was sent to him and then simply asked for more. He sat in his special train in the Black Forest, and had himself shunted into a tunnel every time there was an air-raid alarm. It is almost superfluous to mention that Himmler never visited the front himself, but issued his orders from the safety of the rear.'[24]

Himmler can scarcely be said to have approached his gravely responsible duties on the so-called Vistula front in a realistic spirit. Once more he was appointed in order to improvise, filling the vacuum left by Hitler's spent forces in the face of the final Russian offensive. Guderian, as Chief of the General Staff, had, of course, opposed this unprofessional appointment, but Hitler had remained firm. As Guderian saw it: 'This preposterous suggestion appalled me . . . Hitler maintained that Himmler had given a very good account of himself on the Upper Rhine. He also controlled the Reserve Army and therefore had a source of reinforcements immediately to hand . . . Hitler ordered that Himmler assemble his own staff . . .'[25]

According to Guderian, Himmler surrounded himself with a staff of S.S. men utterly inexperienced for the task ahead of them. His headquarters were 150 miles north-east of Berlin at Deutsch-Krone, and he arrived on 24 January, passing German refugees on the road. The Russians had already over-run East Prussia and reached a line stretching south from Elbing on the Baltic to Thorn, Posen, the old German Army headquarters where Himmler had so often spoken, and Breslau. Northern Germany was at the mercy of the invading armies, and only fragmentary defences existed to stop their further advance.

Himmler's knowledge was also fragmentary. According to Skorzeny, he ordered him to relieve a town barely thirty miles from

Berlin and a hundred miles west of his own headquarters. Either
Himmler had got the name wrong, or believed the Russian forces to
be scattered over widely separated areas of Germany. The Russians
were, in fact, waiting for the supplies their previous advances had
outstripped, but they had already cut off the German forces in East
Prussia, who were in urgent need of relief by Himmler's army and
were in only partial occupation of Posen, the German communication
centre for the region. Himmler withdrew the garrisons at Thorn,
Kulm and Marienwerder, which might, in favourable circumstances
at least, have given him bridgeheads from which to relieve the men in
East Prussia, and replaced the garrison commander in Posen with a
diehard S.S. commander at the head of 2,000 officer cadets. He
also placed police guards along the line of the River Oder to shoot
soldiers seen deserting and put their bodies on display. When he
tried to stage a limited local offensive from Deutsch-Krone in the
direction of Schneidemuehl, his men were defeated, and he had to
re-site his headquarters and withdraw his forces hastily a hundred
miles west to the Oder, ordering the garrison commanders of the
forces he left behind to be court-martialled if they abandoned their
posts. In the north the Russian forces followed on his heels to
establish bridgeheads as far east as the Oder. Himmler, on orders
from Hitler, extended his defences dangerously along the fringe of
the Baltic coast in order to hold as long as possible the U-boat bases
that stretched as far distant as Elbing itself.

By 31 January Russian advance forces were beginning to threaten
Berlin with spearhead advances from the line of the Oder, less than
fifty miles away. Panic set in, but the Russian offensive in this sector
came to a halt.

Himmler's second headquarters on the Eastern front was at the
luxurious villa owned by Robert Ley, head of the German Labour
Front, near the S.S. Ordensburg Crössinsee at Falkenburg.[26] Here
he lived, in effect, the life of a civil-servant who happened to be
administering a war. He got up between eight and nine o'clock,
received treatment from Kersten if he were there or from Gebhardt,
whose nursing home at Hohenlychen was in fact conveniently near.
Between ten and eleven o'clock he received his war reports and took
his decisions. After lunch he rested for a while, then conferred again
with his staff officers. In the evening he was too tired to concentrate,
and after dinner he went to bed. By ten o'clock he was inaccessible.

Hitler, oblivious of the threat to the capital, still planned his principal offensive in the south,[27] but Guderian was convinced that it was necessary to attack the Russian spearheads east of the capital immediately with all the force that could be assembled. He was also sure that Himmler was quite incapable of directing this action, which must be undertaken promptly and skilfully before the Russians had built up their strength for further advances.

Guderian determined to insist on his plan at a staff conference called by Hitler in the Chancellery in Berlin on 13 February. Himmler left his nursing home to be present and, as Guderian expected, opposed the offensive on the grounds that neither ammunition nor fuel could be made available in time. Guderian has recorded the conversation that followed in front of Himmler:

> GUDERIAN: We can't wait until the last can of petrol and the last shell have been issued. By that time the Russians will be too strong.
>
> HITLER: I won't permit you to accuse me of wanting to wait.
>
> GUDERIAN: I'm not accusing you of anything. I'm simply saying that there's no sense in waiting until the last lot of supplies have been issued and thus losing the favourable moment to attack.
>
> HITLER: I have just told you that I won't permit you to accuse me of wanting to wait.
>
> GUDERIAN: General Wenck must be attached to the Reichs-führer's staff, since otherwise there can be no prospect of the attack succeeding.
>
> HITLER: The National Leader is man enough to carry out the attack on his own.[28]

The dispute went on, according to Guderian, for two hours. Hitler became enraged:

> 'His fists raised, his cheeks flushed with rage, his whole body trembling, the man stood there in front of me, beside himself with fury and having lost all self-control. After each outburst of anger Hitler would stride up and down the carpet edge, then suddenly stop immediately before me and hurl his next accusation in my face. He was almost screaming, his eyes seemed about to pop out of his head and the veins stood out on his temples. I had made up my mind that I should let nothing destroy my equanimity and that I would simply repeat my essential demands over and over again. This I did with icy consistency.'

Suddenly Hitler stopped short in front of Himmler and said: 'Well, Himmler, General Wenck will arrive at your headquarters tonight and will take charge of the attack.'

Guderian had never seen Hitler rave so violently. The grim eyes of Bismarck in Lenbach's portrait had stared down on the scene, and Guderian sensed the strength of the gaze from the bronze bust of Hindenburg which was standing behind him.

'The General Staff has won a battle this day', said Hitler, and suddenly gave one of his most charming smiles.

On the same day Himmler's headquarters were moved once more, this time to the woods near Prenzlau, seventy miles north of Berlin and some thirty miles west of Stettin and the Russian front on the Oder. But Himmler returned to Hohenlychen, Gebhardt's nursing home, which was some seventy miles north of Berlin, in a state of nervous collapse, addressing an absurd order of the day to his forces: 'Forward through mud! Forward through snow! Forward by day! Forward by night! Forward to liberate our German soil!'[29] Wenck arrived on 16 February to direct the operations which began that same day, while Himmler summoned Skorzeny to the nursing home, and indulged in day-dreams about the imminent defeat of the Russians. According to Guderian, 'His appreciation of our enemies was positively childish.'

But the offensive was doomed; Wenck broke his shoulder in a car accident while driving through the night to Berlin on 17 February to report to Hitler. On 20 February Bormann wrote to his wife: 'Uncle Heinrich's offensive did not succeed, that is to say it did not develop properly, and now the divisions which he was holding in reserve have to be put in on other sectors. It means constant improvisation from one day to the next.' According to Guderian the attack, which had begun well enough under Wenck on 16 and 17 February, had lost its momentum by 18 February. The Russians regained their lost ground and inflicted heavy casualties on the German armoured divisions.

For a further month Himmler remained in his nominal command during a period involving heavy losses of territory in most sectors in the north-east and the south; the coastal bases were cut off or evacuated; meanwhile the endless, merciless bombing of Berlin continued every night. By the middle of March, the morale of the S.S. divisions in Hungary had collapsed, and they began to retreat against Hitler's absolute orders. In his fury, Hitler demanded that the men of these divisions have their S.S. armbands stripped from them; one of the divisions to be so disgraced was the *Leibstandarte*, which had once formed his bodyguard. Himmler was ordered south to Hungary to supervise the dishonouring of the S.S.

But Himmler had for some weeks lived in a state bordering on collapse. His experiences as a general in the field subject to the raging pressures of Hitler's fanatical command drove him back in March to his bed in Gebhardt's nursing home, which became both his retreat and his headquarters. Wherever he went he could not escape the appalling dilemma of the Russian advances and Hitler's hysterical reproaches. Like Göring, he could not stand the anger of the Führer; he did not have the strength of mind or purpose to oppose him. Like a terrified schoolboy, he retired to bed to escape the wrath of an authority that overwhelmed him. As Guderian saw it: 'I was in a position on several occasions to observe his lack of self-assurance and courage in Hitler's presence . . . His decisions when in command of Army Group Vistula were dictated by fear.'

In consequence of this, Himmler lost the regard of his armies over whom in Hitler's name he endeavoured to establish a reign of terror. During the last days of German rule in Danzig, the trees of the Hindenburg-Allee became gibbets for the bodies of dead youths displayed with placards hung round their necks proclaiming, 'I hang here because I left my unit without permission.'

On the main Oder front, immobile again for a brief while during the middle of March, the still massive armies of Hitler had little armour left with which to fight. Men press-ganged for the front had no equipment with which to repel the invader. Yet they were ordered to fight without thought of retreat, and the practice abandoned almost a century before of thrashing soldiers found guilty of cowardice was revived to curb the defeatism in Himmler's improvised forces, which now included such irregular recruits as foreign conscripts, schoolboys, convicts, exiles from the Baltic, staff from aerodromes abandoned by the Luftwaffe, and old men drafted from the Home Guard.

It was Guderian, according to his own account, who finally managed to displace Himmler from his command, where he had 'proved a complete failure'. No reports were sent in to Army headquarters, and in mid-March Guderian drove to Prenzlau to find out what was happening. He had the impression that the orders sent to Himmler were no longer carried out. When he arrived, Himmler was not there; Guderian was informed he was at Hohenlychen suffering from influenza.

'Can't you rid us of our commander', begged General Heinz Lammerding, Himmler's Chief-of-Staff.

This was what Guderian was determined to do. He drove straight to Hohenlychen, where he was surprised to find Himmler 'apparently in robust health', apart from a cold in the head. Guderian pointed out to him that he was obviously overworked as Reichsführer S.S., Head of the Reich Police, Minister of the Interior, Commander-in-Chief of the Replacement Army and Commander of the Army Group Vistula. Also, 'he must have realized by now that a command of troops at the front is no easy matter'. He ought at least to give up his command in the east. Himmler hesitated.

'I can't go and say that to the Führer', he said. 'He wouldn't approve of my making such a suggestion.' Guderian saw his chance. 'Then will you authorize me to say it for you?' he demanded.[30]

Himmler had to agree, and so lost his command on 20 March. According to Guderian, one of the principal reasons he had retained it, apart from ambition for office, was a desire to win for himself a Knight's Cross.

'He completely underestimated the qualities that are necessary for a man to be a successful commander of troops. On the very first occasion when he had to undertake a task before the eyes of all the world – one that could not be carried out by means of backstairs intrigues and fishing in troubled waters – the man inevitably proved a failure. It was complete irresponsibility on his part to wish to hold such an appointment; it was equally irresponsible of Hitler to entrust him with it.'

Guderian had by now enjoyed the opportunity closely to observe Himmler's character. He describes him as 'the most impenetrable of all Hitler's disciples'. He seemed 'an inconspicuous man with all the marks of racial inferiority. The impression he made was one of simplicity. He went out of his way to be polite. In contrast to Göring, his private life might be described as positively spartan in its austerity.' Yet he also seemed 'like a man from some other planet'. His imagination was 'vivid, and even fantastic . . . His attempt to educate the German people in National Socialism resulted only in the concentration camps.' But Guderian sees fit to add that 'the way the concentration camp methods were kept secret can only be described as masterly'.

The mask of resolution which Himmler chose to wear for the particular benefit of Hitler and the S.S. was dropped to a varying degree when he was faced by men equally determined to stop the war and save what life could be preserved before the final catastrophe. The concentration camps of the east were gradually falling into enemy hands, and Himmler was deeply disturbed by the conditions which the camps inside Germany would reveal should the Allied armies liberate them. Once the desperate task of stemming the Russian advance was removed from his hands by Guderian's intervention, all that was left for him to do in his semi-retirement was to redeem his own personal situation as best he could. It was now that he came more fully under the influence of the peacemakers – Schellenberg, Kersten and the Swedish Count Bernadotte.

Bernadotte has left his own account of his dealings with Himmler from February to April 1945. He acted as a purely private ambassador on behalf of the International Red Cross. In his book *The Fall of the Curtain* he pays tribute to the devious Schellenberg, but never once makes reference to Kersten.[31] Bernadotte was Vice-President of the Swedish Red Cross and he had the distinction of being a relative of the King of Sweden. According to his own statement, he was anxious to intervene largely to rescue from the holocaust of Germany several thousand Scandinavian prisoners of war and a group of Scandinavian women who, although German by marriage, had been widowed during the war and wanted desperately to return to their native lands. Bernadotte was led, either through vanity or illusion, to represent himself in the light of a great saviour and peace-maker fearlessly challenging the leaders of Nazi Germany, and more especially Himmler. That he failed altogether to acknowledge the groundwork achieved in earlier and more difficult times by Kersten is a deliberate omission, and throws some suspicion on his assessment of his personal achievements during the last weeks of the régime.

Kersten, as we have seen, had managed to move his family to Stockholm in September 1943, and, once there, had inspired the tentative peace discussions which Schellenberg had undertaken with Abram Stevens Hewitt, Roosevelt's special representative who was on a visit to Stockholm. He also initiated the first stage of the plan to evacuate Swedes and other Scandinavians who were prisoners of war from German-occupied territory, a plan on which he worked with the Swedish Foreign Minister, Christian Günther. Kersten was also working for the release of Dutch, French and Jewish prisoners. Moving constantly between Sweden and Germany, Kersten had worked on Himmler's conscience with the same assiduous care with which he massaged his body. The initial proposal was that while neutral Swedes might be released, the Norwegian and Danish men and women in the concentration camps should be sent for internment in Sweden.

During the summer of 1944, Kersten had managed to persuade Himmler to consider placing the Scandinavian prisoners in camps where they would be free from the worst bombing and could receive help from the Swedish Red Cross. He also joined with Madame Immfeld to urge the release of 20,000 Jews for internment by the Swiss. In December, when Kersten was attending Himmler on his train in the Black Forest, the Reichsführer had gone further and agreed to release 1,000 Dutch women, together with Norwegian and Danish women and children and certain male prisoners, provided Sweden would organize the transport. He also agreed to transfer to Switzerland 800 French women, 400 Belgians, 500 Polish women and between 2,000 and 3,000 Jews. Before his return to Stockholm on 22 December, Kersten had written a letter confirming the arrangement and explaining that he had discussed the details with Kaltenbrunner in Berlin. He had also implored Himmler to release the Jewish prisoners to the Swiss.

As we have seen, Himmler had begun to transfer some groups of Jews to Switzerland when further evacuations were stopped by Hitler's orders on 6 February. Before this, Himmler had even been negotiating with the Swiss for placing the concentration camps under International Red Cross inspection; Red Cross officials had visited Oranienburg on 2 February. But Hitler's anger was always too much for Himmler; he collapsed like a spent balloon. After the fright he had received on 6 February, he retreated to Hohenlychen as the most peaceful place from which to conduct the military campaign in the east, which at that time was still nominally in his hands.

At Hohenlychen he received a number of important guests. On 14 February, the day after Himmler's humiliation by Guderian in front of the Führer in Berlin, Goebbels arrived in Hohenlychen, having driven through the columns of German refugees from the east in order to visit the Reichsführer who, he gathered, was ill with tonsillitis. Semmler, Goebbels's aide records Goebbels's private remarks during this period about the man who seemed nearest to him now among the Nazi leaders.

'Goebbels obviously disliked Himmler, although in their work they get along together . . . But Himmler's extreme radical point of view and his use of brutal methods to get his own way make him attractive to Goebbels. Sometimes he thinks of the head of the S.S. as a rival . . . Goebbels would have liked the job of Minister of the Interior . . . But Himmler got in first, and since then he has felt prickings of jealousy . . . Except Hitler, no one is entirely without a secret fear of Himmler. Goebbels considers that Himmler has built up the greatest power organization that one can imagine.'[32]

The following day it was Ribbentrop who made contact with Himmler, and probably came to see him at Hohenlychen; Himmler apparently gave his approval to Ribbentrop's plan to send Fritz Hesse to Stockholm on a fruitless peace mission. Hesse left on 17 February, the day after Bernadotte arrived on his mission to Germany.

Bernadotte's principal intention was to visit Himmler and take over the various negotiations initiated by Kersten, whom he appears to have regarded as an interloper. On 18 February[33] Bernadotte had his first meeting with Himmler at Hohenlychen after he had formally visited both Kaltenbrunner and Ribbentrop, whose lengthy speeches during the interview he secretly timed with a stop-watch. Ribbentrop's foreign policy, he observed, seemed to favour some kind of agreement with Stalin for the joint domination of Europe by the U.S.S.R. and Germany – the reverse, that is, of the policy Schellenberg and Kersten were advocating to Himmler, which aimed at linking Germany and the Western Allies in combined opposition to further encroachments by the Red Army into Western Europe. Accompanied by Schellenberg, Bernadotte drove to Hohenlychen, which he discovered to be filled with German refugees from the east. Contrary to what he had expected, he found Himmler in a lively mood. He was dressed in the green uniform of the *Waffen* S.S. and wore horn-rimmed spectacles instead of the pince-nez which Bernadotte had seen in so many portraits of the Reichsführer. Bernadotte's description of Himmler is of particular interest:

'He had small, well-shaped and delicate hands, and they were carefully manicured, although this was forbidden in the S.S. He was also, to my great surprise, extremely affable. He gave evidence of a sense of humour, tending rather to the macabre . . . Certainly there was nothing diabolical in his appearance. Nor did I observe any sign of that icy hardness in his expression of which I had heard so much. Himmler . . . seemed a very vivacious personality, inclined to sentimentality where his relations with the Führer were concerned, and with a great capacity for enthusiasm.'

When Bernadotte, who was aware of Himmler's interest in the Scandinavian countries, gave him a seventeenth-century Swedish book on Scandinavian runic inscriptions, he 'seemed noticeably affected'.

Bernadotte's specific request was for the release of some thousands of Norwegian and Danish prisoners for internment in Sweden; this Himmler refused, but agreed they should be moved to two specific camps, where they might be cared for by the Swedish Red Cross. He even agreed, after a discursive conversation about the dangers to Europe of a Russian victory, that 'if the necessity should arise, he would allow interned Jews to be handed over to the Allied military authorities'. When they parted, he asked Schellenberg for an assurance that a good driver had been obtained to take Bernadotte back to Berlin. 'Otherwise', he added, 'it might happen that the Swedish papers would announce in big headlines: War Criminal Himmler murders Count Bernadotte.'

According to Schellenberg, Himmler was annoyed by this intrusion into the negotiations which he wanted to keep as secret as possible. The fact that Bernadotte's visit was known officially to Ribbentrop and Kaltenbrunner meant that Hitler also would know of it; however, he decided to put the whole matter on an official basis and instructed both Kaltenbrunner and Fegelein, his official representative at Hitler's headquarters, to sound Hitler on the matter. Fegelein reported Hitler as saying: 'You can't get anywhere with this sort of nonsense in total war.' Schellenberg, anxious as ever to put himself in the picture, claims to have advised Bernadotte on the journey out to Hohenlychen to compromise about the Danish and Norwegian prisoners and ask for their removal to a central camp in the northwest by Swedish Red Cross transport rather than their extradition to Sweden for internment. After the interview, he claims that Himmler 'had been very favourably impressed' by the Count, and wanted to maintain close contact with him. No doubt he was encouraged to seize this new lifeline to the future by the failure of the attack on the Russians which had just been carried out in his name by Guderian's nominees.

A week later, Himmler ventured as far as Berlin to attend a reception given by Goebbels at his Ministry. They talked about peace negotiations, but Goebbels had renewed his faith in Hitler and refused to think of such things without the active support of Hitler himself. He even suggested that if such action were ever taken by the Führer, he would much prefer to look to Stalin in the east than the Allies in the west. 'Madness,' murmured Himmler, and walked away.[34] Goebbels was preparing for his role as the stonewall defender of Berlin, the man who with his wife and children was to lay down his life for the Führer.

Kersten returned to Germany from Stockholm on 3 March after further consultations with Günther, the Swedish Foreign Minister, who feared that the Allies would force Sweden to break her neutrality and enter the war if Germany did not withdraw from Norway. He had also met Hilel Storch in Stockholm on 25 February. Storch was one of the leading men in the World Jewish Congress in New York, and he was anxious to use every possible means to secure the safety and the release of the remaining Jews imprisoned in Germany. He knew of Hitler's orders, that both the prisoners and the camps should be destroyed rather than let them be liberated by the Allies. Kersten undertook to negotiate directly with Himmler for the relief of the Jews by the International Red Cross.

He began his new talks with Himmler on 5 March. 'He was in a highly nervous condition,' writes Kersten, 'negotiations were difficult and stormy.'

During the following days Kersten fought to rouse Himmler's conscience and the remnants of his humanity. Schellenberg did the same: 'I wrestled for his soul', he said. 'I begged him to avail himself of the good offices of Sweden . . . I suggested that he should ask Count Bernadotte to fly to General Eisenhower and transmit to him his offer of capitulation.' According to Schellenberg, Himmler gave in and agreed that Schellenberg should continue his sessions with Bernadotte, whom he was unwilling at this stage to meet himself because of his fear of Hitler and of the leadership group in Berlin, who he knew were hostile and had by now an easier access to the Führer than he had himself.

On the same day that Kersten began his desperate discussions with Himmler, Bernadotte arrived from Sweden to make final arrangements for the transportation of the Danish and Norwegian prisoners from camps all over Germany to a central camp at Neuenburg. These negotiations were conducted with Kaltenbrunner and Schellenberg. Difficulties developed on both sides. Bernadotte claims he had overcome Kaltenbrunner's point blank refusal to co-operate. On the other hand, according to Professor Trevor-Roper, Bernadotte himself refused point-blank to accept non-Scandinavian prisoners on the Swedish transport, and wrote to Himmler accordingly.[35] The matter had to be straightened out by Günther and Kersten, and the transportation took place during the last two weeks of March. Meanwhile, Kersten negotiated a further agreement with Himmler of the greatest importance, again working together with Günther. This agreement was signed by Himmler on 12 March, and in it the Reichsführer S.S. undertook to disregard Hitler's orders that concentration camps were to be blown up before the arrival of Allied forces. He agreed to surrender them intact with their prisoners still alive, and to stop all further execution of Jews.

In making this decision, Himmler was no doubt influenced by his discovery on 10 March that a typhus epidemic had broken out in the huge camp at Belsen. The news had been kept from him by Kaltenbrunner, according to Kersten, who at once made use of this new threat to Germany to increase his pressure on Himmler. 'I pointed out that he could not in any circumstances permit this camp to become a plague centre which would imperil all Germany.' He sent orders at once to Kaltenbrunner in which, guided by Kersten, he demanded that drastic measures be taken to stamp out the epidemic. On 19 March Himmler sent further written orders to Kramer, the commandant of Belsen, saying that 'not another Jew' was to be killed and the death rate at the camp, which by now had some 60,000 prisoners, must be reduced at all costs. The state of Belsen was so appalling that even Hoess when he visited the camp was shocked at the sight of so many thousands of dead.

Kersten, who was to leave Germany for Stockholm on 22 March, had now worked Himmler into a pliant mood. In his very full diary for this period, written mainly at Hartzwalde, his old residence near Berlin, Kersten claims that he had managed to persuade Himmler to agree that there should be no fighting in Scandinavia, and also to countermand Hitler's order that The Hague and other Dutch cities were to be blown up by means of V-2 rockets on the approach of the Allied armies, together with the Zuyder Zee dam. On 14 March Himmler had almost reluctantly signed the order that the cities and the dam were to be spared.

'Once we had good intentions towards Holland', said Himmler. 'For us Germanic peoples are not enemies to be destroyed . . . The Dutch have learnt nothing from history . . . They could have helped us and we could have helped them. They have done everything to undermine our victory over Bolshevism.'

Himmler also finally agreed on 17 March, the day before Guderian arrived at Hohenlychen and persuaded him to resign his army command, that he would meet in the strictest secrecy a representative of the World Jewish Congress at Hartzwalde. Kersten suggested that Storch should come to Germany, provided Himmler would guarantee his personal safety.

'Nothing will happen to Herr Storch', said Himmler. 'I pledge my honour and my life on that.'

Kersten, as before, was careful to write Himmler a letter confirming everything that the Reichsführer S.S. had promised to do. Himmler, in his turn, sent an invitation to Storch in which he tried to make out that he had always from the start wanted to draft a helpful and humane approach to the Jewish problem, and had in fact shown his good intentions in recent weeks. He also confirmed his agreements with Kersten in writing, through his secretary Brandt.

On 22 March, the day Kersten flew back to Stockholm to report his various successes to Günther, Himmler received his successor on the battlefront, General Gotthard Heinrici, at Prenzlau, his military headquarters. He had thought fit the previous day to venture seeing Hitler in Berlin, and Guderian saw him walking with the Führer among the rubble in the Chancellery garden. Afterwards Guderian had told him that in his view the war was lost and the wasteful slaughter of men should be stopped at once.

'Go with me to Hitler and urge him to arrange an armistice', Guderian demanded.

This was too much for Himmler.

'My dear Colonel-General', said Himmler very precisely. 'It is still too early for that.' Guderian was disgusted. He could get no further with Himmler, however much he argued. 'There was nothing to be done with the man', he says in his memoirs. 'He was afraid of Hitler.'

On 22 March Himmler's last act as a soldier was to assemble

both his chiefs of staff and his stenographers at Prenzlau and dictate in the presence of Heinrici his summary of what had happened during the period of his command. As he went on talking, this grandiloquent scene of farewell became increasingly absurd. Heinrici's professional opinion was that 'in four months Himmler had failed to grasp the basic elements of generalship'. After two hours' dictation he became so incoherent that the stenographers could no longer make sense of what he had said and, together with the staff officers, they excused themselves from further work. Heinrici, impatient to get to the front, was finally released from this ordeal by the telephone: General Busse, one of the commanders in the field, was in grave difficulties and wanted to report to his Commander-in-Chief. Himmler straightaway handed the receiver to Heinrici.

'You are in command now', he said. 'You give him the necessary orders.'[36]

Before the meeting broke up, Heinrici, like Guderian, tried to sound Himmler on the possibilities of initiating peace negotiations with the Western Allies. Himmler tried to sound inconclusive, but admitted cautiously that he had caused certain steps to be taken.

In the chaos of the last month of the war, many men were salving their consciences by attempting to conduct negotiations with the Allies which might, once the war was over, present them in a more favourable light. Among these was General Wolff, who had been Himmler's liaison officer at Hitler's headquarters until 1943, when he was appointed Military Governor in Northern Italy. Early in March he went to Switzerland and attempted through Allen Dulles to negotiate the surrender of German forces in Italy. However, he failed to meet the emissaries sent by General Alexander to Zürich to discuss terms with him because he dared not admit to Himmler the full nature of his self-appointed mission. He pretended that his sole interest in holding these meetings lay in the exchange of prisoners, a matter which Himmler declared was the concern of Kaltenbrunner. For the moment there was stalemate, but Wolff was only waiting his chance to challenge Kaltenbrunner's growing authority and act again on his own behalf.

It is often difficult to make any sense of the rival negotiations that were taking place behind Hitler's back from motives which were a mixture of desperation and self-interest. According to the evidence given at the Nuremberg Trial by Baldur von Schirach, who was the Nazi Gauleiter of Vienna during the war, Himmler came to Vienna

at the end of March to organize the evacuation of Jews from Vienna
to the camps at Linz and Mauthausen.

'I want the Jews now employed in industry', Schirach reported him
to have said, 'to be taken by boat or by bus, if possible, under the
most favourable conditions and with the best medical care to Linz or
Mauthausen. Please take every care of these Jews. They are my
soundest capital investment.' Schirach gained the impression that
Himmler wanted to 'redeem himself with this good treatment of the
Jews'.[37] It seems, however, that such Jews as survived were in fact
marched on foot to Mauthausen.

During the first part of April Himmler was frequently at Hohenlychen, and it was here on 2 April that he met Bernadotte for the
second time, along with Schellenberg. Himmler appeared nervous
and depressed, but he insisted that the war must still go on. He
agreed, however, to the partial release of the Scandinavian prisoners,
though he said they were not to be released all at once because, as
he put it, 'it would attract too much attention'. Himmler seemed to
be almost completely under the distant control of Hitler, but later
he sent messages through Schellenberg that, should Hitler's position
change, he hoped Bernadotte would get in touch with Allied headquarters on his behalf. Bernadotte warned Schellenberg to get rid of
any illusions either he or Himmler might have that the Allies would
ever enter into negotiations with the head of the S.S., the man whom
the world regarded as a mass murderer.

Goebbels realized by the beginning of April that the concentration
camps were the worst evidence possible for the Allies to discover. 'I
fear that the concentration camps have grown a bit above Himmler's
head', he said, and von Oven duly wrote down this observation:
'Just suppose that these camps should be overrun by the enemy in
their present condition. What an outcry will be heard.' It was in
fact during April that the first contingent of Allied soldiers liberated
Belsen, Buchenwald and Dachau. Himmler believed he had acted
with exemplary humanity in allowing these camps, in which conditions had never been worse, to be entered by the Allies without
their inhabitants first being blown up in the blockhouses where they
lay. The massed overcrowding left both the guards and their prisoners
equally helpless to relieve the barest needs of the dying. An appalling,
hopeless state of inertia faced the Allied units entering these camps
and seeing for the first time what man in the twentieth century could
do to man in the name of racial purity. The first British entered Belsen

on 15 April, after arranging a truce with the S.S. guards three days before. According to Schellenberg, Kaltenbrunner had ordered the wholesale evacuation of Buchenwald which began, probably without Himmler's knowledge, on 3 April; Himmler, says Schellenberg, stopped the evacuation on 10 April as soon as he learned of it from the son of the Swiss President, Jean-Marie Musi, to whom on 7 April he had given his word that Buchenwald should be left intact for the Allied liberation, a promise intended to impress General Eisenhower in Himmler's favour.

Himmler was still nominally a soldier, commander of the *Waffen* S.S. and Commander-in-Chief of the Reserve Army, though in the turmoil of these last weeks such troops as there were left in action came under the direct orders of Hitler. Nevertheless, Himmler saw fit to issue a stern order dated 12 April decreeing the death penalty for commanders who failed to hold the towns for which they were responsible. 'Battle commanders appointed for each town are personally held responsible for compliance with this order. Neglect of this duty by the battle commander, or the attempt on the part of any civil servant to induce such neglect, is punishable by death.'[38]

Kersten meanwhile had been waiting in Stockholm expecting to receive the formal permit for Storch to visit Germany. Bernadotte returned on 10 April, bringing with him a letter for Kersten from Brandt which, although no date was fixed for the appointment, revealed that Himmler had not forgotten his promises. He was, in fact, still very uneasy about the project. On 13 April he said to Schellenberg: 'How am I going to do that with Kaltenbrunner about? I shall be completely at his mercy.' This was one of the occasions when Schellenberg had to wrestle for Himmler's soul; secret arrangements had been made with Professor de Crinis for a detailed report from Hitler's doctor on the Führer's state of health, but this had not yet arrived to help or hinder the Reichsführer S.S. in making up his mind. Himmler took Schellenberg for a walk in the forest near the country house in Wustrow where he was staying, and unburdened himself of his worries:

'Schellenberg,' he said, 'I believe that nothing more can be done with Hitler.'

'Everything he has done lately', urged Schellenberg, 'seems to show that now is the time for you to act.'

Schellenberg goes on to describe their conversation:

'Himmler said to me that I was the only one, apart from Brandt, whom he could trust completely. What should he do? He could not shoot Hitler; he could not give him poison; he could not arrest him in the Reich Chancellery, for then the whole military machine would come to a standstill. I told him that all this did not matter; only two possibilities existed for him: either he should go to Hitler and tell him frankly all that had happened during the last years and force him to resign; or else he should remove him by force. Himmler objected that if he spoke to Hitler like that the Führer would fall in a violent rage and shoot him out of hand. I said, "That is just what you must protect yourself against – you still have enough higher S.S. leaders, and you are still in a strong enough position to arrest him. If there is no other way, then the doctors will have to intervene." '

Eventually Himmler took Schellenberg's advice and arranged a date for Storch to come to Germany on 19 April, during a period when Kaltenbrunner was known to be going to Austria. The message reached Kersten on 17 April, but by this time Storch was unable to go to Germany. He delegated the formidable task of being the first Jew to negotiate direct with Himmler on more or less equal terms to Norbert Masur, director of the Swedish section of the World Jewish Congress in New York. He was to travel incognito in the care of Kersten. On 19 April they flew by the regular service to Tempelhof airport, the only passengers on a plane full of Red Cross parcels. When they arrived, an S.S. guard stood ready to receive them; the S.S. clicked their heels and cried, 'Heil Hitler', but Masur calmly raised his hat to them and said, 'Good evening'. They then drove to Hartzwalde in an S.S. staff car to wait for Himmler, who had spent the day in Berlin conferring with Count Schwerin von Krosigk, the Minister of Finance, an interview at the Count's house arranged by Schellenberg because he hoped the Minister might influence Himmler to take the action they all wanted him to take, 'with or without Hitler'.[39]

Himmler could not meet Masur on 20 April because it was Hitler's birthday. He sent Schellenberg to Hartzwalde during the night of the 19th to prepare the ground for their conversations, which he was ready to begin the moment the birthday celebrations were over. Himmler, according to Schellenberg, had ordered champagne with which to toast the Führer.

But 20 April was no day for celebrations. By now, the Americans were across the Elbe and in Nuremberg; British patrols were approaching Berlin from the west and the full Russian forces were marching in from the east. The American and Russian armies were almost on the point of meeting. Hitler decided to receive his guests in the great Bunker constructed fifty feet under the Chancellery buildings and extending out under the garden. Although Himmler, against Schellenberg's advice, had decided he had better appear and shake Hitler by the hand, he was not invited to confer in private with the Führer along with the service chiefs. Relations were cold by now. He lined up with the rest below ground to congratulate the man he had served as Reichsführer S.S. for fifteen years. Göring, Goebbels, Ribbentrop and Speer were there; so were Doenitz, Keitel and Jodl, all under the watchful eyes of Bormann. It was expected Hitler would now move south and head the great German Resistance which was due to be organized from the Obersalzberg; Himmler joined with the others in urging him to do so. But Hitler reserved his decision, only declaring that if Germany should be cut in two by the forward drive of the armies from the east and the west, then Doenitz should take charge of the defences in the north. The narrow escape route to the south was still open, and once the conference was over the great dispersal took place. Göring travelling with a fleet of cars departed importantly for the safety of Obersalzberg; Speer hurried to Hamburg intent on preserving as much of German industry from destruction as possible; Ribbentrop still hung around Berlin, his advice no longer wanted. Only Goebbels and Bormann remained fast by the side of Hitler, waiting for his decision whether they were to stay and die in Berlin or escape to the south and fight a while longer for survival.

Himmler said goodbye and set off for Wustrow, where Schellenberg was anxiously waiting for him. He was never to see Hitler again.

# VIII

# *Self-Betrayal*

Himmler climbed the curved steps from the lower levels of Hitler's bunker and passed through the passageways and corridors flanked by heavy bulkheads to protect the Führer during the final defence of Berlin. Outside these sealed cells the earth trembled with blast that was slowly disintegrating the remains of the city.

Schellenberg, anxious as ever, had been vainly trying to make contact with Himmler who, after leaving the Bunker, was confined in Berlin by the heavy air attacks which were felling more buildings around him. He did not reach Wustrow, where Schellenberg was waiting for him, until the middle of the night. After some persuasion, he agreed to drive to Hartzwalde, where they arrived between two and three o'clock on the morning of 21 April.

Kersten met him outside the house and urged him to be both friendly and magnanimous with Masur; this was his greatest chance to redeem the honour of Germany and show the world while there was still time that a new and humane policy had at last replaced the repressions and cruelties of the past. Kersten knew that an argument such as this would raise some response from Himmler's professed humanitarianism. As they went in, Himmler assured Kersten that all he wanted now was some agreement with the Jews.

This was the first time since he had come to power that Himmler had met a Jew on equal terms. He greeted Masur formally and said how glad he was that he had come.[1] They sat down, and immediately Himmler began to make a long, defensive statement about the attitude of the régime to the Jews as aliens in Germany, and how the emigration policy he had devised, which, as he said, 'could have been very advantageous to the Jews,' had been sabotaged by the other nations who would not receive them.

Masur was an experienced negotiator and he had come to achieve a particular object. He remained very calm and interposed a few occasional remarks to refute the more extreme of Himmler's arguments. Only when Himmler said that the concentration camps were really training centres where if the work was hard the treatment had always been just, did Masur lose some measure of his patience and refer to the crimes that had been committed in them.

'I concede that these things have happened occasionally', Himmler agreed mildly, 'but I have also punished those responsible.'

He complained bitterly of the false atrocity propaganda that the Allies were making out of the conditions at Belsen and Buchenwald, which he had 'handed over as agreed'. He said:

> 'When I let 2,700 Jews go into Switzerland, this was made the subject of a personal campaign against me in the Press, asserting that I had only released these men in order to construct an alibi for myself. But I have no need of an alibi! I have always done only what I considered just, what was essential for my people. I will also answer for that. Nobody has had so much mud slung at him in the last ten years as I have. I have never bothered myself about that. Even in Germany any man can say about me what he pleases. Newspapers abroad have started a campaign against me which is no encouragement to me to continue handing over the camps.'[2]

Masur urged that all the Jews left alive in Germany should be released at once, and that a stop should be put to the evacuations. But as soon as he was faced with hard facts and terms of agreement, Himmler began to hesitate and avoided committing himself. Masur had to retire with Schellenberg to another room to determine the details of what should be done; since they had met the previous day, Schellenberg knew what Masur wanted. It was easier to reach such agreements apart from Himmler; he only gave way when he was alone with Kersten, who made him promise to implement the agreement he had already made the previous month to release from Ravensbrück for evacuation to Sweden a thousand Jewish women under the cover of their being of Polish origin. Himmler was still openly afraid that Hitler might discover what he was doing.

To the end of the conversation, Himmler attempted to justify what had been done both in Germany and in the occupied countries. Crime had been reduced, he said; no one had gone hungry; everyone had work. Hitler alone had the resolution to resist the Communists;

his defeat would bring chaos to Europe. Only then would the
Americans discover the terrible thing that they had done. With the
help of Schellenberg and Brandt, who was also present, Kersten
achieved the best measure of agreement he could about the number
of Jews to be released and the strict observation of what had already
been accepted by Himmler in the past for the relief of the Jews still
left in captivity. Worried and irresolute, Himmler stayed on the edge
of the conversation, resorting to generalizations about the situation
and the humane things he had done; he withdrew himself from any
discussion of the arrangements that were being undertaken on his
behalf by Schellenberg and Brandt. At about five o'clock in the
morning the meeting broke up, and Kersten took Himmler outside
for a more private conversation.

It was then that Himmler suddenly asked him, 'Have you any
access to General Eisenhower or the Western Allies?'

When Kersten said he had none, Himmler went on to ask if he
would be willing to act as his ambassador to Eisenhower, and go to
him with the suggestion that hostilities against Germany should be
stopped so that war on a single front against Russia could be
undertaken.

'I am ready to concede victory to the Western Allies', he said.
'They have only to give me time to throw back the Russians. If they
would let me have the equipment, I can still do it.'

Himmler could not give up the image of himself as the Supreme
Commander in the German Army. Kersten said he should talk to
Bernadotte about peace negotiations. That was more in his province. Then having reassured himself that the Dutch cities and the
dam were still intact and that Himmler would do all he could to
prevent further bloodshed in Scandinavia, Kersten finally let him go.
By sheer persistence he had won from him everything he could, and
Schellenberg was anxious now to take Himmler on to see Bernadotte
at Hohenlychen; the Count was anxious to talk to him before leaving
that morning for the north.

They went down to the car together; Himmler offered his hand to
Kersten and thanked him for all he had done. It was as if he knew
they would not meet again, and he spoke formally:

'I thank you from the bottom of my heart for the years in which
you have given me the benefit of your medical skill. My last thoughts
are for my poor family', he added, as he said goodbye and drove
away with Schellenberg.[3]

They arrived at Hohenlychen at six o'clock and had breakfast with Bernadotte, who had driven to the nursing home from Berlin the previous evening in order to meet Himmler.[4] Bernadotte was in a hurry to leave and only anxious to get Himmler's consent for the release of the Scandinavian prisoners who had been gathered by the Red Cross in Neuengamme. But Himmler would not give way; he said angrily that the 'tissue of lies' about Belsen and Buchenwald had made him think again about the whole situation, and he ordered the total evacuation of Neuengamme.

'It is outrageous', said Himmler to Bernadotte, 'that this camp which in my opinion was in model shape should have become the subject of these shameless accounts. Nothing has upset me so much as what the Allied press has published about this business.'

Bernadotte noted how tired and nervous Himmler was. He looked 'spent and weary', and said he had not slept for several nights. 'He gave the impression of being unable to remain long in one spot and of darting from place to place as an outlet for his anxiety and restlessness.' Nevertheless, he ate hungrily and as he talked tapped his front teeth with his fingernails – a sign of nerves, as Schellenberg explained in an aside to Bernadotte. He agreed to the women being evacuated from Ravensbrück, and to the Red Cross moving the Scandinavians as far as Denmark, where they must remain under the control of the Gestapo. This was to begin the following day, arranged by the Danes at the request of Bernadotte.

Himmler, worn out, left it to Schellenberg to ask Bernadotte whether he would take a message to Eisenhower. Bernadotte refused. 'He should have taken Germany's affairs into his own hands after my first visit', he said. Schellenberg, who had travelled with Bernadotte part of the way to the airport, returned to Hohenlychen 'filled with a deep sadness', and had scarcely gone to bed to make up his lost sleep when Himmler summoned him. The Reichsführer was lying in bed looking utterly miserable and saying he felt ill. But he decided to drive to Wustrow, the car weaving its way through the columns of troops and refugees that filled the roads. 'I dread what is to come', he said. Just before getting to Wustrow they were attacked by low-flying aircraft, but they escaped uninjured. They dined and then talked far into the night. Himmler dreamed of founding a new National Unity Party unencumbered by the presence of Hitler.

Sunday, 22 April was the day when Hitler, immured in his Bunker and marshalling imaginary troops on territory already lost, finally decided he would stay in Berlin. The Russians had now entered the outskirts of the city. Goebbels and his wife with their six children were all summoned to join him in his concrete grave. Like an angry god in a paroxysm of self-pity, Hitler stormed at the world that had failed him and the traitors at his gates. Let them scatter to the south; he would die in the capital, he and his faithful friends.

Himmler was not among them. He had hurried away from Wustrow, which was also threatened by the Russians. He had gone back to Hohenlychen, where he had heard from Fegelein by telephone of Hitler's intransigent decision. Hitler, he was told, was raving that the S.S. had left him in the lurch.

Gottlieb Berger was with him, as well as Gebhardt. The message touched Himmler's loyalty on the raw, and Schellenberg, who had now gone north to join Bernadotte, was not there to protect him with his subtle advice.

'Everyone in Berlin is mad', he cried. 'I still have my escort battalion – 600 men, most of them wounded or convalescent. What am I to do?'

Berger, a simple man, said outright that the Reichsführer should go with his remaining forces to Berlin and join the Führer. Himmler knew that Schellenberg would oppose this. He telephoned the Bunker again and, after discussion, compromised by agreeing to meet Fegelein at Nauen, a half-way point to Berlin, where the matter could be discussed more fully. This was action of a sort. Had he not said at lunch to Schellenberg before he had gone, 'I must act one way or the other. What do you suggest?'.

Himmler and Gebhardt in two separate cars; Gebhardt wanted to go to Berlin to be confirmed personally by Hitler in a new appointment of some value in the approaching times, that of head of the German Red Cross. For Himmler, Berlin was a place to be avoided, though he still wanted to court the affections of Hitler by offering to send him his escort to die as martyrs among the rubble. But Fegelein failed to meet him at Nauen; he never arrived. The two cars waited at the cross-roads in the darkness of the Sunday night for two hours, while Himmler nursed his uncertainties. Eventually they agreed that Gebhardt should continue the journey to see Hitler in Berlin, taking with him a message from Himmler, who would meanwhile return to the shelter of the nursing-home. So loyalty was satisfied. Gebhardt was received by Hitler late that night and confirmed in his appointment, while Hitler accepted Himmler's generous offer of the blood of his men. It was very simple. Gebhardt asked if there were any message he might take from the Führer to Himmler. 'Yes,' said Hitler, 'give him my love.'

He was followed by Berger, who was about to fly south to keep watch for Himmler on the behaviour of Kaltenbrunner. Berger's simple loyalty was expressed so tactlessly that he had to witness another paroxysm of the Führer's rage – the shouting, the face flushed purple, the trembling limbs, the semi-paralysis of the left side of his body. It was an experience he was not to forget as he flew south along with many others, officials, staff officers, members of the household and secretariat, all hurrying from Berlin with the sound of the Russian guns in their ears. Everyone who possibly could was getting out of the capital through the narrowing territory which still offered an escape-route to the south.

Himmler retired to the comparative safety of Hohenlychen, and turned his mind once more from the Führer to Bernadotte. According to Schellenberg, Himmler had sent him north with a definite message of surrender to the Western Powers offered in his own name. Schellenberg eventually met Bernadotte at Flensburg the following day, 23 April, the day on which Goebbels announced on the radio that Hitler would lead the defence of Berlin and Göring in Obersalzberg was pondering over the best form of words for the message he was to send Hitler, offering to take over the total leadership of the Reich.

It was arranged that Bernadotte and Himmler should meet that night in Lübeck. The conference began by candlelight in the Swedish consulate; the electricity supply had failed, and an air-raid delayed the discussions. They went down to the public air-raid shelter, where Himmler, Minister of the Interior and commander of the Gestapo and the S.S., talked unrecognized to the small group of Germans who came in from the street for protection against the attack. Bernadotte watched him. 'He struck me as being utterly exhausted and at a nervous extremity', he wrote subsequently. 'He looked as if he were mustering all his will power to preserve outward calm.'

When they went upstairs sometime after midnight, Himmler gave his view of the situation. Hitler might already be dead; the capital in any case could not last much longer, and it was only a matter of days before Hitler would be gone. 'I admit that Germany is defeated', declared Himmler. Bernadotte has left a record of the next part of their conversation:

HIMMLER: In the situation that has now arisen I consider my hands free. In order to save as great a part of Germany as possible from a Russian invasion I am willing to capitulate on the Western front in order to enable the Western Allies to advance rapidly towards the East. But I am not prepared to capitulate on the Eastern front. I have always been, and I shall always remain, a sworn enemy of Bolshevism. At the beginning of the World War, I fought tooth and nail against the Russo-German pact. Are you willing to forward a communiqué on these lines to the Swedish Minister for Foreign Affairs, so that he can inform the Western Powers of my proposal?

BERNADOTTE: It is in my opinion quite impossible to carry out a surrender on the Western front and to continue to fight on the Eastern front. It can be looked upon as quite certain that England and America will not make any separate settlement.

HIMMLER: I am well aware how extremely difficult this is, but all the same I want to make the attempt to save millions of Germans from Russian occupation.

BERNADOTTE: I am not willing to forward your communiqué to the Swedish Minister for Foreign Affairs unless you promise that Denmark and Norway shall be included in the surrender.

At the end of their discussions, Bernadotte asked Himmler what he would do if his proposals were rejected.

'In that event', he replied. 'I shall take over the command of the Eastern Front and be killed in battle.'

Himmler set down his proposals in a letter for which Bernadotte had asked so that he might have them in writing to hand to Günther, the Swedish Minister. The letter was carefully drafted by candlelight. This day, said Himmler as he handed the letter to Bernadotte, was the most bitter in his life. Schellenberg and Bernadotte then prepared to return to Flensburg, leaving Himmler to ponder (as Schellenberg told Bernadotte later) whether he should shake hands or not with the Allied Supreme Commander, or merely offer him a formal bow.[5]

In the Bunker, Hitler had received Göring's carefully worded signal as a brutal affront. He called him a traitor and dispossessed him of his rank and offices, ordering his arrest by the S.S. in the south. This sudden defection by Göring, as Hitler was led to see it by

Bormann, who was still anxious to destroy his rivals even during these last moments of the régime, left wide open the problem of a successor. Though he knew nothing of this, Himmler regarded himself by now as the only possible claimant.[6] Hitler is recorded as saying in March that Himmler was not on sufficiently good terms with the Party to succeed him, and 'was anyway useless, since he is so inartistic', a view that echoes the opinion of Goebbels. Himmler, however, was already dreaming of the shadow government with which he might continue as head of state under the Western Allies, and most of the remaining Nazi ministers and war leaders, including Doenitz, Speer and Schwerin von Krosigk, feared that Himmler would usurp the succession.

The next three days, 24 to 26 April, were days of waiting. Fearing that he might be cut off by the Russians at Hohenlychen, Himmler moved to Schwerin, where Doenitz had set up his headquarters for the defence of the north. Each day the front closing round Berlin moved forward on the map like ink seeping through blotting paper, but Hitler stayed on in the Bunker directing forces which were no longer capable of either attack or resistance.

On 27 April, Schellenberg received a message that sent him hurrying to meet Bernadotte at Odense airport in Jutland, where he arrived late because of the bad weather; he had gathered in any case that Himmler's proposals had not been well received in Britain and America, but had decided not to pass this on in case Himmler might relapse once again into faint-heartedness. Bernadotte offered to drive with him to Lübeck to see the Reichsführer. As soon as Himmler heard that his offer had not been eagerly received, he ordered Schellenberg to report to him. With all his subtle plans in a state of collapse, Schellenberg drove south in fear of his life. He took the strange precaution of telephoning Hamburg and arranging to take the astrologer Wilhelm Wulff with him to this dangerous interview. It always calmed Himmler to have his horoscope read.

But it needed more than an astrologer to know what the fates were preparing for Himmler on the other side of the world. The story of the leak to the international press of Himmler's discussions with Count Bernadotte has only recently been told in a detailed statement by Jack Winocour, at that time director of the British Information Services in Washington.[7] Winocour was on the staff attending the three-month session of the United Nations Conference on International Organization, starting in April 1945 at San Francisco. The

British delegation included Anthony Eden, the then Foreign Secretary, who at a private delegation meeting on 27 April is reported by Winocaur to have said quite casually: 'By the way . . . we've heard from Stockholm that Himmler has made an offer through Bernadotte to surrender Germany unconditionally to the Americans and ourselves. Of course, we are letting the Russians know about it.' The British and American Ministers in Washington had reported the offer during the early hours of 25 April to Churchill and Truman, both of whom regarded it as an attempt by Germany to split the Allies, and they arranged at once for Stalin to be informed. A reply was sent that surrender could only be acceptable if it were offered to all the Allies simultaneously.

Winocaur, who was one of the men in charge of British press relations at the conference, knew nothing of this background at the time, but felt that Eden's momentous statement to the delegates should be passed on to the press. After some hesitation, entirely on his own initiative, he gave the news overnight to his friend Paul Scott Rankine of Reuters on the strict understanding that the source should not be revealed. Rankine sent a press cable to London breaking the news in an exclusive statement soon after one o'clock in the morning of 28 April.

While Schellenberg was during the morning of 28 April successfully calming Himmler with the aid of his favourite astrologer, the Allied press was pouring out the news of the Reichsführer's independent attempt at negotiations. Completely unaware of this, Himmler attended a military conference in Rheinsberg convened by Keitel. At this meeting Himmler presided, which showed that he regarded himself as Hitler's deputy and successor.

In the late afternoon Bernadotte heard the news of the negotiations on the clandestine radio, and realized that Himmler was finished as a negotiator. Doenitz also heard the report and telephoned enquiries to Himmler, who immediately denied the story as it had been put in the broadcast, but added that he had no intention of issuing any public statement himself. According to Schellenberg, he then spent part of the day deciding how best to order the evacuation of German troops from Norway and Denmark.

It was not until nine o'clock that night that a monitor report on a broadcast put out by the B.B.C. gave Himmler away to the Führer in the bowels of the Bunker. According to one observer, Hitler's 'colour rose to a heated red, and his face became virtually unrecognizable'.[8]

Then he began to rage at this treacherous betrayal by the man he had trusted most of all. The men and women hemmed in the Bunker were convulsed with emotion, and 'everyone looked to his poison'. Himmler's arrest was ordered; he followed Göring into the limbo of the dispossessed. 'A traitor must never succeed as Führer', screamed Hitler.[9] He took his revenge on the only associate of Himmler he had in his power. This was Fegelein, the brother-in-law of the woman he was about to marry and Himmler's unfaithful subordinate at Hitler's headquarters. He had tried to desert, but he was dragged back, taken upstairs into the Chancellery garden and shot around midnight on the barest suspicion that he had known something of Himmler's treachery.

Hitler ordered Göring's successor as head of the Luftwaffe, Field-Marshal von Greim, to leave the Bunker and fly during the night under Russian fire to Doenitz's headquarters, which were now at Ploen. Greim, who had been wounded in the foot during his hazardous flight into Berlin in a light aircraft, flew north in the same 'plane piloted by Hanna Reitsch, who was a dedicated Nazi. They took off from the avenue leading up to the Brandenburg Gate. This strange pair did not arrive at Ploen, which was on the Baltic coast some 200 miles north-west of Berlin, until the afternoon of 29 April, having landed in the early hours of the morning at Rechlin.

At Ploen they found an uneasy balance of power in force between Doenitz, Commander-in-Chief of the northern armies, and Himmler, Commander of the S.S. and the police. According to Schwerin von Krosigk, Doenitz and Himmler had talked the matter over and agreed that each of them was ready to serve under the Führer's acknowledged successor. Doenitz imagined this must be Himmler, and so, for that matter, did the Reichsführer himself.

During 29 April no official statement reached Doenitz that Himmler had been dispossessed of his rank and power by Hitler, although an ambiguous signal arrived from Bormann at 3.15 on the morning of 30 April: Doenitz was to 'proceed at once and mercilessly against all traitors'. Only Greim had received a definite instruction to arrest Himmler, an order which he was powerless to carry out unaided by Doenitz, who was still certain Himmler would at any moment become his Führer. There is no record of when Greim met Doenitz or what exactly he said to him. Neither of them knew that Hitler's testament was already composed and signed, or that Doenitz was to be appointed Führer with Karl Hanke, Gauleiter of Breslau, as Reichsführer S.S. and Paul Giesler, Gauleiter of Munich, as Minister of the Interior.

The isolation of Hitler in Berlin was now complete. His final craving for vengeance against Göring and Himmler, the men who had served him in their own way for the best part of two decades, was frustrated by the confusion that surrounded the last days of his life. While Göring was kept in nominal confinement in the south by an embarrassed unit of S.S. men, Himmler remained free in the north, a political buccaneer who did not even know until after Hitler's death that his authority had been swept from beneath his feet. With his remaining staff, his escort of S.S. men, and his fleet of cars, he moved in uneasy orbit round the Grand Admiral's headquarters at Ploen with no particular duties to occupy his time except the maintenance of his position and the salvage of his power.[10] It was not until late in the afternoon of 30 April that Doenitz learned in a signal sent by Bormann from the Bunker in Berlin of his unwanted elevation to Führer of a Germany on the verge of disintegration. Bormann's signal was worded evasively and did not even reveal that Hitler had died by his own hand at 3.30 that afternoon: Doenitz merely knew that he, and not Himmler, had been nominated Hitler's successor: 'In place of the former Reich Marshal Göring the Führer appoints you, Herr Grand Admiral, as his successor. Written authority is on its way. You will immediately take all such measures as the situation requires.'

Doenitz, surprised and alarmed, sent a loyal message back to the Leader he did not know was dead. 'If Fate . . . compels me to rule the Reich as your appointed successor, I shall continue this war to an end worthy of the unique, heroic struggle of the German people', he said in the stifled language of loyalty. One of the three copies of Hitler's testament, signed at four o'clock in the morning of the previous day and witnessed by both Goebbels, the new Reich Chancellor, and Bormann, was already on its way. A special messenger had left the Bunker at noon on 29 April, but was, in fact, never to reach Doenitz at Ploen.

Meanwhile, Bormann and Goebbels, without any reference to their new Führer, were trying during the night of 30 April to make favourable terms with the Russian commanders. Bormann sent another evasive signal to Doenitz saying he would try to join him at Ploen and adding that 'the testament is in force'. It was Goebbels who finally sent Doenitz an explicit signal at 3.15 in the afternoon of

1 May, telling him of Hitler's death twenty-four hours after it had happened. He named the principal ministers in the new government, but made no mention of Himmler, or of the fact that he and his wife were preparing to die that night after killing their sleeping children.

Himmler no longer found himself welcome at Ploen. His exclusion from any form of office was a severe shock to him, and Doenitz did not hide his disapproval of Himmler's attempts to negotiate with the Allies. Schellenberg travelled through the night of 30 April along the roads blocked with army transport and refugees only to find Himmler at his new headquarters at the castle of Kalkhorst, near Travemunde. He had just gone to bed. It was then four o'clock in the morning of 1 May. He learned from Brandt what had happened and of Himmler's despair after a late-night conference with Doenitz, during which he had proposed himself as second Minister of State.[11] Doenitz had evaded this offer, though he was still afraid Himmler might use his police escort to regain his lost power. Himmler, says Schellenberg, was 'playing with the idea of resigning, and even talking of suicide'.

At breakfast the following morning he was 'nervous and distracted', and in the afternoon they went together to Ploen. Schellenberg by now was solely concerned to please Bernadotte. He planned to use Himmler's remaining influence to secure from Doenitz a peaceful solution to the German occupation of the Scandinavian countries. By this means he felt he would earn the gratitude of the Allies and secure his own future when he took refuge in Sweden. Himmler, anxious to be present at the conferences called by Doenitz, was prepared to support the peaceful withdrawal of German forces from Norway. He also admitted to Doenitz that he had in fact been attempting to secure peace through Sweden. This finally discredited him in the eyes of the Grand Admiral.[12]

May Day saw the beginning of the surrender of Germany. Mohnke, the commander of Himmler's S.S. regiment which he had sent to cordon Berlin, was captured by the Russians while attempting to escape from the Bunker; at ten o'clock that night a broadcast from Berlin proclaimed officially that Hitler was dead. Kesselring surrendered in north Italy and, on 2 May Doenitz began the first stages of his own surrender to Montgomery without any further consultation with Himmler. Kaufmann, the Gauleiter of Hamburg, in spite of the order he had received, opened up the city to the British forces.

Meanwhile Himmler maintained the façade of power, and it was still formidable. Accompanied by his escort of S.S. men, he moved around in his Mercedes like some medieval warlord. While he was preparing to follow Doenitz on 1 May to Flensburg, on the borders of Schleswig-Holstein and Denmark, he received an unexpected offer from Léon Degrelle, the renegade commander of the Belgian and French fascists enrolled in the *Waffen* S.S., who had retreated from the Russian front with what was left of his men.[13]

Degrelle was determined to make a bold finish to his fighting career in the eyes of Himmler, who no longer wanted to see him, though he was quite prepared to add his men to the diminishing forces at his command. He sent word to Degrelle to join him at Malente, near Kiel, and on the way the Belgian commander in his Volkswagen powered by potato *schnapps* caught up with the Reichsführer S.S. driving at the head of his column of Mercedes and lorries. Himmler, wearing a crash-helmet, was driving his own car, and they broke the journey at Malente. By now Degrelle had little to offer his leader; the Belgian S.S. units had scattered to Denmark. Himmler's sole concern was to keep up with Doenitz, and Degrelle followed the fleet of cars and lorries on the journey north to Flensburg.

As they were approaching Kiel, a daylight raid began. Himmler kept calm and shouted, 'Discipline, gentlemen, discipline', as his staff, both men and women, dived for safety in the mud, in which the girls had the shoes sucked from their feet. Degrelle left the scene as the officers and their aides struggled back with their vehicles after the raiding planes had gone. He went directly north through Kiel while Himmler's convoy retreated in search of some less hazardous route to Flensburg.

That night Himmler was joined on his journey by Werner Best from Denmark.[14] They sat together in the Mercedes which Himmler still drove, and they spent the tedious hours of travel in talk. They were frequently held up by air-raids and did not reach Flensburg until early in the morning of 3 May.

Himmler, as always, was careful what he said. Hitler had not been quite himself, he admitted, during the past six months, and Bormann had increased his hold over him. He had issued Himmler with impossible commands on the Russian front and had refused even to discuss the idea of peace. On the other hand, Himmler said he was certain that if he had been allowed to have only half-an-hour's conference with Eisenhower he could have convinced him of the necessity of joining forces with the Germans to drive back the Russian invaders. Before they parted in the morning, Best said he was going back across the Danish border before his appointment with Doenitz later that day.

'But what are you going to do yourself, Reichsführer?' asked Best.

'I don't yet know', was all Himmler could find to say, but he asked Best to take the S.S. women staff with him over the nearby border into Denmark, where they would be able to wash and get themselves food before returning to their duties.

Himmler's indecision was shown even more in a conversation he had with Schwerin-Krosigk, who had become Foreign Minister in the place of Ribbentrop and therefore retired to Flensburg.[15] He discovered Himmler in a mood of despair, an unwanted adviser at the headquarters of the new Führer.

'Graf Schwerin, what ever is to become of me?' he asked.

Schwerin-Krosigk did not know what was to become of anyone; Germany scarcely had need of a Foreign Minister. It seemed to him that to help organize the evacuation of Germans from the east was the only practical thing they could do for the moment. But he tried to give a serious answer to Himmler's question.

'As I see it, there are three courses open to you', he said. 'The first is to shave off your moustache, disguise yourself in a wig and dark glasses, and try to disappear altogether. I expect, even so, you would soon be discovered, and your end would scarcely be glorious. The second course is to shoot yourself, though as a Christian I can't advise you to do this; you would have to decide such a thing for yourself. What I really recommend is the third course: drive straight to Montgomery's headquarters and say, 'I am Heinrich Himmler, I want to take full responsibility for everything the S.S. has done." As to what will happen then, who can say? But if it proves the end for you, it will at least be the most honourable way out.'

Himmler decided to act as a kind of elder statesman in Doenitz's cabinet at Ploen for as long as he could. He was plainly unable to accept the fact that he no longer held the offices to which he had been formerly attached. His immediate retinue still amounted to some 150 staff officers and assistants. But neither Doenitz nor Himmler knew the full terms of Himmler's rejection by Hitler. The messenger from the Bunker had failed in his mission of bringing the Führer's testament to his successor, and Bormann, as everyone then believed, had been killed while trying to escape from the Bunker on the night of 30 April. Had they been able to read the carefully typed terms of Hitler's denunciation they would at least have known what the Führer had felt about his former Minister: 'Goering and Himmler, by their secret negotiations with the enemy, without my knowledge or approval, and by their illegal attempts to seize power in the State, quite apart from their treachery to my person, have brought irreparable shame on the country and the whole people.' All they knew in fact was what Greim, the wounded leader of the Luftwaffe, and his devoted pilot, Hanna Reitsch, may have told them of Hitler's paroxysms of anger, and what Goebbels's signal indicated about the distribution of the principal offices of state, which neither Bormann nor Goebbels had arrived to take up. Doenitz, concerned only to rid himself of the past and surrender in a manner becoming an Admiral of the Fleet, was most unwilling to have a man of Himmler's reputation serving in any cabinet of his own making. Yet he dared not in the circumstances entirely disregard him, so he put up with his presence at the council table without confirming him in any office.

When on 4 May Montgomery's terms for unconditional surrender were discussed, Himmler's views were aired along with those of Doenitz's other advisers. He felt that the troops in Norway should be surrendered to Sweden to save them from captivity in Russia, and that some concessions might be gained if an offer were made to surrender peaceably the many places outside Germany still held by German troops. Schellenberg, resolutely travelling between Sweden, Denmark and Germany in his efforts to obtain agreement to a peaceful resolution of the German occupation of the Scandinavian countries, turned not to Himmler but to Doenitz and Schwerin-Krosigk when he at length arrived at five o'clock that afternoon after a fearful journey from Copenhagen. The following day, 5 May, he left again for Denmark, saying goodbye to Himmler, in whom he was by now no longer interested.

On 5 May Himmler gathered his own leaders and advisers around him, including S.S. Obergruppenführer Ohlendorff of the Security Office, S.S. Obergruppenführer von Weyrsch of the Secret Police and S.S. Obergruppenführer von Herff, a general of the *Waffen* S.S.; Brandt was also there, as was Gebhardt, who had left his patients at Hohenlychen in the care of the Russians. To them and their colleagues he solemnly recited policies so utterly out of keeping with the situation they can scarcely be credited; only a prolonged blindness to reality through shock can account for them. He, for one, was not going to give up and commit suicide. He would, he said, establish his own S.S. government in Schleswig-Holstein in order to conduct independent peace negotiations with the Western Powers. He then began to distribute new titles to his followers as his partners in founding an entirely new Nazi régime.

Himmler's rejection by Hitler, however, was followed on 6 May by his rejection at the hands of Doenitz, who personally gave Himmler his formal dismissal in writing:

'Dear Herr Reich Minister,
    In view of the present situation, I have decided to dispense with your further assistance as Reich Minister of the Interior and member of the Reich Government, as Commander-in-Chief of the Reserve Army, and as chief of the Police. I now regard all your offices as abolished. I thank you for the service which you have given to the Reich.'

Along with Himmler, Doenitz dismissed Goebbels, who was dead, and other Nazi ministers who still remained like ghosts from an horrific and evil past.[16] He also forbade the continuation of resistance by diehard Nazis of the S.S.

But Himmler would not leave. After 6 May he haunted Flensburg along with his staff, his guards and his equipment, a monstrous survivor without a domain. He told Schwerin-Krosigk he would carefully consider his advice, but he still had obstinate dreams of maintaining his individual power. He went to the Nazi Commander of the German forces in Schleswig and Denmark, Field-Marshal Ernst Busch, in the vain hope of finding in him an ally. But Busch only wanted to get the arrangements for his own surrender concluded. So Himmler returned to the headquarters he had set up in Flensburg from which, one by one, his retinue were melting away.

On 8 May he reduced his fleet of cars to four and made a first gesture of self-abrogation by shaving off his moustache. He wondered where he could go in order to escape unwelcome attention. While Ohlendorff advised him to surrender and answer the world's outcry against himself and the S.S., he considered, naturally without reaching any firm decision, whether he should take refuge with his friend the Prince of Waldeck, an autocratic general who had charge of the S.S. establishment on his estate at Arolsen.[17]

At length, on 10 May, Himmler and his remaining entourage left Flensburg and set out for Marne at the Dicksander Koog on the east coast of Schleswig-Holstein.[18] It took them two days to get there, and they slept either out in the open or inside railway stations during the remaining days of their flight to the south. Himmler could think of only two things, how he could have saved his position and bargained with the Western Allies, and what was happening now to his two families in the south.

Eventually four cars reached the mouth of the Elbe, and it proved impossible to take them further; the distance across the water was about five miles. Reluctantly the little group of S.S. refugees, no better off now than hundreds of thousands of Germans wandering homeless on the roads, abandoned their vehicles and crossed the Elbe; they were ferried over the estuary unrecognized in a fishing boat with other refugees for the price of 500 Marks. There was nothing for them to do now but walk, passing the nights in peasant farmsteads and covering a few miles each day on foot. During the next five days they tramped slowly south through Neuhaus to Bremervörde, which they reached on the morning of 21 May. They had travelled in all little more than a hundred miles from Flensburg.

They were a strange contingent. In addition to Kiermaier, the group still included Brandt, Ohlendorf, Karl Gebhardt, *Waffen* S.S. Colonel Werner Grothmann and Major Macher. They had removed the insignia from their uniforms and pretended to be members of the Secret Field Police, a branch of the Gestapo, making their way to Bavaria. Himmler wore a patch over his eye like a pirate and carried a pass that had once belonged to Heinrich Hitzinger, a man whose identity papers Himmler had kept by him after he had been condemned to death by the Peoples' Court in case they might prove useful.

At Bremervörde they realized they needed travel documents to pass through the check-point set up by the British Military Authority. Kiermaier confirmed this with the local District Councillor. They then decided that Kiermaier should apply to the British for these travel permits while another member of their party stood outside to watch the result and warn Himmler if Kiermaier were arrested. Since the Secret Field Police were in any case on the British Army's black list, Kiermaier was kept in custody. When he did not reappear, Himmler and his companions slipped away.

Captain Tom Selvester was in command of 031 Civilian Interrogation Camp, which was based near Lüneburg.[19] Since large numbers of German troops were trying to make their way home, they were constantly being stopped at check-points set up by the British and held as prisoners-of-war while their documents were examined. If there was any doubt about their identities, they were sent on for further questioning to an Interrogation Camp of the kind Captain Selvester controlled. Here they were paraded outside the Commandant's office, and then sent in singly to account for themselves. After this they were searched, and their possessions carefully listed.

It was at two o'clock in the afternoon of 23 May that a convoy arrived at the 031 Interrogation Camp with a party of suspects who had been arrested earlier on at a check-point on a bridge near Bremervörde. After a while the men were paraded as usual, but around four o'clock Captain Selvester was told there were three men in the party who were giving some trouble and were insisting on seeing the officer in charge without delay. Since the prisoners were usually very docile and only too anxious to create a good impression, Captain Selvester's curiosity was immediately aroused, and he ordered these three men to be sent to him one by one. Captain Selvester has described what followed:

'The first man to enter my office was small, ill-looking and shabbily dressed, but he was immediately followed by two other men, both of whom were tall and soldierly looking, one slim, and one well-built. The well-built man walked with a limp. I sensed something unusual, and ordered one of my sergeants to place the two men in close custody, and not to allow anyone to speak to them without my authority. They were then removed from my office, whereupon the small man, who was wearing a black patch over his left eye, removed the patch and put on a pair of spectacles. His identity was at once obvious, and he said, "Heinrich Himmler" in a very quiet voice.'

Captain Selvester immediately placed his office under armed guard, and sent for an officer from the Intelligence Corps to help him. After he had arrived, the two officers asked Himmler to sign his name in order to compare it with a signature they had in their records. Himmler, thinking he was being asked to present them with a souvenir, appeared very reluctant to write his name, but eventually he agreed to do so provided the paper was destroyed immediately after it had been examined.

The next stage was to search the prisoner; in Captain Selvester's own words:

> 'This I carried out personally, handing each item of clothing as it was removed to my sergeant, who re-examined it. Himmler was carrying documents bearing the name of Heinrich Hitzinger, who I think was described as a postman. In his jacket I found a small brass case, similar to a cartridge case, which contained a small glass phial. I recognized it for what it was, but asked Himmler what it contained, and he said, "That is my medicine. It cures stomach cramp." I also found a similar brass case, but without the phial, and came to the conclusion that the phial was hidden somewhere on the prisoner's person. When all Himmler's clothing had been removed and searched, all the orifices of his body were searched, also his hair combed and any likely hiding place examined, but no trace of the phial was found. At this stage he was not asked to open his mouth, as I considered that if the phial was hidden in his mouth and we tried to remove it, it might precipitate some action that would be regretted. I did however send for thick bread and cheese sandwiches and tea, which I offered to Himmler, hoping that I would see if he removed anything from his mouth. I watched him closely, whilst he was eating, but did not notice anything unusual.'

Meanwhile, word had been sent to 2nd Army Headquarters about Himmler's arrest. While Captain Selvester was waiting for senior Intelligence officers to arrive from Luneburg, he offered Himmler a British Army uniform in exchange for the clothes that had been taken from him. This was all that was available, but when Himmler saw what he was required to put on, he refused; it seemed he was afraid he would be photographed in the uniform of the enemy and that the picture would be published. The only clothing he later accepted were a shirt, underpants and socks; so he was given an Army blanket to wrap round his half-clothed body.

Captain Selvester was obsessed by the thought of the missing phial. For the whole of the time Himmler was in his charge, he watched him as closely as possible. He has described the curiosity this strange man roused in him:

> 'During the time Himmler was in my custody he behaved perfectly correctly, and gave me the impression that he realized

things had caught up with him. He was quite prepared to talk, and indeed at times appeared almost jovial. He looked ill when I first saw him, but improved tremendously after a meal and a wash (he was not permitted to shave). He was in my custody for approximately eight hours, and during that time, whilst not being interrogated, asked repeatedly about the whereabouts of his "Adjutants", appearing genuinely worried over their welfare. I found it impossible to believe that he could be the arrogant man portrayed by the press before and during the war.'

Later that evening, around eight o'clock, Colonel Michael Murphy, the Chief of Intelligence on General Montgomery's staff, arrived to interrogate Himmler. He told him that he intended to search him and his bodyguards. But Himmler re-asserted who he was, evidently expecting to receive special treatment. He had, he insisted, a letter for General Montgomery. Colonel Murphy cannot recollect ever seeing this letter.

Apart from the phial found in the lining of his jacket, no other trace of poison was discovered on Himmler's person. Colonel Murphy decided that Himmler should be taken over to Second Army Headquarters. He was taken there by car, a drive of about ten miles, escorted by Colonel Murphy and another Intelligence Officer. That was the last that Captain Selvester saw of him.

Colonel Murphy writes:

'It was clear to me that it was still possible for Himmler to have poison hidden about him, the most obvious places being his mouth and his buttocks. I therefore told him to dress, and wishing to have a medical search conducted, telephoned my second-in-command at my headquarters and told him to get a doctor to stand by at a house I had had prepared for such men as Himmler.'

Himmler was taken to the interrogation centre which had been set up at a house in the Uelznerstrasse, and put in the charge of Sergeant-Major Edwin Austin, who was not told at first the identity of the prisoner. But, according to his own account which he broadcast the following day for the B.B.C., Austin recognized him immediately he saw him standing in the room to which he had been led.[20] He still wore only the army blanket over his shirt and underpants.

Austin, who had previously failed to prevent the S.S. General Pruetzmann from committing suicide when he had crushed a capsule of cyanide between his teeth, was determined not to allow Himmler to commit suicide by the same means. He pointed at once to a couch in the room.

'That's your bed. Get undressed', he ordered, speaking in German.

Himmler did not seem to understand. He stared at Austin, and then spoke to the interpreter.

'He doesn't know who I am', he said.

'Yes I do', said Austin. 'You're Himmler. Nevertheless, that's your bed. Get undressed.'

Himmler still tried to stare him out, but the sergeant asserted his authority and stared back at him. Himmler dropped his eyes and gave in. He sat down on the couch and started to take off his underpants.

Then Colonel Murphy and Captain C. J. L. Wells, an army doctor, came in to carry out the routine inspection of their prisoner. They still suspected that Himmler was carrying poison. When he had stripped, they searched all over his body – his ears, his armpits, his hair, his buttocks. Then the doctor ordered him to open his mouth, and, in the words of Colonel Murphy, 'immediately he saw a small black knob sticking out between a gap in the teeth on the right hand side lower jaw'.

'Come nearer the light', said the doctor. 'Open your mouth.'

He put two fingers into the prisoner's mouth. It was then that Himmler suddenly turned his head aside and bit down hard on the doctor's fingers.

'He's done it', shouted the doctor.

Both the colonel and the sergeant jumped on Himmler and threw him to the ground, turning him on his stomach to prevent him swallowing. The doctor held him by the throat, trying to force him to spit out the poison. The struggle to preserve his life by using emetics and a stomach-pump lasted a quarter of an hour; every method of artificial respiration was used. 'He died,' said the sergeant, 'and when he died we threw a blanket over him, and left him.'[21]

Two days later, Himmler was buried in an unmarked place near Lüneburg; his body had been wrapped in army blankets and wound in camouflage netting secured with telephone wire. Sergeant-Major Austin, who in civilian life had been a dustman, dug him a secret grave.

# Appendix A:
# Adolf Eichmann's Account of Himmler

Prior to his trial in Israel, Adolf Eichmann voluntarily submitted
to a very thorough examination, during the course of which hundreds
of documents (most of them photostats of affidavits and of R.S.H.A.
files) were sifted and discussed. The examination started on 29 May
1960 and continued in almost daily sessions to 15 January 1961; 76
tapes produced 3,564 pages of typescript, a verbatim account of
the entire interrogation which, through the courtesy of the Israeli
Embassy in London, we were given the opportunity to study.

Eichmann proved eager to co-operate with his interrogators; he
became as obsequious as he must once have been to his former
superiors. He was proud of his punctiliousness in obeying orders, and
he delighted in describing filing systems and other office routine in
considerable detail. He claimed he had originally joined the S.S.
during 1931–2 (he was not sure of the exact date) through the influence of Kaltenbrunner, whom he had known well since childhood.
Later, he had applied to join the S.D. and was appointed a clerk in
the 'Freemason Museum'; subsequently, as we have seen, he became a specialist in Jewish affairs.

During the interrogation, Eichmann emphasized again and again
that it was Hitler who ordered the physical destruction of the Jews,
while Himmler was charged with issuing the necessary orders.
Eichmann first describes Himmler (pp. 38–9) as 'always ready to
oblige the Führer, liable to get bogged down in petty detail, but
then again, quite impulsively, signing some far-reaching decree.'
On p. 146 Eichmann reverts to Himmler's impulsiveness in giving
these far-reaching orders whenever he was struck by some idea; as
often as not such orders would be passed on to any officer who
happened to be with him at the time and later held up by red tape
as soon as they had reached the appropriate official channels.

Eichmann mentions Himmler's aversion to seeing fingers stained with nicotine. Officers ordered into Himmler's presence were advised to use the lemon and pumice-stone available in the washroom of Himmler's special train. Anyone failing to do so risked getting a three or six months' *Rauchverbot*; this meant instant dismissal from the S.S. if he were caught smoking during that period.

In Minsk Eichmann witnessed the mass-shooting of Jews straight into the ditch, and a little later (p. 240) he claims that Heydrich out of sheer bravado gave orders to kill Jews who were already being killed by Globocnik's orders. Heydrich said, 'I herewith authorize you to submit a further 150,000 Jews to the final solution [*der Endlösung zuzuführen*].' Eichmann in fact seemed uncertain whether the figure might not have been 250,000 in this case. In the autumn of 1941 he was sent for by Himmler, along with Mueller, to report about these matters (p. 263). The interview took a mere five minutes.

Eichmann has much to say about the S.S. euphemisms, such as 'final solution' and 'special treatment'. Even at the notorious conference at Wannsee (see page 127) direct references to killing were avoided, Heydrich favouring the term *Arbeitseinsatz im Osten* (labour assignment in the East). Another point frequently mentioned by Eichmann (for example, on pages 135–6, 1020, 2028, 2167) is the fact that Himmler considered the camp at Theresienstadt very much his own domain, insisting on giving all the necessary orders for this place personally. As previously mentioned, he was very keen on maintaining the myth of Theresienstadt as the *Altersghetto*, suggesting it was a place where elderly Jews could live out their lives in peace and comfort, and was very angry whenever news leaked through of inmates from Theresienstadt being sent to the gas-ovens in Auschwitz and other extermination camps. Yet since the camp's maximum capacity was 10,000, he did nothing to stop hundreds of thousands of victims from Theresienstadt being 'evacuated'. He merely insisted on the strictest secrecy so as not to offend world opinion.

At all times Himmler was specially interested in 'prominent' prisoners; hence (p. 2608) we find him giving special orders for Fray Glück, the sister of La Guardia, the Mayor of New York, to be taken out of a mass transport and to be transferred to the camp where Léon Blum, Odette Churchill and other important prisoners were held.

On pp. 2456 et seq. Eichmann shows his surprise at documentary evidence of Himmler having devoted much time during the difficult years of 1943–4 to such petty details as the question of two or three Jews in one case and five or six in another being exempted from extermination on account of their expertise in metallurgy and diamonds respectively, experts in that field being required for the armaments industry and for the production of the highest grade of Knight's Cross.

There are several references (such as those on pp. 1249, 1290 and 1318) to Himmler's orders of October 1941 stopping any emigration of Jews, 'except in isolated instances beneficial for the Reich' (which refers to Jews wealthy enough to pay a minimum of 100,000 Swiss francs). In July 1944 Himmler issued an order that the emigration of certain Hungarian Jews to Palestine must be stopped 'because they are biologically potent, so their survival is not desirable in the interests of the Reich.' But in April 1942 (p. 478) Himmler wrote to the Chief of the S.D. stating that while the Führer's orders for the 'final solution' must be carried out ruthlessly, he wanted those Jews and Jewesses still capable of work to be exempted for the time being and set to work in the concentration camps. In July 1942 neither Eichmann not his chief Mueller dared to decide about the fate of French Jewish children still cared for by French welfare organizations (p. 701–2). Mueller asked Himmler for a decision, and the Reichsführer's personal order came for 'sending all of them East', that is, having them killed. On pp. 660 *et seq.* there are details about Himmler's personal orders for a *Grossabschiebung* (mass removal) of French Jews eastwards for the 'final solution'.

The last time Eichmann saw Himmler was during the spring of 1945, when Himmler told him that in the case of future negotiations with Eisenhower he wanted some 200 to 300 prominent Jews 'for hostage purposes'. Eichmann was to collect them in various camps, and see Gauleiter Hofer in Innsbruck about allocating some evacuated villages for them. Eichmann dutifully reported the Reichsführer's order to Kaltenbrunner, who, according to Eichmann, 'showed little interest, since nothing really mattered any longer'.

# Appendix B:
# The Frankfurt Trial 1964-5

By the time this book is published, the Auschwitz Trial at Frankfurt will have been in session for almost a year, and yet be nowhere near its end. Similar trials (such as that of Eichmann's associates, Hunsche and Krumey, in Budapest) have been or are running concurrently in Frankfurt and elsewhere, while others are being prepared.

The long delay in holding these trials by the German Public Prosecutors is due to the fact that the relevant files have only been handed over in recent years by the Allies, who took possession of them after the war. The Public Prosecutor's Office specially set up to deal with German war crimes only began to function round 1957 in Ludwigsburg, near Stuttgart. Another cause of delay has been that many of the men now being indicted have lived in hiding using false names: others have fled abroad, and negotiations for their extradition have been prolonged – some, like those concerning the notorious Dr Mengele, with little hope of success.

Twenty-three men finally stood in the dock at Frankfurt in 1964. Evidence has been produced which shows that they have been guilty of the most appalling crimes. The character of the men employed by Himmler and his staff is revealed, for example, in the behaviour of Oswald Kaduk, whose noted fondness for children extended to issuing Jewish children in the camp with toy balloons (an 'organized' issue, to quote from the terms of the evidence) before they were 'squirted' (*abspritzen*) with a phenol injection in the heart at the rate of ten children a minute. 'Papa Kaduk', as he was later known because of his love for children, had worked as a male nurse after the war until his identification and arrest.

When a former S.S. Judge was heard as a witness, he appeared both elegant and at ease as he enunciated his slick, evasive answers to the questions put to him by the President and the Prosecutor, reviving once again the verbiage of death: 'special treatment', 'desettle-ment', 'the general line' and even 'sovereign acts beyond the reach of the judiciary', all S.S. terms for murder. Then suddenly one of the less intelligent men in the dock, Stefan Baretzki, asked leave to speak. It was obvious he could no longer stand this evasion of the truth. The President gave him leave to come forward. We had to do the dirty-work, said Baretzki in effect, while these men talked, and when we complained about being ordered to kill children we were told to be silent about something we could not understand, and obey our orders. He then walked back to his seat.

This outburst reveals the process of Nazi genocide. The men who carried out the killings were encouraged not to think what they were doing, but to accept it as a necessary mission for the Führer and the German people. After this, the readiness to be tough, ruthless and efficient in the destruction of people regarded as subhuman was the virtue most to be valued in those chosen to carry out their Führer's orders.

# *Notes*

The primary published sources to which we have constantly turned during the
preparation of this book are Gerald Reitlinger's *The Final Solution* and *The S.S.*,
*The Kersten Memoirs*, and *The Schellenberg Memoirs*, and also the transcript of
the Trial of the Major War Criminals in Nuremberg; the edition of the latter
referred to below as I.M.T. is that published by H.M.S.O. in London in twenty-
two volumes. We have also drawn extensively on the documents used in evidence
at the trial in the edition in German published in Nuremberg, and in the American
edition in English known as *Nazi Conspiracy and Aggression*, referred to as
N.C.A. below. Important secondary sources include Willi Frischauer's *Himmler*,
Charles Wighton's *Heydrich*, H. R. Trevor-Roper's *The Last Days of Hitler*,
Rudolf Hoess's *Commandant of Auschwitz*, Edward Crankshaw's *Gestapo*, and
Mitscherlich's and Mielke's *The Death Doctors*.

Throughout this book we have drawn on material from the copious files
originating from Himmler's headquarters and preserved now variously at the
German Federal Archives in Koblenz, the Institut für Zeitgeschichte in Munich,
the Berlin Document Centre, the Tracing Centre in Arolsen, the Rijksinstituut
voor Oorlog Documentatie in Amsterdam, and the Wiener Library in London.

In these Notes the authors are referred to individually by their initials, R.M.
and H.F.

CHAPTER I

We are grateful to Gebhard Himmler, the elder brother of Heinrich, who was
our principal source of information for this initial period. We have also studied
the microfilm of the surviving portions of Himmler's early diaries kindly loaned
us by the Library of the Hoover Institution at Stanford in California, and
consulted the most valuable analysis of these diaries made by Werner T. Angress
and Bradley F. Smith in the *Journal of Modern History*, Vol. 31, No. 3, Sept.
1959. The quotations from the diaries are in some instances derived from their
translations, but in most cases we have used our own.

Other sources of information concerning Himmler's youth include evidence
from men who knew him as a student, in particular Dr Riss, head of the Erding
law court, and Colonel Saradeth of Munich.

1. During Himmler's infancy the family home was frequently changed. Himmler
   was born in a second-floor apartment at 2 Hildegardstrasse, Munich. In
   March the following year the family moved to a comfortable apartment
   over Liebig's chemists' establishment in the Liebigstrasse, a pleasant street
   in the city. From March 1902–4 the Himmlers were in Passau, a town near

Munich, after which they returned to Munich and lived until 1913 at 86 Amalienstrasse. It was in this house, therefore, that Himmler's boyhood was spent. From 1913–19 the family was in Landshut; from 1919–22 in Ingolstadt; then back again in Munich from 1922–30, when Himmler's father retired at the age of 65. He died five years later, in 1935; Himmler's mother died in 1941.

2. These are, of course, German pounds. Himmler's weight at birth was 3.7 kilos.

3. Diary-writing was not common among the boys of the period, but Himmler was no doubt encouraged to keep one because his father was a meticulous diarist. A list of books noted by Himmler as read during his last years at school include Thomas Mann's *The Magic Mountain*, and works by Dinter and Bierbaum, which put the case both for and against the Teutonic ideal. Strangely enough, Himmler makes no comment about any of these books, merely listing their titles.

4. He made this claim to Count Bernadotte. See *The Fall of the Curtain*, p. 57.

5. These recollections are principally those of Dr Riss and Col Saradeth. Dr Riss was a member of the Apollo.

6. Dr George W. F. Hallgarten was later to emigrate from Germany to the United States where he works as an historian and sociologist. He published a pamphlet in German giving his recollections of Himmler at the school in Munich at which his father taught. He confirms Himmler's diligence, his primness of nature, and his pathetic determination to succeed in sport and gymnastics, for neither of which he had any aptitude. For example, he could not complete a single 'pull-up' at the cross-bar. The school served as a preparatory establishment for the Pagerie, a school reserved exclusively for the sons of the Bavarian aristocracy who were eligible for service as pages in the Bavarian Court. Hallgarten claims that Himmler felt great resentment that he was not eligible by birth to attend the Pagerie. This however has been denied to H. F. by both Herr von Manz and the Baron Waldenfels, who knew the Himmler family and attended the Pagerie. For Prof. Hallgarten's recollections see *Mein Mitschüler Himmler* (Wiener Library).

7. See Note 22, p. 211 of the article by Angress and Smith mentioned above.

8. Each state in Germany had, and still has, its own provincial parliament for the conduct of local affairs, to which deputies are appointed from the parties after local elections. The Reichstag represented, and still represents under its new name the Bundestag, the federal parliament, dealing with national policy and legislation. Deputies were elected to the Reichstag (as now to the Bundestag) on the basis of proportional representation, the various parties selecting their own deputies to fill the number of seats due to them after each election.

9. Gebhard Himmler recollects that the motor-cycle was a second-hand Swedish machine of which Himmler was inordinately proud.

10. We drew this conclusion from evidence originally given us by Otto Strasser when he was interviewed by H.F. in connection with our book, *Doctor Goebbels*.

11. See Kurt G. W. Ludecke, *I Knew Hitler*, p. 267.

12. See *The Early Goebbels Diaries*, pp. 78, 94, 116.

13. Otto Strasser told the story to H.F. that Himmler came into his office shortly before his marriage and solemnly admitted that he had lost his virginity. Strasser congratulated him. According to Gebhard Himmler, it was Marga's blonde hair that was her outstanding attraction for Himmler. Himmler's first meeting with her at Berchtesgaden came about through his clumsiness in pouring melting snow all over her frock when removing his Tyrolean hat with too generous a flourish as he entered the hotel lobby. His apologies led to making her acquaintance, and this in turn to long walks and longer conversations.

14. The initials S.S. also stood for Saal-Schutz, that is, 'hall protection'. This is a reminder that the original duty of the S.S. was to act as 'chuckers-out' at political meetings.

*Additional Note*

Among the superfluity of personal papers meticulously preserved by Himmler and now held in the Federal Archives, there is an early essay written by Himmler as a very young man and revealing his idea on the economic and ideological aspects of agriculture. The date of this essay cannot be exactly determined, but according to the style and content there can be no doubt that he wrote it while studying at Munich. This impression is confirmed by his brother Gebhard. The essay is naïvely idealistic and visualizes what Himmler regarded at that time as a model farming community, entirely self-supporting, that is, living on the fruits of the soil and by their own labour, and having no use for money within the community itself. Money would only be required to repay the initial cost of machinery and other capital expenditure, and this would be obtained from the sale of surplus products from the land. When writing at this time Himmler deliberately used archaic terms such as *Meister, Geselle* and *Lehrling* for the hierarchy of his community; he advocated chastity and a deep communion with the soil, together with the revival of ancient folklore, folk-dancing, traditional music and so on. It is interesting to compare his concept for community living on the land with the economy and ideology of the contemporary Israeli kibbutz.

CHAPTER II

We are grateful to Frau Lina Heydrich, widow of the S.S. leader, for giving us facts concerning her husband's early career and initial meeting with Himmler.

1. Darré's conception of inferior races extended to the Latin peoples, Negroes and Asiatics. When the Rome-Berlin axis was widened to include the Japanese, this caused Himmler and the other racialists considerable embarrassment.

2. The text of the code appeared as document PS-2284 at I.M.T.

3. The word *Sippe* is a deliberate archaism which has no exact English equivalent, the nearest word being possibly 'clan'. In using it, Himmler was anxious to stress the Teutonic ideals of ancestry.

4. In the evidence she gave H.F., Frau Heydrich denies the familiar story that the girl with whom Heydrich was previously in love was with child by him. She also denies that Heydrich had any Jewish blood in his ancestry; even so, the suspicion of it hung over him throughout his career in the Party. See also Chapter IV, note 3.

5. This account of Heydrich's introduction to the Nazi Party and to Himmler was given us by Lina Heydrich. It is supported by Werner Best in evidence he gave H.F.

6. Frau Heydrich has stressed how extremely poorly paid her husband was, as well as other S.S. leaders. Since neither she nor Heydrich had significant private means, they lived very humbly. Frau Heydrich's family gave them furniture and linen. They could afford no servants for several years. Frau Heydrich has also given us a number of interesting sidelights on Himmler's character at this time. He insisted that she address him as Reichsführer, and not as Herr Himmler, which she thought more appropriate for a woman. She found him fussy, and still remembers with some amusement how, when he came to stay at her house, he carefully hung up his face-cloth to dry, and that it had a red rose embroidered upon it. He refused to eat potatoes, rice or spaghetti.

7. The term *Junker* is mostly misunderstood outside Germany. It is an archaic term implying descent from noble stock, an *élite* class. A *Junkerschule*, therefore, is an institution for the upper class, or so Himmler implied.

8. Nevertheless, Himmler seemed at first to welcome the idea of the return of Roehm, his former commanding officer, and not to see it as a threat to his own position. Roehm and Himmler corresponded while Roehm was in Latin America; during 1930 Himmler wrote to him at least twice, complimenting him on his escape from danger in campaigns against the Indians, and joking about him being an old hand at revolutions. He also urged him to raise money for the S.S. among the wealthy Latin Americans of German descent and said how he looked forward to their future co-operation on Roehm's return to Germany. The letters are preserved at the Federal Archives at Koblenz.

9. Herr Riss, a friend of Himmler during his student days, told H.F. that when he met Himmler during 1931 and complimented him on becoming a Reichstag deputy, Himmler merely laughed at the 'talking shop' and claimed the Nazi deputies were only there to make use of the occasion for their own ends. What he was proud of, he said, was being Reichsführer S.S.

10. See Lüdecke, op. cit., p. 433.

11. See Gerald Reitlinger, *The S.S.* p. 27, William L. Shirer, *Rise and Fall of the Third Reich* pp. 144–5, and Nuremberg Case XI, transcript of judgment 28, 440–7; 28, 599; and 28, 794. Keppler was later to support Himmler's so-called research into Aryan history by forming a circle of businessmen-patrons called 'Friends of the Reichsführer S.S.'. Himmler is stated by Schroeder himself to have accompanied Hitler when he attended the famous Hitler-Schroeder meeting. See Alan Bullock, *Hitler* (Edition, 1952), p. 220 and Schroeder's testimony at Nuremberg in N.C.A. II, 922–4.

12. I.M.T. XX, p. 246.

13. Later, in 1936, he was to become head of the uniformed police (O.R.P.O.) and, after the assassination of Heydrich in Prague in 1942, Heydrich's successor as Reich Protector.

14. This and subsequent accounts of Hoess's extraordinary career and relationship to Himmler are taken largely from his own autobiography written in prison after the war – *Commandant of Auschwitz*.

15. See I.M.T. II, p. 361.

16. See I.M.T. documents PS-778; also Trial II, pp. 371–2. And compare Shirer, op. cit., p. 272.

17. Himmler worked fast; he became Chief of Political Police in Bavaria in April 1933, then in Hamburg the following October, and in Mecklenburg, Lübeck, Wuertemberg, Baden, Hessen, Thüringen and Amhalt in December. In January 1934, he assumed the same office in Oldenburg, Bremen, Saxony and Prussia. (Taken from the official file listing Himmler's offices preserved at the Berlin Document Centre.)

CHAPTER III

1. Gebhard Himmler explained to H.F. that the boy Gerhard, who was a year or so older than Gudrun, was never formally adopted by his brother. He was the son of an S.S. officer called von Ahe who had been killed before the war, and he was brought up in Himmler's household.

2. The estrangement was neither formally recognized nor privately acknowledged, even when Himmler much later set up a second household with his mistress Hedwig, who bore him the two children of whom he became the legal guardian. His love for his wife Marga cooled after a period of years, and his visits to Gmund became less and less frequent, though he was always deeply concerned over the welfare of Gudrun. Himmler and his wife continued to conduct the mere business of marriage throughout the rest of their lives, though Marga tacitly accepted Himmler's relationship with Hedwig and all affection died between them. Marga's term of address for her husband in her letters became *Mein Lieber Guter*, an untranslateable phrase which combines a kind of old-fashioned feminine effusiveness, with possessive sentimentality. As we shall see, Himmler's relations with Marga's interfering sister Bertha became very strained. It should be added that on rare occasions Himmler did allow Marga to accompany him on state occasions. For example, he took her to Italy; it is typical of him that, on this occasion, he insisted that all her expenses should be charged to his private account.

3. Himmler's good relations with Roehm rapidly changed when his former superior officer stood in his way. It should, however, be realized that what finally drove Hitler to discard Roehm, of whom he was genuinely fond, was the implacable opposition to him and the S.A. that had developed among the very people whose support he felt at this stage he most needed – the generals and the industrialists. Hitler's promise to Eden to reduce the S.A. fitted in well with this policy. These considerations, and not solely the pressure brought to bear on him by Göring and Himmler led to Hitler's decision to strike down Roehm and destroy the influence of the S.A. For

Frick's affidavit see N.C.A. V, pp. 654–5. See also Reitlinger, *S.S.* p. 62 for further evidence from Roehm's legal adviser that Himmler twisted every circumstance he could in order to incriminate Roehm in Hitler's eyes.

4. Gisevius, the former Gestapo official who joined the resistance movement and whose book, *To the Bitter End*, is one of the most revealing and colourful sources of information about the Nazi régime, claims to have seen the report on this incident prepared by Daluege on orders from Himmler. Daluege was much more amused than concerned about the hole in the windscreen, which his report claimed was made by a stone thrown up by a passing car. This explanation was also given to H.F. by Bodenschatz, who was present at the ceremony. According to Gisevius, Himmler, 'white, trembling, excited', held up the interment while he insisted that forty Communists should be shot at once as a reprisal; later he had two S.A. brigade leaders executed for making an attempt on his life. Frischauer, in his biography of Himmler (p. 64) is inaccurate in claiming that Himmler was travelling to Carinhall in the same car as Hitler after their conference on Roehm in Berlin, and that he was actually wounded in the arm.

5. I.M.T. XX, p. 249.

6. This was Papen's own view as he expressed it to H.F.

7. I.M.T. XII, p. 278.

8. The oath demanded of the S.S. officers was more exacting: for example, the oath for a Lieutenant-General ran: 'Being an S.S. Lieutenant-General, I undertake to see to the best of my ability that, with complete disregard of whatever merits his parents or ancestors may have, only such men are to be accepted into the S.S. who comply fully with its high standard. I will see to this even if it means rejecting my own sons or daughters or those of my *Sippe*. I further undertake to see to it that in every year one quarter of S.S. candidates consists of men who are not sons of S.S. men. I swear to live up to these obligations in loyalty to our Führer Adolf Hitler and to the honour of my ancestors: so help me God.' The text of this oath is preserved in the Federal Archive at Koblenz. It is significant because it reveals Himmler's deep distrust of aristocrats exploiting the 'merits of their ancestors'.

9. Schellenberg's *Memoirs*, p. 10.

10. See I.M.T. III, p. 130.

11. A considerable file of correspondence survives in the Federal Archive dealing with the coats-of-arms the S.S. officers were expected to produce for formal emplacement at Wewelsburg. Since for the most part S.S. men were of middle-class origin, they had some difficulty in concocting 'authentic' coats-of-arms to satisfy Himmler's Teutonic snobbery. See below, Chap. IV, Note 12.

12. A letter is preserved in the Federal Archive in which a schoolboy called Fritz Brüggemann wrote in January 1937 directly to Himmler for an authoritative statement as to whether or not Jesus was a Jew. Himmler sent the answer through a member of his staff: 'Most certainly, dear boy, Jesus was *not* a Jew.' Himmler favoured adapting Christian ceremonies and festivals to Teutonic forms – for example, ceremonies for christening and

burial stressing the affinity between the individual and the nation. He turned Christmas into a Teutonic feast, and he gave a Teutonic form of candlestick, called a *Jul-Leuchter*, as his normal Christmas present.

13. *Ahnenerbe* first appears as an official organization in an order signed by Himmler at Gmund on 9 August 1937. A record of this is held at the archives at Amsterdam.

14. Hoess, the future commandant of Auschwitz, records that Himmler held 'a grand inspection' of Dachau in 1936, and adds that 'Himmler was in the best of spirits because the whole inspection has gone off without a hitch. Dachau . . . is also going well.' Himmler asked after Hoess's family, and shortly afterwards promoted him an S.S. Second Lieutenant. Following his usual practice at these inspections, Himmler picked out a few prisoners and interviewed them in front of the Gauleiters and high Nazi officials who accompanied him.

15. For Frick's attempts at intervention, see I.M.T. XII, pp. 203–6, 266.

16. Höttl, Behrends and Schellenberg.

17. The police under Himmler were divided into the uniformed police (O.R.P.O.) and the secret, plain-clothes police (S.I.P.O.). Himmler's security police were placed under Heydrich, and embodied the Gestapo, their colleagues in *Kripo* (the criminal police, or C.I.D.) and the Security Service, the S.D., which was still a Party, not a state, organization. In September, a further stage was reached in merging the S.S. and the Police by making S.S. leaders of each district the Chief of Police for their areas, and the operations of the Gestapo, which were still nominally confined to Prussia, extended to the whole of Germany. It was not until two years later, however, in June 1938, that all members of the Security police had to become members of the S.S., so closing the gap in Himmler's dual control in the state. (See Crankshaw, *Gestapo*, p. 90.)

18. In his speech, Himmler described the strategy of the Saxon duke called Henry the Fowler, who became Heinrich I, founder of the German state. He made a pact with the Hungarians, who threatened his newly-formed kingdom, in order to give himself time to prepare to resist them. Himmler did not share the normal German admiration for Charlemagne, whom he regarded as representative of an inferior race.

19. It is necessary in connection with the *Lebensborn* movement to make it quite clear that the homes were no more than large maternity establishments to care for mothers some of whom were bearing legitimate and some illegitimate children. The rumour soon got around that they were stud farms where suitable men and women were mated in order to breed even more suitable children. This was not so, though there are records of women applying to the *Lebensborn* homes saying that they 'wanted to give the Führer a child'. One of the official replies to such women reads: 'We are *not* a matrimonial agency.' The *Lebensborn* movement was officially founded 'by the will of the Reichsführer S.S.' in 1936, and registered in Munich on 24 March 1938. For further details of *Lebensborn*, see the Bulletin of the Wiener Library, July 1962, p. 52. Cp. Chap. IV, Note 13.

20. In 1944 Himmler was to be formally recognized as the father and official guardian of his illegitimate son and daughter. See Chap IV, Note 14. Himmler's relationship with Hedwig, who was known affectionately as Häschen, amounted to a form of bigamous marriage, and there is no doubt that she represented the lasting love of Himmler's life. Frau Heydrich told H.F. that Himmler's whole manner changed when he developed this relationship with Hedwig; he became for a while more relaxed and human. As a result of her situation, Hedwig lived a very enclosed life, but she was both liked and respected by all who came in contact with her. At one stage, Himmler wanted to divorce his wife and marry Hedwig, but she refused to let him do so for Gudrun's sake. In conversation with H.F., Schwerin-Krosigk, Hitler's Minister of Finance, reported that Hanna Reitsch, the famous Nazi woman aviator, had told him of her experiences immediately after the war when she was confined for questioning along with Hedwig. Himmler's mistress told her how much she had loved Himmler, and how good he had been to her. Hedwig is now married and wishes to forget the past; her two children by Himmler were given other surnames.

21. The five 'required' sports which caused so much trouble for the older men who were expected to qualify in them, just as Himmler desired to do, were sprinting, swimming, long-distance running, the high or long jump, and putting the shot or javelin. Achieving a sports badge was made obligatory for all S.S. men, and Himmler, after months of training mostly at the *Junkerschule* at Bad-Toelz, had to be deliberately deceived by his subordinates that he had in fact passed the necessary tests. When men, such as Baldur von Schirach, regarded as valuable over-strained themselves to fulfil Himmler's sports requirements Hitler became annoyed with the idea.

22. See Kersten's *Memoirs*, pp. 294, 306.

23. See N.C.A. IV, pp. 616–34 for the text of this speech.

24. In our book *Hermann Göring*, we followed Wheeler-Bennett in his *Nemesis* in placing this challenge as being sent *after* the hearing. It seems more likely, according to Reitlinger, that the challenge was sent during February. The story of the challenge came originally from Otto John.

25. *Memoirs*, p. 32.

26. It is possible that Eichmann was already in Vienna. See Reitlinger, *The Final Solution*, pp. 25–6, and Lord Russell, *The Trial of Adolf Eichmann*, p. 186.

27. During the winter of 1938–9, Himmler formed two companies, *Deutsche Ausruestungswerke* and *Deutsche Erd- und Steinwerke* for this purpose. They were administered by the business management department of the S.S. under Oswald Pohl, who had been a Paymaster-Captain in the Navy. See Reitlinger, *The S.S.*, p. 257.

28. See Henderson, *Failure of a Mission*, p. 111.

29. See I.M.T. III, pp. 191–2.

### CHAPTER IV

1. Gisevius in *To the Bitter End*, Kersten in the *Memoirs*, and Hoettl in *The Secret Front*, pp. 44 et seq.

2. After the war, H.F. interviewed Madame Kitty in Berlin to obtain further details of this exclusive and specialized establishment. By no means all the women who worked there were high-class professional prostitutes; some were young society women who volunteered for service, posing as patriots. Kitty told H.F. that though Ribbentrop was a frequent visitor, Goebbels only came once; he exuded charm, viewed a lesbian display, but declined to patronize any of the girls. Neither Himmler nor Göring thought fit to visit a place of this kind.

3. In conversation with H.F., Werner Best, who also had to work closely with Heydrich, confirmed his insatiable ambition, his intelligence and his ruthless energy. He is certain Heydrich aimed to supplant Himmler, and even possibly Hitler himself. He deliberately set out to terrorize his subordinates, and he was always making sarcastic remarks to Best on account of his legal training. However, he made something of a confidant of Best and spoke to him on one occasion about his supposed Jewish ancestry. There was, said Heydrich, a man called Süss among his forebears, but he claimed, quite reasonably, that Süss was not an exclusively Jewish name. (See also Chapter II, note 4). Wolff's view of Heydrich given to H.F. during an interview, is that he was able and efficient, but a most unpleasant man.

4. Frau Heydrich has denied to H.F. that she ever had intimate relations with Schellenberg. Nor does Schellenberg himself claim as much. No doubt it was one of Heydrich's sadistic exercises to try to make it seem that his wife was unfaithful and his subordinate guilty. Though at the start of his career, Schellenberg may have been associated with interrogations involving torture, he managed after the war to dissociate himself completely from the worst excesses of the S.S. and Gestapo. Nevertheless, when he was sentenced in 1949 to six years' imprisonment dating from 1945, he was regarded by his judges as involved in the execution without trial of a group of Russian prisoners. He was released in 1951 because of his ill-health, and died of a kidney disease in Turin in 1952. He began to write his lengthy memoirs while in hiding in Sweden after the war, and resumed them again as soon as he was released. His wife negotiated their posthumous publication in England in 1956, and H.F. read the original typescript which ran to some 3,000 pages. The memoirs as published have had much inessential and repetitive material deleted.

5. Not to be confused with R.U.S.H.A., the original S.S. marriage office, which was later also concerned with kidnapping children of Nordic blood for German upbringing.

6. For the origin of the *Einsatzgruppen* in Heydrich's S.D. offices as early as 1938, see Crankshaw's *Gestapo*, pp. 146–52, Reitlinger's *S.S.*, p. 126 et seq,. and Shirer, op. cit., pp. 958–64.

7. Himmler was frequently forced to discipline the greed for land of these new German settlers, uprooted from their homes and anxious to win the most they could out of their new circumstances.

8. See Cohen, op. cit. pp. 106–8. The figure of 60,000 was Brack's own estimate for Germany. The Czechoslovak War Crimes Commission estimated some 275,000 mental patients and old people exterminated. For the details of procedure in Germany, see *The Death Doctors*, p. 236 et seq.

9. See Shirer's *Berlin Diary*, pp. 569 et seq.

10. See *The Death Doctors*, p. 265.

11. Himmler's famous edict exhorting S.S. men to procreate before leaving for the front was issued in printed form on 28 October 1939. 'Let us never forget that victory by our swords and the blood shed by our soldiers make no sense at all unless they are succeeded by the victory of our children and the occupation of new earth', said Himmler. Throughout the war, Himmler was deeply concerned about the sex relations of his S.S. men. Documents held at the Federal Archive at Koblenz show that in 1942 he would only permit sexual relations between S.S. men and Polish women provided the women were officially assigned to a brothel and that there was no question of procreation or emotional entanglement. This is stated in a secret order signed by Himmler and dated 30 June 1942. On 7 March the following year, he signed a further top secret order given by the Führer himself that any S.S. man caught in homosexual activities with another S.S. man would be liable to the death penalty. On the other hand, an increase in the number of illegitimate children of the right stock was favoured; there could not be too many of them. But orphaned children of racially undesirable parents were, by an order signed by Himmler on 1 June 1943, to be taught 'obedience, diligence and unconditional submission to their German masters', and given only sufficient low-grade education to make them useful as unskilled labour. Himmler also developed very early on a horror of venereal disease developing among his men, primarily because it might bring on impotence. Everything was done to encourage men with the disease to submit themselves for early treatment.

12. Himmler did not consider designs for his own Reichsführer S.S. seal until the beginning of 1944, when drawings were submitted to him for both a large and a small seal combining the Reich eagle, the S.S. death's head, oakleaves and gothic lettering. See above Chapter III, Note 11.

13. The files concerning *Lebensborn* held at Arolsen, now the centre of the International Red Cross Tracing Service for Lost Persons, show that these homes were a constant source of trouble, gossip and scandal. The women, for example, complained officially that their excess milk was siphoned off and that this might spoil the shape of their breasts and make them less desirable. There was trouble over the chocolate allocations, about the medical care, about the way the women were addressed (*Frau* was the rule), about artificial insemination, about gratuities for especially prolific mothers, and endless fuss about illicit relations and racial impurity. (Compare Chapter III, Note 18). Underlying everything was Himmler's sentimental attachment to blond children. On one occasion he excused a man who had blocked his way on the road because his car was full of beautiful, fair-haired progeny.

14. In order to regularize as far as possible his fatherhood of Hedwig's children, Himmler in a legal document dated 12 September 1944 acknowledged himself their father and became co-guardian with Hedwig of the boy Helge, then aged two, and the baby girl, Nanette Dorothea. Nanette's birth certificate, dated 20 July, names Himmler as the father, and adds that he had

already appeared before an S.S. judge on 25 June to claim official recognition of his paternity.

15. Schellenberg is exaggerating when he claims that Himmler actually lived with Hedwig. Rather, he set her and her children up in their own establishment and visited them just as he continued to visit his wife and daughter in Gmund. Nor need he have gone short of money with which to maintain these households. It was only his own meticulous honesty in matters of finance that prevented him from using expense-accounts, let alone accumulating ill-gotten wealth like the other Nazi leaders. He lived strictly within his official income.

16. For the text of this speech at Metz, see N.C.A. IV, pp. 553–8.

17. Many of these were used in evidence during the Doctors' Trial, and are quoted in *The Death Doctors*, from which our own quotations are derived.

18. See *Ribbentrop Memoirs*, pp. 81–2.

19. See I.M.T. VI, p. 179.

20. N.C.A. V, p. 341.

21. See I.M.T. IV, pp, 29 and 36. For Wolff, compare Frischauer op. cit. p. 149.

22. See below Chap. V, p. 150, and Chap. VI, p. 184.

23. See *The Final Solution*, pp. 21–2, 76–9, and the Dutch edition of Kersten's *Memoirs, Klerk en Beul* (1947), pp. 197–8.

24. See Manvell and Fraenkel, *Göring*, p. 244.

25. See Russell, *The Trial of Adolf Eichmann*, p. 205.

26. I.M.T. III, p. 278.

27. See Hoess's *Memoirs*, written in captivity after the war.

28. See Cohen, op. cit., p. 114.

29. For our account of this last phase of Heydrich's life we have relied mainly on Wighton's biography and Schellenberg's *Memoirs*.

CHAPTER V

1. These instructions, as far as we know, have not previously been published. They exist as a three-page typescript, marked secret, with marginal corrections in Himmler's hand, and they are held now at the Federal Archives.

The pedantic instructions exactly match Himmler's style; he details, for example, the exact distance at which the execution squads should stand from the prisoner, and whether or not his eyes should be bandaged or his face turned to the wall.

2. I.M.T. XVII, pp. 19–20.

3. See Reitlinger's *The S.S.*, p. 263. Official S.S. statistics showed that between June and November 1942, 136,700 prisoners had been taken into the camps, and that 70,610 had died, 28,846 had been 'transferred out' (i.e., gassed), 9,267 executed, and 4,711 released.

4. See N.C.A. III, pp. 467–9.

5. A vivid description of this repulsive hoard is given by Reitlinger in *The Final Solution*, p. 453.

6. Files of correspondence and memoranda held in the Instituut in Amsterdam, for example, set down the hard deals which the S.S. were negotiating for the sale of Jewish liberties, the minimum price of which was eventually increased from 50,000 to 100,000 Swiss francs.

7. For the text of this speech, see N.C.A. IV, pp. 558–78.

8. Various terms were used to camouflage genocide. These included *Aussiedlung* (desettlement), *Abbeförderung* (removal), and *Auflockerung* (loosening-up). Such terms were in keeping with the fiction that ghettoes such as that at Theresienstadt had the status of an '*Alters-Ghetto*', that is, a place of pleasant retirement for elderly Jews, and so called in order to give a favourable impression. Himmler was very angry when he heard that the true nature of the ghetto at Theresienstadt had leaked out.

9. This story has been most eloquently told by John Hersey in his book, *The Wall*. A full account of the revolt appears in *The Final Solution*, p. 274 et seq.

10. The bare notes for this speech have, however, been preserved. See I.M.T. documents, PS 910, and *The Final Solution*, p. 256.

11. I.M.T. document, PS 1061.

12. See *The Final Solution*, p. 490. For comparison, it may be of interest to note that in a speech fourteen months later, on 25 May 1944, Himmler quoted to an audience of legal men, including the principal judges, the numbers in the concentration camps as 50,000 Germans and 300,000 aliens.

13. The facts for this brief survey of the fate of the Jews in various parts of Europe over which Germany exercised control is derived from *The Final Solution*.

14. In conversation with R.M. in Stockholm, Frau Irmgard Kersten recalled how she accompanied her husband and Himmler to Italy on this occasion; this was the only time she had any direct dealings with Himmler, whom she always tried to avoid. After lunch one day in Rome, Himmler made a

special point of talking to her about the need to be rid of the Jews and the Jehovah Witnesses, and even delayed his departure on an official journey to continue the lecture he gave her. He evidently felt the need to make an ally of Kersten's German wife of whom he saw so little.

15. Hoess's *Memoirs*, p. 148.

16. The Jehovah Witnesses, apart from their pacificism, exacted some response in Himmler's nature. He openly admired their fanaticism, their sobriety and their desire for hard work. It irritated him profoundly that such good people should refuse to co-operate.

17. Himmler never used his special train as a centre for self-indulgence after the manner of Göring. The surviving record of the food taken aboard on 12 December 1942 is extremely modest: it's cost amounted to 20 marks, 75 pfennigs.

18. In a recent book which makes a study of Hitler's medical record, it is only fair to point out that the document seen by Kersten testifying to Hitler's alleged syphilis is not mentioned. See Dr Johann Rechtenwald, *Woran hat Hitler gelitten*. Indeed, it now seems certain that Hitler was not suffering from the after-effects of syphilis but, as has often been stated, from Parkinson's disease (*paralysis agitans*).

19. Another intimate adviser was, of course, the former S.S. General, Karl Wolff, who acted as Himmler's liaison officer at Hitler's headquarters until 1943, when he was appointed Military Governor of Northern Italy. Prior to his recent sentence he was held in custody at Stadelheim prison in Munich, and there H.F. was allowed to interview him on several occasions. He is a man of some charm and humour, and Himmler always addressed him affectionately as Wölfchen.

20. Officially, Mueller has for some time been regarded as dead, but an excavation of his grave during 1963 has revealed that it contained the remains of three men, all younger than Mueller at the time of their deaths. This deception seems only to confirm the original suspicion that he has escaped to Russia.

21. Schellenberg in his *Memoirs* (pp. 395 and 432) writes as if he responded quite independently of Himmler to an invitation from Kersten to visit Stockholm and discuss peace proposals with Hewitt. When Kersten reported his discussions to Himmler, he was, says Schellenberg, 'aghast'. Later, however, he encouraged Schellenberg to maintain contact with Hewitt.

22. Hitler's and Himmler's racial prejudices lost the Germans, until it was too late, the opportunity to draw on Russian reinforcements alleged to amount to some 800,000 men of the Cossack *élite* regiments. Led by the Ukrainian General, Vlassov, their price would have been equality with the German soldiers and independence for the Ukraine. Hitler failed to develop the Ukraine into an anti-Stalinist, pro-German stronghold. See also Chapter VII, p. 203.

23. Himmler's new position in fact gave him few additional powers to those he already held; his control over Frick had always been tight. Bormann, according to that acute observer of Nazi character and intrigue, Albert

Speer, 'did not take long to stalemate Himmler as Minister of the Interior'. If the regional police came under Himmler, the civilian authorities, the local Gauleiters, were responsible to Bormann. This was the source of Bormann's power in the nation itself, just as his position as Hitler's personal secretary was the root of his power at the Führer's headquarters.

24. Dornberger's initial encounters with Himmler are described in his book, *V.2*, pp. 172 et seq.

25. We are grateful not only to Dr Otto John but to the former S.S. General Wolff for giving us evidence on the Langbehn-Popitz attempt to approach Himmler. Both agree there was only one meeting between Popitz and Himmler, not two as has been frequently alleged. Wolff confirms that Langbehn stayed talking with him while Popitz went in to see Himmler. Otto John told H.F. that Popitz explained to him that he began the interview with Himmler by voicing his anxiety about Göring's indolence, and then vaguely hinted that, for the sake of the fatherland, even the leadership at the top required shaking up.

26. Another very important group of high-minded members of the resistance who had links with the *Abwehr* – Dietrich Bonhoeffer, Joseph Müller and Hans von Dohnanyi – had been arrested in April 1943.

*Additional Note*

We have received useful information about Himmler from Doris Mähner, who at the age of twenty-two joined Himmler's secretarial staff in 1943, her particular recommendation being that she, like Himmler, was Bavarian. She was well treated, but paid only 300 marks a month. She was expected to live on Himmler's special train for days and nights on end. He dictated to her fluently in his broad Bavarian accent, but irritated her by plucking at his left eyebrow with his left hand. As a man she found him utterly unimpressive, but he was always very considerate, giving the girls who worked for him small presents on their birthdays and at Christmas. He had a careful system of reminders to keep him up to the mark. Similarly, his correspondence, which was voluminous, was carefully docketed to ensure he received the replies he asked for. Frl. Mähner noticed his love for Hedwig; he kept her photograph hidden in his desk and often looked at it while he was working. The girls joked about his obsession concerning blond men and women; Frl. Mähner often watched him studying the photographs of prospective S.S. brides before making a decision as to their suitability for his men.

CHAPTER VI

The references in this chapter are all to Kersten's *Memoirs* (Hutchinson, London, 1956). The many sheets from Himmler's desk diary that survive in the Federal Archive at Koblenz show how much time Himmler spent in the care of his captive masseur; he normally set aside as much as two hours at a time, morning or afternoon, for the treatment that became increasingly essential to him. It should be remembered that Kersten was by no means popular with such men as Müller and Kaltenbrunner; he was, too, regarded as 'interfering' by some of those who were seeking to bring about peace through neutral Sweden. There was, no doubt, a certain element of vanity in Kersten's nature. His negotiations were bitterly resented by Count Bernadotte, who wanted to keep all the credit for the attempts to bring about peace for himself. Since the war, Kersten's leading protagonists have included his biographer Kessel, Professor Hugh Trevor-Roper and Achim Besgen, who published a book on Kersten, *Der Stille Befehl*, in 1960. At one stage after the war, Kersten was being actively considered in Sweden for the Nobel Peace Prize.

1. *Memoirs*, pp. 311–12.

2. *Memoirs*, pp. 256–7.

3. *Memoirs*, pp. 257–8.

4. *Memoirs*, p. 177.

5. *Memoirs*, p, 178.

6. Himmler did not want to be considered an agnostic. He invented a special term for the form of belief he favoured – *gottgläubig*, implying belief in a form of godhead distinct from anything Christian. Himmler was against priesthood as a profession. He did not want, he said, a new form of 'popery' to grow up in the S.S.

7. *Memoirs*, p. 120.

8. *Memoirs*, pp. 306–7.

### CHAPTER VII

1. The full story of the attempt on Hitler's life and of the failure of the military *coup d'état* on 20 July 1944 is told in the authors' book *The July Plot*.

2. Himmler said this to von Krosigk, who later repeated it to H.F.

3. The list of 161 proven victims who were executed is given in Wheeler-Bennett's *Nemesis*, p. 744.

4. See *The S.S.*, pp. 300–1.

5. See *The S.S.*, p. 268. According to evidence submitted at the I.M.T., Himmler formally witnessed the execution of Russian officers at Mauthausen during September 1944. See I.M.T. V, pp. 170, 174, 231.

6. See Dulles, *Germany's Underground*, p. 163.

7. The evidence at Koblenz, Amsterdam and Warsaw (which H.F. visited during 1963) in particular carries innumerable documents which testify to the commercialization of the Jewish persecution. These include the sale of emigration permits which in Amsterdam, for example, goes back to April 1942. Elderly Jews were favoured who represented no security risk and who were willing to hand over money, securities or industrial plants. Other documents list in painstaking detail the disposal of looted treasure which was to be distributed among various Army, Navy and S.S. units.

8. See Schellenberg's *Memoirs*, p. 430.

9. See *The Final Solution*, p. 462. Becher's affidavit was produced during the hearing of Case XI at Nuremberg, Doc. No. N.G. 2675.

10. Eichmann refused to obey orders received from Himmler by telephone to stop the deportations; he claimed he must have them in wirting. See *The Trial of Adolf Eichmann*, p. 170.

11. See I.M.T. XI, p. 306.

12. See *The S.S.*, p. 385.

13. Quoted by Milton Shulman in *Defeat in the West*, p. 218.

14. See Dornberger, *V.2*, pp. 187–201.

15. See Guderian, *Panzer Leader*, p. 355.

16. For the dispute surrounding this episode, see *The S.S.*, p. 377.

17. For Vlassov and the significance of Himmler's refusal to make use of him, see above, Chapter V, note 22.

18. Werwolf, the so-called German resistance movement against the Allies, was largely a propaganda device prepared by Goebbels and Himmler.

19. See *The S.S.*, p. 381.

20. According to von Oven, *Mit Goebbels bis zum Ende* (Vol. II, p. 161) Goebbels proposed to Hitler that Himmler should be made officially Minister of War.

21. For quotations, see *The Bormann Letters*.

22. Fegelein and Burgdorff, these men with whom Bormann seems so friendly, have their modest place in history. Fegelein, Himmler's uncertain representative at Hitler's headquarters, was married to Eva Braun's sister, but nevertheless was executed by Hitler for desertion during the last days of the war. Burgdorff's claims to distinction include the sinister fact that it was he who handed Rommel the poison with which he was required to kill himself.

23. See Westphal, *The German Army in the West*, p. 172.

24. Westphal, op. cit., p. 188.

25. Guderian, op. cit., p. 403.

26. An interesting picture of Himmler as commander-in-the-field is given by the well-known German journalist, Jürgen Thorwald, in his two books, one on the Vistula campaign, *Es begann an der Weichsel,* and the other on the Elbe campaign, *Das Ende an der Elbe.*

27. The German synthetic oil industry had suffered severely from Allied bombing. Hitler believed that at all costs he must preserve the Austrian and Hungarian oil wells which were still in his hands.

28. Guderian, op. cit., p. 413.

29. See *The S.S.*, p. 406.

30. See Guderian, op. cit., p. 422.

31. Count Bernadotte, in *The Fall of the Curtain*, a book largely ghost-written by Schellenberg who took refuge with him after the collapse of Germany, deleted all Schellenberg's references to Kersten. Nor are there any references to the work of the Swedish Foreign Minister, Christian Günther, who had planned the negotiations which Kersten so resolutely carried through with Himmler. See the attack on Bernadotte's attitude to Kersten made by Trevor-Roper in his Introduction to *The Kersten Memoirs*. Dr de Jong, director of the Rijksinstituut in Amsterdam and a distinguished historian, who knew Kersten personally, assures us that while Kersten undoubtedly did good, he was a man of great vanity who tended to exaggerate his influence, an example being his claim that he practically saved the entire Dutch nation from evacuation to the East. Kersten and Bernadotte were unable to tolerate each other.

32. See Semmler, *Goebbels, the Man next to Hitler*, pp. 178–9.

33. In *The Fall of the Curtain*, the date of the final meeting with Himmler is given on p. 41 as 12 February. This is plainly an oversight, since on page 20 Bernadotte states he flew to Berlin on 16 February. Schellenberg states (p. 435) that he took Bernadotte to see Himmler two days after the meeting with Kaltenbrunner. In *The Last Days of Hitler*, Prof. Trevor-Roper wrongly accepts 12 February as the date of the meeting, and Reitlinger variously gives it as 17 February in *The Final Solution*, p. 462 and 18 February in *The S.S.*, p. 415.

34. See *The S.S.*, p. 414. The source is von Oven, op. cit. II, pp. 252–4.

35. See Prof Trevor-Roper's Introduction to *Kersten Memoirs*, pp. 15–16, and *The S.S.*, p. 416.

36. See Thorwald, *Das Ende an der Elbe*, p. 25, and *The S.S.*, p. 413.

37. See I.M.T. XIV, p. 374, and *The Final Solution*, p. 446.

38. Quoted by Shulman, *Defeat in the West*, p. 280.

39. During the course of this talk, Count Schwerin-Krosigk said that he felt the only justification for the sacrifices which Hitler had imposed on the German people would be to break the alliance between the Western Allies and the Russians. Himmler agreed and, according to Schwerin-Krosigk, openly admitted that great mistakes had been made. As for the Jews, they had now become very important as 'barter in all future negotiations'. Himmler was not prepared to say anything disloyal about Hitler; he merely said that 'the Führer had a different conception'. Speaking of himself,

Himmler added that 'while his reputation was that of a gay and godless person, in the depths of his heart he was really a believer in Providence and in God'. It was God who had spared the Führer on 20 July last; it was God who had brought a thaw to the frozen waters of the Oder and delayed the Russian crossing at the moment when he had been in despair about the collapse of their defence; it was God who had taken Roosevelt's life at the very moment when the Russians were closing in on Berlin. (See Shirer, *End of a Berlin Diary*, p. 197 et seq.)

*Additional Note*

Frau Heydrich has given us a striking picture of Himmler at the turn of the years 1944–5. She was still living in the castle near Prague, but by now she was sheltering many refugee German women and their children from East Prussia, all of them connected in one way or another with the S.S. Himmler visited her unannounced some time after she had written to him for advice on what she should do. He was evasive, as usual, about the situation, and referred vaguely to Hitler's miracle weapons (*Wunderwaffen*). When he stroked her son's blond hair and said with a sigh, 'Ach, Heider', she sensed there was nothing to be done but resign herself to her fate. When she spoke to him about the problems of evacuation, all he said was that there were plenty of edible mushrooms in Bavaria. He shook hands with the women at her request, and after he had gone (it was the last time she was to see him), Frau Heydrich organized the evacuation of her household and the refugees in three lorries.

CHAPTER VIII

In this chapter we are specially indebted to Colonel Michael Murphy and Captain Tom Selvester, the British officers who had charge of Himmler, to Josef Kiermaier, Himmler's bodyguard, and to Dr Werner Best, for the special evidence they have given us concerning the last days of Himmler's life.

1. 'Let bygones be bygones', he is reported to have said to Masur.

2. *Kersten Memoirs*, p. 288.

3. Kersten managed to get a flight from Tempelhof to Copenhagen the following day, 22 April; after this he travelled surface to Stockholm and reported to Günther on the evening of 23 April.

4. The account of this meeting between Himmler and Bernadotte is taken primarily from Bernadotte's own account in *The Fall of the Curtain*.

5. Himmler was so pre-occupied that, according to Bernadotte, he drove his car straight into some barbed wire. He frequently preferred to drive himself rather than be driven, even during these last days of strain.

6. For the various opinions on Himmler's claim to the succession, see Trevor-Roper, *The Last Days of Hitler*, pp. 101, 182–3; Semmler, op. cit., p. 178, Alan Bullock, *Hitler*, pp. 705, 709, and, for Schwerin-Krosigk, Shirer's *End of a Berlin Diary*, p. 203.

7. This statement by Winocaur was published for the first time in 1963 in *Amateur Agent*, by Ewan Butler. Ewan Butler also tells the story (pp. 157 et seq.) of the forged German stamps printed in London and valued at 20 pfennigs; they bore the effigy of Himmler instead of Hitler, and agents were instructed to put them into use in Germany during the last months of the war. American collectors after the war were offering $10,000 for cancelled copies of these stamps. Ewan Butler himself 'borrowed' through an agent 150 pages of typescript of Schellenberg's diary, items for which he posted daily from Germany for safe-keeping in Sweden. The sheets were microfilmed, and Butler translated the diary for the Foreign Office in London. (See pp. 182-3).

8. Hanna Reitsch. See Shirer, *End of a Berlin Diary*, p. 168-9.

9. In the will he dictated and signed during the small hours of 29 April, Hitler referred expressly to Himmler's treachery: 'Before my death I expel from the Party and from all his offices the former Reichsführer S.S. and Reich Minister of the Interior, Heinrich Himmler. In his stead I appoint Gauleiter Karl Hanke as Reichsführer S.S. and Chief of the German Police, and Gauleiter Paul Giesler as Reich Minister of the Interior.'

10. Doenitz and Himmler met during the morning of 30 April to consider the best action to take to prevent Kaufmann, the Gauleiter of Hamburg, from surrendering the city to the British. Doenitz in the end sent his own messages to Kaufmann, considering Himmler's too pathetic and impractical.
    Doenitz's own guarded account of his dealings with Himmler is given in his autobiography, *Zehn Jahre und Zwanzig Tage* (1958), p. 439 et seq. He refers first of all to a meeting with Himmler on 28 April at Rheinsberg, at which Himmler openly asked him if he would be 'available' in case Himmler were appointed Hitler's successor; Doenitz replied he would be for any legal government out to stop bloodshed. He also claims that he received a signal from Bormann on 30 April which referred to Himmler directly: 'New treason afoot. According to enemy broadcasts Himmler offered capitulation via Sweden. Führer expects you to deal with all traitors fast as lightning and hard as steel. Bormann.' Doenitz observes that he was in no position to cope with Himmler, who was still surrounded by S.S. men and police. He says that he met Himmler again on 30 April at a police station in Lübeck, because, he says, 'I wanted to know what he was up to'. Himmler kept him waiting and seemed to behave as if he were already the Führer. But the meeting remained friendly; Himmler denied that he had had any dealings with the Allies. Only after this meeting was concluded did Doenitz learn from Bormann that he was to succeed as Führer.

11. This meeting, according to Doenitz, took place at Ploen at midnight. Himmler arrived with six armed officers. Doenitz claims to have received him with a loaded gun hidden under his papers. Himmler was appalled at the news that he had been displaced.

12. Hanna Reitsch records a conversation she had with Himmler after the news of Hitler's death in which she claims she challenged him to his face with high treason. Himmler seems to have made no attempt to deny that he had undertaken the negotiations; on the contrary, she says that he stated Hitler was insane and that history would interpret the negotiations as an attempt to save Germany from further bloodshed. See Shirer's *End of a Berlin Diary*, pp. 171-2.

13. Degrelle has left his own account of this meeting in his book, *Die Verlorene Legion*. See also *The S.S.*, pp. 442-3.

14. Best gave his own account of this meeting in conversation with H.F. Himmler's act of thoughtfulness on behalf of his women secretaries was confirmed to H.F. by Doris Mähner. She also recalls the moment when he said goodbye a few days later. He thanked her, and told her to go back to Bavaria and rest. Soon, he said, they would meet again, and then there would be a great deal of work to do.

15. Schwerin-Krosigk in conversation with H.F.

16. The copy of this note was found in one of Doenitz's files.
    According to Prof. Trevor-Roper, it remains uncertain whether the original was actually delivered to Himmler, or whether Doenitz told him of his dismissal personally. (See *The Last Days of Hitler*, p. 246, note.) Doenitz does not clarify this point in his memoirs, but he claims that had he known about the atrocities in the concentration camps he would never have let Himmler go free. (See pp. 466–8) 'Now, most clearly', he writes, 'I recognized the evil side of National Socialism and so changed my attitude to the form of state created by it.'

17. Arolsen has now become the headquarters of the International Red Cross Tracing Service financed by the Bonn government.

18. For details of this journey we are grateful to Josef Kiermaier, who accompanied Himmler almost up to the time of his arrest by the British. Kiermaier recalls suggesting to Himmler that they fly south while they still had an aircraft at their disposal; then at least, said Kiermaier, they could see their womenfolk before the end came. Himmler turned this suggestion down on the grounds that in times as adverse as these, no man should indulge his personal desires.

19. Information on the following events from Colonel Michael Murphy and Captain Tom Selvester.

20. The following account is taken from the B.B.C. broadcast by Sergeant-Major Austin in a programme introduced by Chester Wilmot from Luneberg on May 24 1945, shortly after Himmler's death.

21. Colonel Murphy writes that as part of the effort to keep Himmler alive he 'shouted for a needle and cotton, which arrived with remarkable speed. I pierced the tongue and with the cotton threaded through held the tongue out.' There seems no doubt that, since the normal action of cyanide produces a quick death, Himmler's long death agony was caused by the interference with the penetration of the poison into his system. After Himmler's death, Colonel Murphy says that it was some twenty-four hours before the Russians sent their representatives to view the body and agree, 'grudgingly', that 'it *might* be Himmler'. Only after this examination was Himmler's body buried. Gebhard Himmler, who was in the south, was not brought in to identify the body, as Frischauer claims in his book, p. 257. Gebhard Himmler, in conversation with H.F., has confirmed this.
    Colonel Murphy has some interesting comments to make on the poison capsule. Himmler, he said, had not eaten in his presence, 'and there is no doubt in my mind that from the time I met him to the time of his death the capsule was in his mouth. So far as I can remember from the one taken from his clothes, this was of thin metal – strong enough to withstand careful mastication and liquids, especially if the other side of the mouth was used, but not strong enough to withstand a decision to break it. I think the time of

death was midnight May 23–4, but I cannot be sure. Himmler was sure of himself and arrogant to the end. He was quite convinced that he would be taken to see Montgomery and was surprised at the firm treatment I gave him in getting rid of the bodyguards and searching him. I should have received a German General with more courtesy'!

*Additional Notes*

[1] We are grateful to Karl Kaufmann, the former Gauleiter of Hamburg, for giving us an account of his own observation of Himmler's arrest. During the morning of 23 May, Kaufmann, along with Brandt and other prisoners stood at the barbed-wire fence of Camp 031 at Kolkhagen, near Nienburg on the river Weser. They were watching lorries from Fellingbosdel Camp (Lüneberg Heath) driving up. Among those who got out was Himmler, minus his moustache and with a patch over one eye. He stood in the right wing of the group, wearing boots, field grey trousers and some sort of civilian jacket. He did not recognize Kaufmann and the others, but they saw him suddenly disappear behind a nearby rhododendron bush, where he removed the eye-patch. He reappeared almost instantly putting on his glasses; he was immediately recognizable. This was the time he decided to give himself up, in Kaufmann's opinion. A few minutes later there was quite a commotion; extra guards with tommy-guns and machine guns appeared; extra sentries were posted at the gate. Soon the cause of the excitement was being passed through the grapevine of the camp. The British soldiers seemed overjoyed that Himmler was among their prisoners.

[2] We are indebted to Count Schwerin v. Krosigk for some additional facts he recalled when reading the first impression of this book. On the evening of 1 May, at Himmler's urgent request, the Count went to see him at his H.Q. between Plön and Eutin. Himmler had learned that next day Schwerin was to be appointed Foreign Secretary; and he earnestly tried to convince him that at no time was that office more important than just then. By joining the Western Allies they would have a splendid chance of expanding their eastern borders as far as the Urals; they had, in fact, never been so near to that most desirable aim of German foreign policy. Himmler seemed utterly unable to grasp realities; he was convinced that his own future as 'the second man in the Dönitz administration' was assured. 'All I want', he added, 'is a brief chat with Montgomery and Eisenhower. It should be easy enough to convince them that I and my S.S. are an indispensable *Ordnungsfaktor* [guarantee of law and order] in the struggle against Bolshevism.'

# Selected Book-List

This bibliography contains only those books which are of special interest for the study of Himmler; only those general histories of the Third Reich which are important in the understanding of Himmler are included. Of the published official records, we have drawn specially on *The Trial of the Major War Criminals:* Proceedings, Vols. I-XXIII; Documents in Evidence, Vols. XXIV-XLII (Nuremberg, 1947–9). The Proceedings were also published by H.M.S.O. in London in twenty-two volumes, and this is the edition quoted and referred to in this book. Translations into English of some of the documents used in evidence were published by the U.S. Government Printing Office under the title *Nazi Conspiracy and Aggression* in eight main volumes and two supplementary volumes. When quoting from the British edition of the Proceedings we use the abbreviation I.M.T.; when quoting from *Nazi Conspiracy and Aggression,* we abbreviate as N.C.A.

## (i) HISTORICAL AND GENERAL STUDIES

BARTZ, KARL: *Downfall of the German Secret Service.* (London: Kimber, 1956.)

BAYLE, FRANÇOIS: *Croix gammée ou caducée.* (Freiburg, 1950.)
— *Psychologie et éthique du national-socialisme.* (Paris, A 1953.)

COHEN, ELIE A.: *Human Behaviour in the Concentration Camp.* (New York: Norton, 1953.)

CRANKSHAW, EDWARD: *The Gestapo, Instrument of Tyranny.* (London: Putnam, 1956.)

CYPRIAN, T. and SAWICKI, J.: *Nazi Rule in Poland 1939–45.* (Warsaw: Polonia, 1961.)

DARRÉ, WALTHER: *Neuadel aus Blut und Boden.* (Munich:Eher Verlag, 1934.)

DATNER, S., GUMKOWSKI, J. and LESZCZYNSKI, K.: *Genocide 1939–45.* (Warsaw: Wydawnictwo Zachodnie, 1962.)

DULLES, ALLEN: *Germany's Underground.* (New York: Macmillan, 1947.)

EISENBACH, A.: *Operation Reinhard* (*Mass Extermination in Poland*). (Poznan: 1962.)

*Experimental Operations on Prisoners of Ravensbrück Concentration Camp*. (Warsaw: 1960.)

FITZ GIBBON, CONSTANTINE: *The Shirt of Nessus*. (London: Cassell, 1956.)

*German Crimes in Poland*, Compiled by the Central Commission for Inter-Investigation of German Crimes in Poland. (Warsaw: 1946.)

KOGON, EUGEN: *The Theory and Practice of Hell*. (London, Secker and Warburg, 1951.)

MITSCHERLICH, A. and MIELKE, F.: *Doctors of Infamy*. (New York: 1949.)

— *The Death Doctors*. (London: Elek, 1962.)

PECHEL, RUDOLF: *Deutscher Widerstand*. (Zurich: Rentsch, 1947.)

POLONIA PUBLISHING HOUSE: *Poland under Nazi Occupation*. (Warsaw, 1961.)

— *We Have Not Forgotten*. (Warsaw, 1961.)

RECKTENWALD, JOHAN *Woran hat Hitler Gelitten*. (Munich: Reinhardt, 1903.)

REITLINGER, GERALD: *The Final Solution*. (London: Valentine Mitchell, 1953.)

— *The S.S.; Alibi of a Nation* 1922–1945. (London: Heinemann, 1956.)

RITTER, GERHARD: *The German Resistance*. (London: Allen and Unwin, 1958.)

— (Shortened version of original German edition, *Karl Goerdeler und die Deutsche Widerstandsbewegung*. (Bonn, 1954.)

SHIRER, WILLIAM L.: *The Rise and Fall of the Third Reich*. (New York: Simon and Schuster, 1960.)

SHULMAN, MILTON: *Defeat in the West*. (London: Secker and Warburg, 1949.)

SOSNOWSKI, K.: *Tragedy of Children under Nazi Rule*. (Warsaw: Zachodnia Agencja Prasowa, 1962.)

TAYLOR, A. J. P.: *The Origins of the Second World War*. (London: Hamish Hamilton, 1961.)

THORWALD, JÜRGEN: *Es Begann an der Weichsel*. (Stuttgart: Steingrüben Verlag, 1950.)

— *Das Ende an der Elbe*. (Stuttgart: Steingrüben Verlag, 1950.)

WHEELER-BENNETT, J. W.: *The Nemesis of Power*. (London: Macmillan, 1953.)

Note: The official account of Eichmann's pre-trial interrogation has been published in six mimeographed volumes by the Police d'Israel, Quartier Générale, 6ième Bureau. (Jerusalem, 1963.)

## (ii) MEMOIRS, DIARIES AND BIOGRAPHIES

BERNADOTTE, FULK: *The Curtain Falls.* (New York: Knopf, 1945.)

BEST, S. PAYNE: *The Venlo Incident.* (London: Hutchinson, 1950.)

*The Bormann Letters.* Edited by H. R. Trevor-Roper. (London: Weidenfeld and Nicolson, 1954.)

BUTLER, EWAN: *Amateur Agent.* (London: Harrap, 1963.)

BULLOCK, ALAN: *Hitler.* (London: Odhams, 1952.) Revised 1964.

BESGEN, ACHIM: *Der Stille Befehl.* (Munich: Nymphenburger Verlagshlandlung, 1960.)

*Ciano's Diary, 1937–38.* (London: Methuen, 1952.)

*Ciano's Diary, 1939–43.* Edited by Malcolm Muggeridge. (London: Heinemann, 1947.)

DEGRELLE, LEON: *Die Verlorene Legion.* (Stuttgart: Veritas Verlag, 1955.)

DIELS, RUDOLF: *Lucifer ante Portas.* (Zurich: Interverlag, 1949.)

DÖNITZ, KARL: *Zehn Jahre und Zwanzig Tage.* (Bonn: Athenäum Verlag, 1958.)

DORNBERGER, WALTER: *V.2.* (London, 1953.)

*Hans Franks Tagebuch.* (Edited by Stanislaw Piotrowski.) (Warsaw: Polnischer Verlag der Wissenschaften, 1963.)

FRISCHAUER, WILLI. *Himmler.* (London: Odhams, 1953.)

GISEVIUS, H. B.: *To the Bitter End.* (London: Cape, 1948.)

GOEBBELS, JOSEPH: *My Part in Germany's Fight.* (London: Paternoster Library, 1938.)

— *The Goebbels Diaries.* (London: Hamish Hamilton, 1948.)

— *The Early Goebbels Diaries.* Edited by Helmut Heiber. (London: Weidenfeld and Nicolson, 1962.)

GUDERIAN, HEINZ: *Panzer Leader.* (London: Michael Joseph, 1952.)

HALDER, FRANZ: *Kriegstagebuch.* (Stuttgart: Kohlhammer, 1962.)

*The von Hassell Diaries, 1938–44.* (London: Hamish Hamilton, 1948.)

HEIDEN, KONRAD: *Der Führer.* (London: Gollancz, 1944.)

HENDERSON, SIR NEVILE: *Failure of a Mission.* (London: Hodder and Stoughton, 1940.)

HESSE, FRITZ: *Hitler and the English.* (London: Wingate, 1954.)

*Hitler's Table Talk.* (London: Weidenfeld and Nicolson, 1953.)

HOESS, RUDOLF: *Commandant of Auschwitz*. (London: Weidenfeld and Nicolson, 1959.)

HÖTTL, WILHELM: *The Secret Front*. (London: Weidenfeld and Nicolson, 1953.)

— *Hitler's Paper Weapon*. (London: Hart-Davis, 1955.)

KERSTEN, FELIX: *Totenkopf und Treue*. (Hamburg, 1953.)

— *The Kersten Memoirs*. (London: Hutchinson, 1956.)

KESSEL, JOSEPH: *The Man with the Miraculous Hands*. (New York: Farrar, Straus and Cudhany, 1961.)

LÜDECKE, KURT G. W.: *I Knew Hitler*. (London: Jarrolds, 1938.)

MANVELL, ROGER and FRAENKEL, HEINRICH: *Doctor Goebbels*. (London: Heinemann, 1960.)

— *Hermann Göring*. (London: Heinemann, 1962.)

— *The July Plot*. (London: The Bodley Head, 1964.)

MASUR, NORBERT: *En Jud talar med Himmler*. (Stockholm: Hoffmann und Campe, 1946.)

MÖLLER, KURT DETLEV: *Das Letzte Kapitel*. (Hamburg, Hoffmann und Campe, 1947.)

OVEN, WILFRED VON: *Mit Goebbels bis zum Ende*. (Buenos Aires: Dürer Verlag, 1949–50.)

PAPEN, FRANZ VON: *Memoirs*. (London: André Deutsch, 1952.)

*The Ribbentrop Memoirs*. (London: Weidenfeld and Nicolson, 1954.)

*The Rosenberg Memoirs*. (New York: Ziff Davis, 1949.)

RUSSELL OF LIVERPOOL, LORD: *The Trial of Adolf Eichmann*. (London: Heinemann, 1962.)

*The Schellenberg Memoirs*. (London: André Deutsch, 1956.)

SCHMIDT, PAUL: *Hitler's Interpreter*. (London: Heinemann, 1951.)

SEMMLER, RUDOLF: *Goebbels, the Man Next to Hitler*. (London: Westhouse, 1947.)

SHIRER, WILLIAM L.: *Berlin Diary*. (New York: Knopf, 1941.

— *End of a Berlin Diary*. (New York: Knopf, 1947.)

*The Report of Jurgen Stroop*: an account of the Warsaw Ghetto Rising. (Warsaw: Jewish Historical Institute, 1958.)

SKORZENY, OTTO: *Geheimkommando Skorzeny*. (Hamburg, 1950.)

TREVOR-ROPER, H. R.: *The Last Days of Hitler*. (London: Macmillan, 1947.)

WESTPHAL, SIEGFRIED: *The German Army in the West*. (London: Cassell, 1951.)

WIGHTON, CHARLES: *Heydrich*. (London: Odhams, 1962.)

WULF, JOSEF: *Heinrich Himmler*. (Berlin: Arani Verlag, 1960.)

# Index

.